THE JOYS OF
JEWISH COOKING

By Stephen and Ethel Longstreet

THE JOYS OF JEWISH COOKING
A SALUTE TO AMERICAN COOKING

THE JOYS OF JEWISH COOKING

by Stephen and Ethel Longstreet

with illustrations by Stephen Longstreet

Weathervane Books New York

To our dear Friend
and
Benevolent Taskmaster
SHIRLEY BURKE
With much Thanks
For many Good Deeds

PREFACE

> There is nothing better for a man, than
> that he should eat and drink . . .
> *Ecclesiastes 2:24*

This cookbook is the result of a research poll done for another text we wrote, A SALUTE TO AMERICAN COOKING, selected by two book clubs. During the writing of it, we questioned many people in our travels, both here and abroad, and discovered at least seventy percent of those who had a liking for what is called Jewish food were non-Jews with many dissimilarities in diet. It was not merely an interest in bagels and lox, chopped liver, a delight in strudel, the blintz, or gefilte fish as a tidbit at cocktail time. Or an addiction to borsch, or the legendary chicken soup with mandlen. No, we discovered households serving Austrian-Jewish Salzburger Nockerl, Rothschild Garnieter Schnitzel, the Bialystok version of carp Polonaise, and kasha (buckwheat groats) as a substitute for rice or potatoes.

On further study, we found there was no full text, no satisfying world Jewish cookbook. What was available was narrow, limited, specializing mostly in loose American versions of Jewish cookery, often unauthentic, ignoring the sauces and the more genuine savory recipes.

We became aware of the wider, deeper sumptuous appeal of Jewish cookery by our interests and travels in the last thirty years—when as co-authors, we researched material and cultures in various parts of the world for the genre histories on which we collaborated, particularly at one time, books on the lives of modern Jewish artists, such as Soutine, Modigliani, Chagall, Pascin, Lipchitz, and others.*

We agreed with James Boswell, "Man is a cooking animal." For our research was not our first introduction to Jewish world cooking. We had both been raised to appreciate the nuances of ethnic appetites at their highest home achievements, and our families' kitchen daybooks (Tante Longstrasse kept a daybook for forty years), private journals, and letters going back several generations, listed such items as seloka in smetana (herring in sour cream), the Hungarian szekely gulyas (goulash) a cold rheinlachs (salmon) with remouladen sauce. Food was listed

* (*Young Men of Paris, Man of Montmartre, The Burning Man.*)

more often than the state of affairs during the Great War, Mr. Loeb
of Kuhn, Loeb & Co., Franz Josef's newest mistress, the first Benz
car bought by a German great-grandfather, or a distant Russian tea
merchant uncle buying a first Picasso in Paris in 1910. Food interested
our sources. One of the compilers of this book had files of unused
material from when he was for fifteen years a contributing editor of
Gourmet magazine.

Both of us in our many travels—as dedicated feeders—("Appetite
is the best sauce") took time to try the often full cuisines during our
wanderings into various parts of the world. In thirty years, we discovered we had piled up filing cases of Jewish world recipes, local
cookery histories from merchant princes to village tailors and artisans.
Also a collection of handwritten manuscripts by cooks famous and
unknown, by chefs and grandmothers—rabbis' wives, out-of-print texts
on foods and the memory of old folk. Friends of our families.

"There German-Jewish families . . . were a cohesive, knit, and
recognizably distinct part of New York society. They were also the
closest thing to Aristocracy—Aristocracy in the best sense—that the city,
and perhaps the country, has seen." So Stephen Birmingham overstates
his case in his history, *Our Crowd*. Even if he meant the families of the
members of the elite New York City Jewish club, the Harmonie (Harmonie Gesellschaft), where the language was German, and a portrait of
the Kaiser probably hung on the wall. The Century Club at White
Plains kept out all Jews, but for a few "token Gimbels." But its menus,
wrote an uncle, "didn't excite me." The Harmonie Club was famous
for its food. ("Particularly celebrated was the club's herring with sour
cream, which it put up in jars and the ladies carried home.")

An old long-time member of the club wrote in a letter to us: "It
was fine Jewish European food for Temple Emanu-El families there.
You'd find in the dining rooms Cullmans, Lehmans, Zissers, Sachses,
two, three generations of Loebs, Seligmans. The Seligmans, they bred
with the Loebs, spawned like salmon. All there eating Partridge with
Sauerkraut, and Dampfnuden—the fine steamed dumplings, Sour
Cherry Kompot, and the wine maître d' serving not a bad Burgundy,
and only a fair Port. The club members weren't really up on it about
the best wines.

"They all tried to get a French chef, English butler, Irish maid,
German governess; but you should see them smile when they bit into a
crunchy kosher garlic pickle, brought up from downtown, from where
the Russian, Polish Jews still obeyed the dietary laws. I'd take parties to

Second Avenue to try the peroshkis and the sorrel soup, the Krevski cutlets . . ."

We both grew up aware of fine cooking and hearing Hebrew folk
wisdom, "Fill the table and the quarreling will stop." And from the
Talmud, "Eating should be done in silence lest the windpipe open
before the gullet."

Moderation in eating, of course, makes for getting the most out of
good food. The Talmud, in about 200 B.C., gave a proper formula.
"In eating, a third of the stomach should be filled with food, a third
with drink, and the rest empty." The drink mentioned is a mild wine
and, at that, half or two thirds diluted with water. As Randle Cotgrave
added, in 1611, "Eat at pleasure, drink by measure."

In rechecking details of the Yiddish and Hebrew background, and of
some of the rituals, holidays, and traditional humor, we want to ac-
knowledge our thanks to *Judaism, A Historical Presentation,* Isadore Epstein; *Why I Am a Jew,* D. de S. Pool; *The Joys of Yiddish,* Leo
Rosten; *Yiddish Language and Literature,* A. A. Steinberg (Encyclo-
paedia Britannica); *This Is My God,* Herman Wouk.

CONTENTS

THE JOYS OF
JEWISH COOKING

INTRODUCTION

Is There Actually Such a Thing as
Jewish Cooking?

The answers are YES there is. NO there isn't.

The ancient Jews of Old Testament Judea, the Hebrews who existed before and after the Babylonian exile, the Roman-Jewish wars, and the destruction of the Temple, were a nomadic desert people, mostly shepherds. They ate cereals (their *corn* mentioned in their ritual texts is actual wheat). They had grapes and made wine. They gathered dates—wrote of a "land of milk and honey," and, of course, had lamb and mutton and could, if rich, provide a prodigal son with a fattened calf. While the Old Testament mentions the Fruit of the Tree of Knowledge in the Garden of Eden, which later scholars were to translate as an apple, and in the Song of Songs sings: "Comfort me with apples for I am sick of love," most likely the fruit was *not* an apple, but a pomegranate. They may have gotten peaches from Persia, and certainly the melon. There was the dove to eat. "The voice of the turtle-[dove] is heard in the land." St. Paul was a fisherman, and Christ addressed fisherfolk on the Sea of Galilee. So to this diet add a flat pita-type bread, garlic and onions, and that pretty much was the *original* Jewish food. It was not an educated palate and bears no resemblance to the delicacies, the pungent dishes, the cunning spicing of yesterday's and today's Jewish cookery . . . "Man does not live by bread alone." (*Deuteronomy 8:3.*)

Jewish cooking as we know it and as it has developed since Diaspora, the Exile, and the razing of the Temple, is an evolutionary process—part epicure, part survival—of adopting native foods, improving, refining them, or simplifying the fitting of them into the ritual dietetic rules of the People of the Book. So Jewish cooking, must, as we do in this book, be divided, hyphenated, into Russian-Jewish, German-Jewish, Hungarian-Jewish, North African-Jewish, Latin American-Jewish, and so on, ending with the biggest hybrid of all, American-Jewish dishes, where, in the words of a Jewish-descended philosopher, Michel de Montaigne; "A man should not so much respect what he eats as with whom he eats." Whether to make this a Jewish cookbook *or* a kosher cookbook was the first question we asked ourselves.

Is Jewish Cooking Kosher Cooking?

To understand the problem let us define *kosher* and *Jewish*. Kosher food is that food that is prepared according to ancient dietary laws set down in Leviticus and Deuteronomy. It permitted the use of only certain parts of certain animals, fowl, and fish. The slaughtering of these animals and fowl is performed only by an Orthodox official called a Shochet. The meat had to be drained and salted in a certain way, liver broiled on an open flame. The mixing of dishes containing milk, cream, or butter with dishes of meat or fat was forbidden. Shellfish were taboo, as were pigs and most wild game, including a long list from the camel and rabbit to owls and eagles. Certain fish were allowed ("A land with lots of herring eaters can get along with few doctors." Polish village rabbi).

Jewish cooking was *once* mostly kosher, it observed the dietary rules up until the challenge of Orthodox Hebrew beliefs in the middle of the nineteenth century by Conservative Judaism and by Reform Judaism. By the end of World War I, the Conservative and Reform branches had begun to replace the Orthodox Jewry and their shuls with more liberal permissive attitudes and rituals and with Temples. The women now sat with the men, music was introduced, folk dancing, art shows, guest Christian clergy. Many Jews relaxed their insistence on ritually approved kosher procedures, even if they might still shun the shellfish, and keep pork from their home kitchens—not mix meat dishes with dairy ones.

Today, not only in America but in many parts of the world, the Ortho-dox are a declining minority and most Jewish families are Conservative and Reform temple subscribers. Few are strict kosher advocates, and shrimp and even bacon are eaten, coffee sipped with cream, after a roast, butter at all meals is common.

Kashrut (Kosherness)

Franz Kafka, considered by world critics as most likely *the* important Jewish writer of modern times, wrote, "Yearly the leopards broke into the temple and drank the wine from the sacred chalice; eventually it became part of the ritual . . ."

Some students of ritual anthropology think in this manner did the rites of kashrut enter Hebrew life, and came down to the Orthodox Jews of today. . . . As to sacred texts: in Genesis animal blood is "forbidden to the seed of Noah." Moses added to the no-no list, suet, the flesh of animals that had died and not been slaughtered in a ritual manner. Then some quote the Talmud's line that forbids foods that "pollute the body and mind."

This Is a Jewish Cookbook

It is *not* a kosher one. It, however, does not include any shellfish recipes, and almost no meat dishes cooked with butter or cream. Such non-Jewish cookery can be found in any of many good cookbooks planned along other ethnic lines.

Leo Rosten, a much respected Jewish scholar, sums up the situation: "The strict observation of *kosher* laws has declined drastically among Western Jews . . ."

Are There Exclusive Jewish Foods?

> Outside of Hungary if there is any life
> it is not the same.
>
> *Ferenc Molnár*

Special Jewish foods? Not in the sense that there are vegetables, fruits, spices that *only* Jews know and use. Even the sacred matzo of Passover now comes in packaged supermarket mutations as "egg matzo," and "chocolate matzo." The herring, which many once suspected as being strictly a Jewish delight, is actually adopted from the North Sea and Baltic people: Scandinavians, the Dutch, Germans, Russians. *Lax,* the Swedish name for salted salmon, became in America the lox of Bagel and Lox. But it was *unknown* to Eastern Jews! The potato latke (pancake) was actually a late-comer into Europe. "Only the Irish and cattle would eat the potato or South American tuber up until the near middle of the 18th century." And there was a German potato pancake created at the same time as the latke. What makes Jewish cooking Jewish in concept is that it adopted, with its own variations, the cuisine of the country it helped settle and make prosper, often *improved* certain dishes by the elimination of hog lard (lard is now recognized as a deadly creator of cholesterol and has disappeared from much of modern cooking). Jewish dishes *refined* the spicing and introduced a *better* use of the onion, a daring touch of garlic, a skill in the use of chicken and goose fat, and the more pungent so-called kosher salt (which you can buy in the better food shops and is superior for much cooking to the usually overrefined commercial salt).

How Healthy Is Jewish Food?

It was cleaner, more healthy, in most recipes—but it didn't know about calories, yet furnished vitamins—unknowingly. Its insistence on separate sets of pots and pans and dishes for milk and the meat dishes lessened danger of food contamination. And it was, best of all, cosmopolitan; in a Europe of bad roads, of savage times, and nationally enforced restrictions, it moved its delicacies across borders, brought new dishes to the attention of stay-at-homes, expanded the diet. Red-bearded Jews (as seen in Chinese Tang pottery seated on camels) brought back tea from Asia, the noodle, the filled dumpling, all from far-off China, the Middle Kingdom. Corn meal, mamaliga, was spread by Jewish travelers from Romania (after Indian maize appeared in Europe) into Russia and Poland and became in time the polenta of Italy, the corn balls of North Africa, fried in peanut oil.

The roasting of the holiday chicken or goose became a special art, and no historian of food can really get to the core, to that moment a dish comes over from Jewish cooking into a national cuisine, and just *when* the recipes made the journey from the peasant's hut and the duke's palace into the ghetto of a Polish Pale or to the mansion of the Jewish barons, de Hirsch, de Rothschild, or de Günzberg. (It was Edmund de Rothschild who quoted the old saying, "Cooks are made, roasters are born.")

Are There Separate Ethnic Jewish Variations of Cooking?

At the turn of the century, Jewry was those Spanish Jews who went into exile and had settled in Holland, France, Italy, and called themselves Sephardic Jews; the German Jews, called the Deutsche Yehudim, next in self-importance, in good eating, and the largest group the Jews of the Ashkenazim faith, Eastern European Jews, mostly of Polish-Russian, Romanian backgrounds. Basically, the ritual laws made the cooking of all three groups similar. Yet each group brought with them in their journeying around the earth, the flavors and seasoning, the adoption of the native dishes from those places where they had often spent centuries as doctors, teachers, bankers, artisans, traders, weavers, shopkeepers, farmers.

The Pale (palisade or enclosure)
of Settlement

What helped keep the Jews stay bound together as a collection of people, and creators of their special cuisine, were the brutal orders of the Czars that confined the Jews to isolated places, a people not allowed to move about; abused by a power, an absolute power that held them captive in twenty-five provinces of Holy Russia. To go outside, to live away from the village, special permission was needed, as we have noted. Some skilled workers, businessmen, professional figures, did manage to get such permits, even if by purchase and bribery. But the majority of the Jews lived in restricted areas until World War I. They could be brutally moved on, with only what they could carry away, at the whim of some official or governor. These Jews, barred from most higher education, land-holding, government positions, became peddlers, shopkeepers, fish-

sellers, cobblers, tailors, truckers, milkmen (also a few artists, writers, bankers). Their villages were called shtetls or shtetlach, and in confinement the Jews bred as pious, superstitious folk, stubborn to change. They persisted, as pogroms came and went, with extra taxes, brutal exploitation.

All this only intensified their own precious culture, their love of their holy texts, their rites. *And* a taste for their food and cooking at a time when some actually starved to death in bad years.

Besides an interest in food and its preparation that hungry, exploited people have—their isolation as groups was always menaced, always in danger; their food in their huddled life took on an originality. Ritual food feeding a people engaged in eternal debate and paradox; rueful, wary, witty. A style that extended to their Friday-night candlelighting, the realistic delight in chopped liver, a good fat herring, the smell of a properly roasted goose. Even a dish of boiled flanken, or a simple plate of soup.

When the First World War ended the confinement of the Pale, many Jews went to the cities, to the streets and factories of Petrograd, Odessa, to the worldly debates and universities of Moscow and Kiev. Polish Jews trooped to Warsaw and Lodz. Jews entered the ranks of visionaries, as unionists, social democrats, the false dreams of Marxist-Leninist revolution. It was a complete break from the pious village life of the past, a life perhaps medieval in style, isolated in danger. Now free, torn by ambivalence, a new generation lost much of its shtetl respect for ritual and tradition, even for the Jewish Cook-Mother Syndrome. The respect for kosher food began to weaken. Only the older Orthodox still tried to keep the kashrut.

But it is interesting that what survived, almost whole, *was* the Jewish cuisine; modified, changed some, expanded, yet the basic dishes, special foods, and ways of preparing them remained with many of the released Jews. And with those who had earlier managed to find a place in the cities.

Holidays at Table

Jewish holidays were in the main days of memory, sorrow, joy in creation, celebrations of survival, and thanks for God's assistance in times of trouble or turmoil. Each holiday has some special dish, a baking, a pungent delight.

ROSH HASHONAH (Day of Judgment, starting the Ten Days of Penitence) is the beginning of the New Year. To sweeten the hope of a happy year, after the ram's horn (the Shofar) is blown, the honey cake is popular; date-nut torte, poppy seed candy, macaroons (in Latin America even a banana cake), and various forms of the fruit stew tzimmes were expected.

YOM KIPPUR (Day of Atonement) calls for a day of fasting (no washing or wearing shoes) and prayer. But the food that is served before the sun goes down on the preceding day has to be substantial to last out the twenty-four-hour period until the next sunset. As drinking of water is also forbidden, the seasoning must be kept bland, and no thirst-producing dish be presented. Boiled chicken is served, a mild chicken soup, the braided bread (the challah), stewed fruits, sponge cakes, and *lots* of tea. And in the United States, celery tonic and soda water (seltzer) from pressure bottles.

SUCCOTH (Festival of Tabernacles or Feast of Booths) lasts for seven days in Israel and among the Reform; eight days for the Orthodox. Once celebrating the harvest times—some eat today in an outdoor booth (succah). It could be called the Jewish Thanksgiving (even if some Jews were in the Western Hemisphere [Mexico] *before* the Pilgrims). It is the happiest of holidays; viewing the stars, the flowers and fruit decorating the booth. A sense of celebration and joy was the proper note of Succoth, in a hut suggesting the forty years' wandering in the wilderness. Meals are big; appetizers of chicken wings, boiled beef, kreplach (the filled dumplings) much in evidence, and stuffed cabbage steaming hot, sweet and sour, with fillings of rice and chopped meat. All to aid the great Hosanna—(Hoshanah Rabbah) a procession of chanting.

CHANUKAH (Festival of the Lights) for the Jewish heroes, the Maccabees' victories, took all of eight days and was a time of comparing gifts. Cheerfulness and good food was the rule, besides loud gaiety. Cakes and cookies were of the richest egg and butter content, pastries filled with raisins, nut meats. The pancake was almost ritual; both the potato pancake of brown crispness, and the cheese pancake, rich, and eaten very hot.

To fully understand Chanukah, the Feast of Dedication, which comes on the twenty-fifth day of Kislev in the Hebrew calendar (usually in December) and is the only important Jewish holiday *not* mentioned in the Bible (but only in the books of the Maccabees that are part of the Apocrypha, and also found in the text of the Greek historian Polybius, 204?–122? B.C.), one can begin with the death of Alexander the Great in 323 B.C. His generals then divided his empire among themselves. Judea, after several generations of fighting, became the property of Greek-thinking Syrian kings. In 175 B.C. (sorry about all these dates) Antiochus IV ruled the Jews. He objected to their distinctive way of life, the respect they showed not to him but to the holy of holies, their Temple. Seeking a more direct control of the Jewish population, he removed the Hebrew high priest Onias from power and raised in his place Onias' more co-operative brother, Joshua. Joshua, like Antiochus, was Greek-oriented as to their culture, philosophy, hedonism. He changed his name to Jason, then proceeded to attempt the Hellenization of the Jews. He got many of them to wear Greek costumes, and he led the younger priests from the services in the Temple to enter into Greek sports and habits. Assimilation took place; Judaism grew feeble. But a group who called themselves the Pietists (Hasidim) went underground to keep the old true form of their faith alive.

In 168 B.C., Antiochus, sensing this defiance, decided to break the stiff-necked zealots who still obeyed the laws of Moses and of the God of Sinai. The king established a national church into which *all* the religions of his subjects were to merge in a worship of the Greek Zeus, and he the king was proclaimed—by himself—to be a splendid deity—incarnation on earth as Epiphanes—God Manifest. On pain of death all Jews were

forbidden to set themselves aside as ritual Jews, and the Temple services were ordered to be set up for Zeus worship.

In the town of Modin (today Ara'in), an old Hebrew priest, Mattathias, refused the new order of things and set up resistance. The king had caused the Jewish towns to be looted, burned, pillaged. Men were slain, and women and children sold into slavery. Mattathias and his five sons, the Maccabees, escaped into the mountains, there to mount a revolt. A war of Judaic rebels against the great Syrian empire; a condition somewhat like that in Vietnam in the last few years.

Judah, third son of Mattathias, trained a guerrilla band, and armed them as best he could. Opposing him were not only the trained, well-fed armies of Antiochus' generals, but also many renegade Jews who had been assimilated. Yet in furious fights, magnificent actions, the Maccabees won four great battles. At the pass of Emmaus, the enemy was sent fleeing in a great military rout. Yet before the battle of Mizpah the Syrian general was already selling futures in captive Jews as slaves—those he hoped to take in the battle. Judah, however, took a great victory, moved on to capture the Temple. He broke the pagan altars, and then, to the great rejoicing of the people, rededicated the place to the God of Israel. The anniversary of this restoration and eight days of festival and dedication is what is celebrated among the Jews today as Chanukah. The nine-branched candlestick is ritual. The war itself went on for years. The Maccabee brothers were killed or assassinated, all but Simon, the last brother. Simon, in 142 B.C., won complete freedom for the Jews to serve their own God. He became the leader of Judah and its high priest.

Chanukah is actually a holiday celebrating the victory of Jewish values over Greek ones. Jehovah against Zeus, of Hebrew ideals bound by the Torah to moral ways of life set against Greek hedonism delighting in the pursuit of sensual and aesthetic pleasures. To make it very simple: the Greeks saw their godhead in beauty, the Hebrews' interpretation of beauty meant living by divine law. The Maccabeean revolt was in the end a battle to safeguard the actual identity of the Jew. It made clear that to tamper with the Temple, with traditional religious rites, would always mean a destruction of the Jews' distinctiveness, a dissolution of his identity. So Chanukah remains the most popular of all holidays.

PURIM, Feast of Lots (Rescue of the Jews from a massacre in Ancient Persia) a day of happy meetings, reunions, masquerades, dances. Talking over old times and new prospects and devouring an ancient historic item like the prune-filled hamantaschen (named for the tyrant Haman, whom the Jewish Queen Esther caused to be hanged), or the knish, and poppy seed cakes.

PASSOVER (Festival of Deliverance from Egypt) is the housewives' time of hard work and ritual searching out of crumbs. The two sets of dishes and pots, cutlery, used every day (one for meat foods, one for dairy foods) are to be put away, and closets and kitchens washed, scrubbed, and made pure. New sets of dishes, pots, pans, for eight days of Passover, and even cutlery brought out of storage, washed and purified and then stored after use for the eight-day period. Bread is forbidden of course, and every last bit in any hidden corner searched out and removed from the house. Forbidden also is yeast, baking soda, to symbolize the hasty flight from Egypt when there was no time to let the bread rise. (We shall describe a ritual Passover Seder below.) For the week of Passover feeding, there is roast fowl, gefilte fish, the matzo ball in rich chicken soup, the blintz, the knish, the borsch (hot or cold, cabbage or beet), and *always* fried matzo (matzo-brie).

Passover folklore states the first Hebrews as having tribal beginnings with patriarchs leading them in wanderings into many parts of the ancient world. They were as yet without the religious revelations to come from Sinai. Many were assimilated by the people of Canaan, but a large group, according to the Bible, called the people of Jacob, moved south to the land of Goshen (now Wadi Tumilat) in the eastern Nile Delta, in the middle of the second millennium, much in the manner of Americans homesteading in the nineteenth century. In Egypt, they lived a pastoral existence, the life of herdsmen and harvesters.

Then, as is written, "A Pharaoh arose," who oppressed them into serfdom and slavery. They were forced to make bricks, existed under harsh taskmasters in hard manual labor. For the Pharaohs were great builders of huge, nearly useless monuments to their vanities. Who was this Pharaoh? Some Bible historians have identified him as Thutmose III, others as Rameses II. No matter who, the oppression went on until the nineteenth Dynasty, in the thirteenth century B.C., and the slogan of the Jews was to be: Remember your bondage in Egypt where we ate the bread of affliction.

It was the time of the Exodus and the appearance of the imposing figure of Moses, to lead them toward the one God, and the establishment of a Jewish nation. Moses "created" the Hebrew people. We all know the Moses story, of how a daughter of the Pharaoh found him, an abandoned baby in the rushes, hidden there by his mother to keep him from being slain. How he grew up as a favorite in the royal court, and yet was sad at the bondage of the Jews. One day, witnessing the flogging of a Hebrew serf, he killed the taskmaster and fled to the desert, where he came to know God as Yahweh, and so went back to save his people.

Also well known is the Exodus, the escape from Pharaoh, the crossing of the Red Sea. Moses led the Jews to Mount Sinai, where they received their sacred religious responsibilities, their moral and social codes. Slaves just yesterday, now they were a people with souls. They had God's laws; hard, stern, desert laws, fitted to the principles of nomad living, the wandering for many years before settling to raise up a nation when at last they came to Canaan. Moses died before the final settling, and the tradition is that God kissed him as he died "and no man knows his sepulcher."

The philosopher Ahad Ha'am called Moses "A pillar of light on the doorstep of history." And so the Passover celebrates the journey, the release from bondage, and escape from Egypt, the coming over as a people with a godhead and a nation. It also celebrates the beginning of the early harvests. For the Passover is actually more than an event connected with the deliverance from Egypt. It also expressed the knowledge of the value of arriving at Sinai, the acceptance of a special mission as a people moving from darkness to light; from pagan shame and ignorance to a glory and a destiny that was to produce the Psalms of Praise to God. . . . For, as Exodus related it, God will come to Israel as a lover singing to his beloved and win her as his own. So Passover celebrates not only that journey from Egypt, but a continuing experience involving all generations right up to today; for the people have been on *many* roads, escaping from other tyrants, and needing divine sustenance. And understanding that deliverance comes not just from God, but also by one's own efforts.

The Seder ceremony of Passover night is not only the recalling of what once was, what happened, but in a larger sense it is an inspired way of bringing together the past, the present, and what will be the future. Binding all three into one solid experience. It can be read as saying that all Jews, not just those who fled the Pharaoh, move toward a Red Sea, and all are set on a journey called eternal time. All are *always* at Sinai in the Presence of God. The clarifying text is there in the Haggadah: "Every man in every generation must look upon himself as if he himself had come forth out of Egypt. It is not our fathers alone that the Holy One redeemed, but ourselves also did he redeem with them." It is the significance of the Exodus that *is* the Passover. Whatever historic reality it ever had is still being re-enacted.

THE FAMILY SEDER AT PASSOVER. The most ritual and cherished of all
Jewish holidays, it recalls at table in the text of Exodus, the deliverance
of the Jews from Egypt, from slavery over 3200 years ago. The first and
second nights of Passover (Pesach) are celebrated by a family gathering
called the Seder ("order-of-procedure" is a feeble translation). It is a
meal of feasting *and* of a religious service. A feasting on unleavened
food eaten on plates used only for this holiday.

Gathered are the sons and daughters, sons-in-law, daughters-in-law,
all the children, old aunts and uncles, grandparents, invited strangers, to
mark the people of the Disapora with holy rites (da Vinci's painting,
"The Last Supper," with Christ presiding, was of a Passover Seder.)

Set out on the best family tablecloth, in the golden glow of candles, is
the symbolical meal of the Exodus and the slavery. The unleavened
bread of flight (the matzo); harsh herbs and horseradish for bitter generations of slavery; a baked or roasted egg and a lamb bone to suggest
offerings once brought to the Temple. And the charoseth, a mush of apples, chopped nuts, and cinnamon all wet with wine to take the place of
the clay with which Hebrew slaves made bricks. Added as a dish was
salt water (for tears). This symbolic still life is not for eating. Nor is the
green sprig of parsley to signify this is a spring holiday.

Wineglasses stand at each place, even the small children will get a
few drops of wine and much soda water. The head of the house reclines
on a pillow (an echo of Roman banqueting), and looks over his family
and the invited strangers. A prayer is said over the matzos and all the
adults remember old sorrows and past dangers of their wandering for
generations.

To re-enact the Passover and explain it, the youngest child asks the
"Four Questions" (Fier Kashehs). In a usually piping voice, he asks his
father: "*Why* do we eat unleavened bread? *Why* the bitter herbs? *Why*
dip them in salt water? *Why* do we recline at table?"

The father begins the history: "Slaves were we unto Pharaoh . . ."
The Haggadah, a historic text, is also read, a narrative of events leading
to crossing the Red Sea. When the ten plagues that God sent down on
the Egyptians is read aloud, everyone spills out a few drops of wine from
his glass as each plague is named.

That done, the holiday food is served. After the feasting on chopped
herring, liver, the fish, meat, fowls, the fruit stews, the cakes, a large
glass of wine is set down in the open doorway. This is for the Prophet
Elijah, and a chant of welcome is added. For it is written that Elijah is
the herald who will announce the Messiah, he who will someday pro-
claim God's Appearance on this earth.

After 1878, a song, "Hatikva," was usually sung—written in that year it became the anthem of the Zionists, and later the national anthem of the State of Israel.

SHAVUOTH (Festival of the Torah) lasts for two days. It is a dedication to the basic dogma and ritual of the Hebrews, as expressed in the sacred scrolls, the Torah. It calls for light dairy eating for most, the cold schav (sorrel soup), the various blintzes with cheese or jam fillings, also meat patties of assorted kinds. A time of tzimmes, and fillets of herring taken from the brine, and soaked or pickled, fried, or baked.

Holidays That Call for Fasting

Other holidays that call for fasting are TSOM GEDALIAH, and ASERETH B'TEBET. So the best food is provided for the family and guests *before* the sunset of the preceding day. . . . A fast for all past disasters is the holiday of TISHA BOV, commemorating the Destruction of the First Temple in Jerusalem (586 B.C., by Babylonians), and the razing of the Second Temple (A.D. 70, by Romans). Tisha Bov comes after the nine days of mourning, during which meat cannot be eaten, nor marriages performed. In some modern temples a text on the Hitler catastrophe has been added to other communal lamentations.

Prayer and Food

To the Jew eating and drinking are true religious acts. For, it was said, in the process of feeding ourselves we partake of God's bounty. So each meal for the pious Jew begins with a benediction of thanks, and is finished with the saying of grace. (St. Paul, by the way, in the Acts of the Apostles, also asks Christians to give up the blood from meat, and the flesh of strangled animals.)

So complex became the dietary laws, that only a shrewd learned rabbi could in time explain all the nuances of what food could be eaten, how to prepare and cook it. What may also have begun as a method of sanitation in iceless and prerefrigeration times, in eras of unsanitary procedures, has persisted into modern times. Some see in kashrut a way for the Jew, individually and as a group, to keep his identity and his people intact, attached to a creed.

All primitive people have food taboos, rites of animal sacrifice, themes of purification and propitiation, and see some symbolic strengths in what they eat. Wrote Rabbi Eli Secundus in 1969, "Kosherness gave to food the proper respect of it as God's gift. Much of this is lost today in prepackaged TV dinners and adulterated, dyed products. The chemically-doctored, preserved, plastic-enclosed packaging. The Jews may well have been the first organic food addicts."

Friday Night—The Sabbath

The European Jew, living for centuries among bigoted peasants and cruel ruling classes, was officially an outcast, always in danger of death by mob and government instigations. He had one bright weekly moment; he looked forward to Friday night, the beginning of the Shabbes ("rest from labor" in Hebrew). Shabbes, the Sabbath, was also called "the Queen [or the Bride] of the week."

Friday, from dawn on, was baking and cooking, plucking fowl, chopping liver and fish. Cooking done by a mishpocheh (family and relatives), mother, daughters, daughters-in-law, an aunt, an advice-giving bubbe (granny), all were usually part of the bustle of preparing for the Shabbes. No matter how poor the family, the goal would be an attempt to provide the gefilte fish of pike or carp, the chicken soup with mandlen or knaidel (baked dough or dumplings), a tzimmes of stewed fruits, a steaming potato kugel, the braided bread (the challahs), painted with egg yolk to shine like gold in the light of the brass candlesticks.

One bathed before dusk, put on fresh garments as the Shabbes began.

In the villages there was whispering that on this night angels were near, that the stars were brighter. Some even saw holy figures seated in the sky on golden thrones. Isaac Bashevis Singer remembers the Friday-night mood in candlelight and the scent of spices as "an atmosphere of wonder and miracles."

Jews in mortal danger, even being condemned to death, had cried out, "The saviour of the Jews is the Sabbath."

It was the Jewish mother—her one moment as a priestess—who lit the candles and offered the benediction. She shut her eyes and made passes over the burning candles with her hands. She recited, "Blessed art Thou, O Lord, our King of the Universe, Who has sanctified us . . . has commanded us to kindle the Sabbath lights." She also asks God to bless the food, to preserve the family, grant health and peace.

The two challahs are covered with a decorated cloth; near by the Kiddush cup of wine stands ready to sanctify the Shabbes. A few more prayers come from the father, perhaps even a verse to his wife from

"Eshes Chayil" ("A Woman of Valor"), which comes over rather lamely into English:

> She is clothed in strength and honor
> She speaks with a mouth of wisdom
> Her children stand, and call
> Her blessed
> And her husband speaks in praise of her . . .

After which there is only the time of satisfaction in eating, talking over the week, questioning the children. But *no* talk of business or money affairs.

The devout Jew could not carry cash on the Sabbath, ride, bake, plow(!), or carry *any* object not of a ritual nature. The very pious didn't even carry a handkerchief, but pinned one to their outer garments.

As the Friday candles guttered, and the last dish was removed, walnuts cracked, the atmosphere retained its warmth, its intimacy. Usually present was a poor man or a stranger, or a student, the hospitality guest, called the family's oyrech. Not to have an oyrech to Friday-night dinner was to abuse an ancient custom. It was a habit that made Jews into a universal group; none were ever strangers in a strange place.

The Recipes

Great care and much time went into this book. Each recipe has been prepared with admiration and care and presented in detail. Each is a dish we have ourselves eaten, some prepared in our home, mostly all observed in their place of origin.

There is a difference, to a serious cookbook compiler, in a dish found in cold print, or seen on a TV show, and actually sitting at table while the wife and daughters, the cook, are busy in the kitchen, and a well-filled table of guests greets each dish with a cheerful comment or a smile. Often there is a story relating to the dried mushroom soup, or a rich uncle's heartburn after a bride's first cholent.

Measurements and oven temperatures have been worked out with care, sometimes translated from world and European units. Certain overexotic dishes have been eliminated, such as goose blood soup. Most of the cooked brain, heart, gizzard, lung dishes, too, remain in our files; just one or two show how these actually savory, tasty items can be prepared.

No ingredients have been included that cannot be bought in most markets, and certainly in city specialty shops. It is assumed that when baking is called for, you will preheat the oven to the temperature listed; that you will understand "pinch of salt and pepper to taste" is geared to your own sense of taste and smell (much pleasure in food comes directly from the nose); and that you have established a personal ideal salt-and-pepper balance in your cooking. Cooking oils that can be used are corn oil, peanut oil, soybean oil—or shortening (white refined vegetable oil in solid form). In some cases we have given the modern equivalents for the original ingredients, such as a few frozen or canned items available in vegetables or fruits, even packaged noodles. Use blenders, foils, canned beef, and chicken stocks, too, *if* you so desire.

It may be you need to train your butcher to chop, saw, cut, and shape properly the meat you buy. We no longer pluck or gut our own fowl. Some gourmets insist liver and fish chopped by hand is superior to grinders or blenders.

Portions and Other Items

Each recipe notes how many can sit down and get a fair share of each dish. This is the only loose information we give. There are *large* eaters, and *small* eaters, gluttons and lip smackers, dieters and calorie beaters. Prepare about a third more than you figure, if you have more fressers (gourmands) than gourmets on your dinner list. Martinis and highballs, shots of bourbon and scotch, slivowitz or cognac, do numb the taste buds a bit. Save the "L'chayim" for *after* dinner. Margarine can be used in place of butter and the other way round, chicken fat for oil, oil for chicken fat. Many canned or frozen products, if not too watery, are tasty and healthy, *but* fresh vegetables and fruit are still superior in taste and texture. We have found the cast-iron skillet or frying pan cooks food a little better, but needs special care. Most processed cheeses and sausages sold in this country are inferior if mass produced—and often diluted with filler. They merely photograph prettily.

Don't reject an ingredient, such as animal brains, lungs, clarified chicken skin, because you've never tried it before or because your culture doesn't eat it too often.

RUSSIA

> The Lord shall scatter thee among all people,
> from one end of the earth to the other . . .
>
> *Deuteronomy 28:64*

Contrary to such popular entertainment as *Fiddler on the Roof, not* all Jews in Imperial Russia were locked away in small shtetlach (restricted villages). There were in the larger cities, St. Petersburg, Kiev, Odessa, Moscow, important Jewish banking houses such as the Günzburgs', one of whose heirs, Baron Dmitri Günzberg, backed Serge Diaghileff's famous Ballet Russe. The ballet featured Nijinsky in a dance theater and its greatest artist was the Russian Jewish designer Léon Bakst. Jewish tea merchants, Shchukin, Morosov, journeying to Paris to eat at Maxim's, bought the first paintings of Picasso and Matisse before their fame was international, prior to World War I, and the collectors, well fed, brought modern art to Russia, even before Chagall and Soutine left the Czar's domain.

Jewish lawyers, merchants, doctors, dentists (these teeth-fillers often women), made up a society of professional or well-off Jews, existing sometimes on the edge of danger, but usually, by offering gifts to officials and by providing services that strange nation needed, they were not too far from the center of gourmet living. Accounts exist of them entertaining, giving great dinners, mingling on the fringe of a society of middle class hedonism in gypsy cafés. And at home blending the older forms of Orthodox Jewish cuisines with the more traditional Russian recipes. From the herring barrel ("Of all the fish in the sea, herring is king," J. Howell, 1659) to the epicure's caviar, an enterprising Russian Jew felt he was in the Lord's hands when trouble came.

The Barons Günzburg did a great deal to soften the hardships for Russian and Polish Jews. The grandfather was Yevzel Günzburg, a native of Vitebsk, who founded the great Jewish-Russian Y. E. Günzburg Bank of St. Petersburg, the first private banking house of Russia. For the founder of the "Russian House of Rothschild," who ate Orthodox food, the Czar Alexander II acceded to Yevzel being accepted as a Hesse-Darmstadt Baron Günzburg.

When Imperial Russia found itself short of funds to build modern railroads, the Günzburgs secured investing European capital to lay fourteen thousand miles of steel rails, *and* lost some of the dietary laws.

Horace, Baron Günzburg, the son, got important concessions for Jewish merchants of the first guild and permission for Jewish artisans to live and work outside the Pale. He was rather shy about taking the same credit for Jewish prostitutes who also at that time got freedom to move about in their trade.

The grandson was so Russianized that he carried with ease his Slavic name, Dmitri. But even at Monte Carlo with the Ballet Russe, or at the Savoy in London, dining with Fokine, Massine, or Diaghileff, he was several times heard to mention the virtues of the fried matzos of his childhood that a Jewish governess made for him.

There were very prosperous Russian-Jewish farmers with good land-holdings, like the father of Leon Trotsky (his true name was Bronstein), who was a millionaire agriculturist. The surviving core of life that saved the Jews from complete assimilation was remaining in the Russian villages, where the restricted struggling Jews survived with their rituals and their foods. The Jews were not Johnny-come-latelies, but had come into the land before it was a Russia, when it was still pagan steppes, when there was no Russian Orthodox Church, and the first Romanoff was not yet on the throne. Already there were Chinese Tang (A.D. 600) statues of red-bearded Russian-Jewish traders on camels in Asia— bringing back, most likely long before Marco Polo, recipes for noodles (lokshen) and the filled dumpling (kreplach) and, of course, tea (Tchai).

There were Jews in the land in A.D. 986, when the heathen Grand Duke Vladimir, seventh ruler of Russia, almost accepted Judaism, but in the end decided on the Church, and so Jews were not permitted to enter or settle the country. After the Crusades, a time of great German per-secution of Hebrews, the German Jews began to emigrate into Russia and Poland with pots and recipes. By the fifteenth century, five million Ashkenazic Jews (German in *Hebrew*) were making Jewish-Russian cooking a special cuisine, the bedrock of much of what is today called Jewish cooking.

In 1791, Catherine (called the Great), once a German ruling the Russias, established the Pale of Settlement, confining her Jewish subjects to certain shtetlach areas, and restricted conditions. The rest is history neither pleasant nor part of this book.

In long centuries of existence, the Russian Jews perfected their pungent dishes, created new ones, from Russian tradition in food, which they converted to the Orthodox ritual manner in the preparing of their food. This almost right up to the Revolution of 1917. Generations of Jews delighted in Kievski cutlets, orechnevaia kasha (buckwheat groats). From Romania they imported, made the popular mamaliga (ground corn meal). The cooks became experts in not breaking ritual laws in their use of tvorozhniki (cottage cheese), smetana (sour cream), and avoiding mixed dairy and meat dishes. Herring became an edible delight—schmaltz, matjes, herring in various combinations, pickled, fried, in salads, were made a table art. The garlicky kosher dill pickle in brine survives in every supermarket today. The strict ritualists shunned the sturgeon and its caviar, all shellfish, oysters, clams, lobsters, and crabs. But the city Jews in many cases saw caviar as a social status, and a *very* appetizing part of the zakuski (hors d'oeuvres).

Improved were soups of beets, cucumbers, cabbages. The various borsches, hot or cold, became Jewish delights, for they took on a difference, slight, but yet important to the palate. The wives made their own versions of the pirog and piroshki, and they perfected the potato latke and the potato kugel, the fruit-and-the-vegetable tzimmes, calf's foot jelly (petcha), the cold sorrel soup (schav), and the proper use of the chicken. Also the duck and the goose, to dominate the table for the family or its guests on High Holidays, social events, or just to get together.

Jewish life was *not,* as popular tradition has made it, a chicken fat culture; the prime ingredient of the backwater villages. There was much more. Great and small Russian-Jewish families have left us memoirs, journals, handwritten kitchen daybooks, recipes that show to what delectable heights Jewish cooking could reach when in harmony with the Russian cuisine. Sholom Aleichem added a few footnotes.

The samovar steamed nearly at all times (not on the Sabbath). At the Jewish fetes, weddings, bar mitzvahs, anniversaries, some greetings of honored guests, native or from abroad, the wine was—if affordable—often imported from France. Tokay from Hungary, the best of the Rhine valley vineyards. The native stuff was Caucasian and Crimean, *not* the best of Europe's vintages. In the cities there was drinking of vodka, then distilled from potatoes, but in the villages the Jews enjoyed most a tot of slivowitz (a Polish plum brandy) after Sabbath services, a bris (circumcision), or one for the road. There were few heavy Jewish drinkers, but a great interest in food. "A wife who could braid challah [a Friday-night bread], make matzo balls soft as a feather bed was a prize above rubies." (Tante Longstrasse's kitchen daybook.)

The modern bagel was not to be invented until 1863, and in Vienna at that, but the baranki was there, a round flat dough cake baked and sprinkled with poppy seeds. The house where the pancake called blini (of buckwheat flour and yeast) was served as a platform for salt herring, or caviar, covered with grated onion, sour cream, was the true sign a Russian Jew had arrived socially.

Meat

RUSSIAN-JEWISH CHOPPED CHICKEN LIVERS

The basic shtetl recipe on which most variations around the world are based.

4 Spanish onions, chopped fine
1 cup rendered chicken fat, with grieben (rendered skin)

1 pound chicken livers
½ teaspoon each, salt, pepper
4 hard-boiled eggs

Put onions in a skillet over medium heat. Cover skillet, allow onions to steam in their juice until almost dry. Add ½ cup of chicken fat, and sauté onions until golden brown. When onions are done, remove from pan, leaving excess fat. Put chicken livers in pan, season, and sauté 4 minutes. Sprinkle with salt and pepper. Put onions, livers, and grieben through meat grinder, with hard-boiled eggs. Add pan drippings. Mix well with spoon. Taste and correct seasoning. Add rest of fat. Pack into 1-quart jar, top with a little chicken fat. Will keep for 2 weeks.
Makes 1 quart.
10–12 servings.

CHOPPED BEEF LIVER

Chicken livers may be the queen of all chopped livers, but heretics speak highly of the beef livers in a Jewish pâté.

1 pound beef liver
1 medium onion, cut up
1 green pepper, cut up

2 hard-cooked eggs
15 dry crackers
Salt, pepper to taste

Slice liver into cubes and place in skillet. Barely cover with water, cover, cook until liver is tender. Remove liver from water and add onion and green pepper. Cover, cook until vegetables are tender. Grind liver, cooled, with vegetables, eggs, crackers. Season to taste with salt and pepper. Add water from vegetables to give consistency. Mold. Chill 4 hours.
4 servings.

PETCHA (CALF'S FOOT JELLY)

Russian Jews, in exile, sometimes bring tears to their eyes when they speak of this dish. Actually it's not too difficult to make, if care is taken to follow directions.

2 calf's feet, chopped into
    fragments
2 onions
4 cloves garlic

1 tablespoon salt
½ teaspoon freshly ground pepper
3 quarts water
4 hard-boiled eggs

Your butcher will chop up the feet if you charm him. Pour boiling water over feet. Soak 5 minutes, and then scrape them with a knife. Put feet in a saucepan with onions, garlic, salt, pepper, and water. Bring to a boil, cook over low heat 3½ hours. Strain, reserve the soup. Cut all the meat from the bones. Put the soup and meat into a casserole and chill overnight. Sprinkle with pepper and slices of hard-boiled egg, and serve with grated horseradish.
6 servings.

CHANUKAH PICKLED TONGUE

1 (4-pound) smoked tongue
2 cups white wine vinegar
2 onions, sliced
½ cup sugar

2 tablespoons pickling spice in
 cheesecloth
2 bay leaves

Place the smoked tongue in a large kettle, add water to cover, bring slowly to a boil, skim the surface. Simmer tongue, covered, over low heat for 3 hours, until it is tender: Let tongue cool in the stock. Skin the tongue, trim off end and gristle—slice the tongue very thin. Chill the stock, remove the fat. In a saucepan combine 2 cups of the stock with white wine vinegar, onions, sugar, and pickling spice. Bring the mixture to a boil and simmer for 5 minutes. Discard spice bag. Pour over tongue. Garnish it with bay leaves. Chill the tongue on a flat serving platter.
8 servings.

HOME CORNED BEEF WITH VEGETABLES

3 pounds beef brisket
1 clove garlic
1 teaspoon saltpeter
2 tablespoons salt
4 potatoes, peeled

½ head of cabbage, washed,
 cored
6 carrots
2 tablespoons pepper
1 tablespoon ginger

Put the beef in 4-quart pot and add whole garlic clove and saltpeter. Pour cold water in pot to cover. Let this stand 10 days in refrigerator. Simmer in its salted water for 2 hours until tender. Add potatoes, cabbage, carrots, pepper, ginger, and cook 45 minutes until tender.
6 servings.

BOEUF OREL

3 pounds chuck roast
Salt
1 carrot, diced
1 onion, chopped
2 stalks celery, diced
1 sprig parsley
3 cloves

¼ teaspoon coarse black pepper
Pinch each, sage, rosemary,
   marjoram, sweet basil, bay leaf
3 cups California burgundy or
   other red dinner wine
3 tablespoons margarine

Begin to season roast on both sides with salt. Put the meat in a bowl. Add all other ingredients except margarine. Cover, refrigerate 2 days, turning once a day. Drain meat, reserve marinade. Brown meat on both sides in margarine, add wine marinade. Simmer 2½ hours until meat is tender. Serve with mamaliga (corn meal pudding).
4 servings.

BEEF WITH HORSERADISH SAUCE

4 pounds top round steak, cut in
   2-inch cubes
½ cup chicken fat
2 large onions, thinly sliced
2 teaspoons curry powder
1 teaspoon ground ginger
1 teaspoon salt

½ teaspoon freshly ground
   pepper
1 cup cider
2 tablespoons prepared
   horseradish
2 tablespoons freshly chopped
   parsley

Preheat oven to 300°. Brown meat in 4 tablespoons chicken fat; remove to casserole. Brown onions in remaining fat. Add to casserole along with curry powder, ginger, salt, pepper, and cider. Bake, covered, in slow oven 3 hours, till meat is tender. Just before serving, combine horseradish and some of the pan juice; stir into meat with parsley.
5 servings.

PEPPER BEEF BRISKET

3½ pounds boneless fresh beef
  brisket
1 tablespoon whole black
  peppercorns
1½ teaspoons salt

⅛ teaspoon allspice
½ clove garlic, crushed
2 tablespoons fine dry bread
  crumbs
1 onion, sliced

Wipe meat, put on board. With heavy object, pound meat on both sides. With a knife, score meat lengthwise and crosswise, both sides. Put peppers in a small cloth and crush with hammer. Sprinkle meat with crushed peppers, salt, allspice, garlic, and crumbs. Roll lengthwise; tie tightly with string. Put in kettle, add onion, cover with hot water. Cover. Simmer 3½ hours, until tender.
6 servings.

ROAST OF VENISON TROTSKY

We came by this recipe through an old Siberian exile from the Czar's days, a Jewish Marxist who served time in the wilderness with Leon Trotsky. We make no historic claims for it, but venison was a favorite dish of radicals exiled in Siberia's deer-filled forests. Many were Jews— before the heaven of the workers turned anti-Semitic. Whatever its source, we have tried the dish and it is fine eating. In this version, chicken fat has replaced the original bacon drippings.

1 (3-pound) fillet of venison

THE MARINADE:

2 cups dry red wine
1 bay leaf
2 cloves

Pinch of thyme
5 whole black peppercorns

2 tablespoons chicken fat
Salt, pepper to taste
2 onions, chopped
2 carrots, chopped

1 celery stalk, chopped
1 bay leaf
1 cup Chicken Soup

Wash meat in cold water and dry. Put in deep bowl, cover with
marinade. Cover, refrigerate for 48 hours. Remove and dry. Save 1
cup of marinade. Heat chicken fat in a pot, add the meat seasoned with
salt and pepper. Cook over high heat until browned on all sides. Set
meat in roasting pan and put the onions, carrots, celery, and bay leaf
around it. Roast in a 350° oven 30 minutes. Mix the reserve marinade
and soup and baste while meat is cooking. Repeat every 15 minutes
for 1 hour more. Remove roast, slice thin. Set on heated platter. Put pan
with juices and vegetables on top of stove. Reheat, strain, serve in a
gravy boat.
6 servings.

DROVERS' LEG OF LAMB

½ cup mustard   1 clove garlic, sliced
1 (6-pound) leg of lamb   ½ cup dry sherry
Salt, pepper to taste   ½ cup water

Preheat oven to 325°. Smear mustard over lamb. Season with salt
and pepper. Make small slits in lamb, insert garlic. Place lamb in roasting pan and roast at 325° for 2½ hours. Halfway through pour off fat.
Mix sherry and water, pour over roast, baste often. Serve with gravy
below.

LAMB GRAVY

Pan drippings, fat removed   1 cup Chicken Soup
½ cup flour   Salt, pepper, sugar to taste
1 cup water

Heat pan drippings, stir in flour. Gradually add water, soup, and cook
and stir until thickened. Season to taste with salt, pepper, *and* sugar.
Simmer 3 minutes.
8 servings.

CASPIAN SEA LAMB CHOPS

6 (1 inch thick) shoulder lamb chops
1 cup flour
1 teaspoon salt

2 tablespoons oil
2 onions, sliced thin
4 turnips, peeled, sliced
½ cup beef broth or soup

Preheat oven to 325°. Dip lamb chops in flour mixed with salt, set aside. Heat oil in skillet, add onions and cook until tender, *not* brown. Put onion slices in casserole. Set turnips over onions. Brown chops in skillet, both sides. Arrange chops on turnips. Add broth to skillet, heat and scrape off brown bits. Pour over chops. Cover and bake at 325° for 1½ hours until meat is tender. Remove cover last 15 minutes to crisp.
6 servings.

KREPLACH (MEAT-FILLED DOUGH)

The original was most likely Chinese, a recipe brought back centuries ago by Jewish tea traders who went to Asia.

The dough is the same one we give for Soup Noodles. Roll out the dough but do *not* allow it to dry. Shape dough into 2-inch squares with a knife.

THE FILLING:

1 pound beef chuck, in chunks
2 large onions, sliced
2 tablespoons chicken fat

1 egg
Salt, ground black pepper to taste
3 quarts salted water

Fry meat, onions, in fat—force through grinder—add egg, salt, pepper. Mix. One teaspoon of meat goes on each square of dough. Fold over into triangle, pressure-seal edges. Boil in 3 quarts salted water 22 minutes. Serve as is, or put into clear soups.
6 servings.

HOLISHKES (SWEET AND SOUR CABBAGE ROLLS)

The Poles and the Romanians also claim holishkes as *their* own. The Jews have made it world-famous. Rimski-Korsakov and Moussorgsky were reported to like the Jewish version, and, according to Gertrude Stein, the Jewish artist Léon Bakst fed it to the dancers of the Diaghileff ballet.

1 medium head green cabbage, washed, cored	1 (1-pound) can tomato purée
1 pound ground beef chuck	1 lemon, sliced
1 large onion, grated	Juice of 1 lemon
1 large egg	½ cup raisins
½ cup water	1 cup dark brown sugar
Salt, pepper to taste	1 large onion, sliced

Put the cabbage in a large pot, cored side *down,* cover with boiling water. Bring to boil, lower heat, cook 15 minutes more. Drain in colander, cored side *up.* Run cold water all over cabbage to loosen leaves for separating. Drain and separate leaves one by one. Remove some of the thick membrane near core-end of leaf with a sharp knife.

FOR FILLING: In a large bowl mix the meat and grated onion, egg, ½ cup water, salt and pepper to taste. Place a tablespoon of mixture on each cabbage leaf and roll up like a very fat cigar, folding end in, until all meat is gone. Chop remaining cabbage leaves into slices for sauce. In a 4-quart pot with a tight lid, bring to a boil the tomato purée, chopped cabbage leaves, sliced lemon, lemon juice, raisins, brown sugar, pepper, salt, sliced onion. Put rolls of cabbage into sauce, simmer covered for 60 minutes.

6 servings.

CABBAGE STEW

2 medium-sized onions, chopped	½ teaspoon curry powder
2 tablespoons oil	¼ teaspoon pepper
1 pound stew meat, already cooked	1 medium head green cabbage, washed, cored
1 teaspoon salt	3 tomatoes, chopped

Fry the onions in oil, *light* brown. Add cooked meat, salt, curry powder, and pepper. Add water and cabbage. Cook until soft for 20 minutes. Add the chopped tomatoes. Stir all together, heat through and serve.

4 servings.

SWEET AND SOUR STUFFED PEPPERS

6 green peppers
1 pound rough ground beef
½ cup cooked rice
1 onion, grated
½ teaspoon salt
⅛ teaspoon pepper

2 eggs
1 cup tomato purée
Juice of 1 lemon
3 tablespoons brown sugar
Pinch of paprika

Preheat oven to 350°. Cut off stem ends of peppers, remove seeds, membranes. Place in boiling water, simmer 5 minutes. Drain. Combine beef, rice, onion, salt, pepper, and eggs, and stuff the peppers, not too firmly. Place in casserole, add water, 2 inches (keep adding if need be), to cover bottom of dish. Cover, and bake 40 minutes. In pan combine tomato purée, lemon juice, brown sugar, and paprika. Simmer 15 minutes. Pour sauce over peppers, continue to cook uncovered for 10 more minutes.

6 servings.

SWEET AND SOUR BEETS

1 pound beets, cooked, sliced
4 tablespoons sugar
4 tablespoons butter
Salt, pepper to taste

4 tablespoons flour
2 teaspoons vinegar
1 cup sour cream

First drain beets well. Put sugar, butter, salt, and pepper in saucepan. Heat until butter melts. Add flour. Blend in vinegar, cook for 30 seconds. Add beets and heat for 2 minutes. Stir in sour cream. Heat, do *not* boil.

6 servings.

CHOLENT

There is nothing like this dish in any other culture, according to its admirers. Tante Longstrasse in her kitchen daybook wrote: "It [cholent] has killed more old Jews than the best doctors in Vienna, Berlin and St. Petersburg." She had a grand distrust of doctors and lived to a very ripe old age. As far as we know, *she* never served cholent in her own gracious house. But she may have eaten it in her youth, when she traveled with her father, who had something to do with building railroad systems.

To most Eastern Jews, the cholent was the dish that, on Friday afternoon, was carried to the town baker and placed in his oven overnight. At noon Saturday, it was carried home, its clay pot steaming and smoking. Everyone agreed it was a hearty tasty dish. People with no old-fashioned village baker and his oven can use a modern stove.

1 pound dried large lima beans	1 teaspoon paprika
3 large onions, chopped	1 pound potatoes, pared,
¼ cup chicken fat	quartered
3 pounds beef brisket	⅓ cup flour
1 clove garlic, mashed	2 cups Concord grape wine
Salt, white pepper to taste	

First soak the lima beans in water overnight. In a 5-quart pot with a tight lid, brown the onions in fat; remove onions. Rub meat with garlic, salt, pepper, and paprika. Brown on all sides in the hot fat. Add onions, potatoes, lima beans. Sprinkle with flour, add wine, and enough boiling water to cover. Bring to a boil; cover tightly, place in oven. Bake in hot oven (450°) for ½ hour and then turn down to 250° for an hour. It can also be made on top of the stove; simmer slowly 4 hours. Serve in deep soup plates.
6 servings.

One cholent enemy wrote: "The only way to avoid heartburn is to remove the dish from the oven . . . open the kitchen window about ten inches, and dump the cholent into the garbage can."

MEAT BORSCH

Borsch was a dish that played no favorites; the poor tailor, the rich tea or tobacco merchant, all ate basically the same borsch; the well-off and the rich, of course, had *more* meat in theirs. In the eighteenth century, the St. Petersburg Imperial Palace Guards had a Jewish borsch cook who was said to be a genius.

6 quarts water	Salt to taste
2 pounds brisket of beef	3 tablespoons brown sugar
½ pound beef bones	Juice of ½ lemon
8 beets, grated	2 eggs, beaten
2 onions, diced	

In a deep saucepan combine half of the water, meat, and bones. Boil 5 minutes. Drain in colander and wash well under cold water. Return meat and bones to pot. Add 3 quarts water, bring to boil. Add beets, onions, salt. Cover, cook over medium heat 2 hours. Add brown sugar, lemon juice. Cook 30 minutes. Taste to correct seasoning. Beat eggs. Gradually add to hot soup, beating to prevent curdling. Cut meat into slices, serve with soup and with hot boiled potatoes.
8 servings.

ROAST STUFFED DERMA, OR KISHKA (BEEF GUT)

It was the food you could make merry jests about. Yet it was a must item once at Orthodox Jewish weddings. It was a dedicated taste and its lovers described it almost in poetic terms. Sometimes a turkey or goose neck was used instead of a beef casing. No matter, it was a festive delicacy. The kosher butcher knew how to prepare the gut, how to clean it and present it ready to stuff.

2 cups ground beef fat	1 whole beef casing sides sewed,
2 cups flour	ends open
1 cup farina	1 onion, grated
1 large onion, diced	1 clove garlic, crushed
2 tablespoons finely chopped	1 teaspoon paprika
fresh parsley	2 onions, sliced
Salt, freshly ground	1 cup apple cider, or dry white
pepper to taste	wine

Preheat oven to 350° and mix the beef fat, flour, farina, diced onion, parsley, salt, pepper. Stuff skin. Sew openings closed. Rinse under cold water. In a small bowl put grated onion, garlic, paprika, salt and pepper to taste. Mix and rub well on sides of casing. Take a shallow roaster, make a bed of sliced onions, place stuffed kishka on top. Pour apple cider over kishka. Place foil over pan, but see it does not touch the kishka. Roast for ¾ hour. Remove foil. Baste with pan juice, add more if needed. Place in oven for 1 hour, basting every 15 minutes. Remove and allow to stand on platter 2 minutes, then slice. The daring eat the baked casing as well as its contents.

8 servings.

Fowl

NABOB CHICKEN KIEV

"To the village Jew, a Nabob was any member of his race rich enough to own more than two feather beds and a watch chain that didn't turn green . . ."

Isaac Babel, in a letter

4 chicken breasts, skinned, boned
2 tablespoons lemon juice
Salt, white pepper to taste
½ cup margarine
1 teaspoon lemon juice
1 clove garlic, crushed
½ teaspoon dried tarragon
1 teaspoon dried chervil
1 tablespoon freshly chopped
  parsley
3 egg yolks
¼ cup flour
1 cup bread crumbs
1½ quarts vegetable oil

Take up chicken breasts and sprinkle with lemon juice. Season with salt and pepper. Mix the margarine, lemon juice, garlic, and herbs together. Place 1 tablespoon of it on each chicken breast. Roll up the breast, tuck in the sides. Beat egg yolks. Make separate mounds of flour and bread crumbs. Dip chicken breasts in the flour. With a pastry brush dipped in egg yolk, paint the chicken breasts thickly. Roll breasts in bread crumbs. Put oil into a heavy pot with a deep-frying basket. Heat the oil to 370° (use a deep-frying thermometer). Put in chicken breasts two at a time, cook 4 minutes. Heat oven to 250°. Place the fried chicken breasts in a pan in oven for 15 minutes. Serve hot with lots of kasha.

4 servings.

CHICKEN FAT AND GRIEBEN
(RENDERED CHICKEN SKIN)

Chicken fat and the small squares of clarified chicken skin are as vital to much Jewish cooking as olive oil and garlic are to Italian cuisine, chili to Latin American cookery, paprika to certain Hungarian dishes. The layers of yellow fat and the skin of the fowl are removed from the chicken with a sharp knife (the same process is also used for clarifying duck and goose fat).

1 pound unrendered chicken fat and chicken skin
1 small onion, sliced

Take up the chicken fat, cut it into 1½-inch squares, place in a saucepan over low heat. In 5 minutes add the onion. Continue over low heat until onion and bits of skin are brown. Strain into a jar. It keeps indefinitely in the refrigerator. Keep the brown grieben after the chicken fat has been rendered. Reheat crisp and hot, they make a cocktail tidbit, or a spread on a slice of rye bread.
Makes about a pint jar.

PHEASANT SOUVAROFF

The Nabob Jews, the rich, the socially politically protected, who aided the Czar with banking, importing, the building of railroads, did not all observe the ritual laws about Orthodox cooking. Game birds were a problem to local rabbis. Most said *no* to Russian Jews eating them. But the Baron Günzburg, Trotsky's father (Bronstein), and many other well-off folk enjoyed the pheasant in the following Jewish manner, which avoids the usual bacon and pork fat in the recipe.

2 (2 pounds each) pheasants	8 medium truffles
1 cup thick chicken fat	2 ounces Madeira wine
Salt, pepper to taste	2 cups chicken stock
8 ounces pâté de foie gras	1 ounce cognac
½ cup beef fat, sliced	

Preheat oven to 400°. Tie up the birds, pour on chicken fat. Sprinkle with salt and pepper. Roast in oven for 30 minutes. Stuff the birds with foie gras and beef fat. Remove to casserole, adding truffles already boiled in Madeira. Drain fat from the pan in which pheasants were roasted. Flambé chicken stock with cognac, add Madeira in which truffles cooked. Pour sauce over the birds. Place lid on casserole. Put in oven and heat 45 minutes.
4 servings.

HOLIDAY GAME HENS

4 Cornish game hens, thawed	¼ teaspoon salt
Salt, pepper to taste	Pinch of pepper
5 oranges, peeled	½ cup margarine, melted
2 slices day-old bread torn in small pieces	Allowing 1 hen for each guest is best

Preheat oven to 350°. Remove giblets. Season inside and out with salt and pepper. Cut 3 oranges into sections, mix with bread pieces, season with ¼ teaspoon salt, and a pinch of pepper. Spoon mixture into cavities of birds. Close with skewers. Place hens breast side up in a shallow roasting pan. Brush with margarine. Bake uncovered at 350° 1 hour. Squeeze juice of 2 oranges and use to baste frequently. In last 10 minutes of cooking, increase heat to 400° to brown birds. In high gourmet circles the rule was—remove orange stuffing and discard.
4 servings.

NOTE ON A CHICKEN CULTURE

Russian Jews didn't keep dogs, they kept *chickens*. Every housewife had a few pullets sitting on eggs for hatching, and the flock often ran free, pecking and scratching the ground, earning their own living and gobbling house leavings. In bigger towns, the hens lived in coops, and even in the house itself. There was usually a captive goose being force-fed for a High Holiday roasting. But the chicken was the creature close to the average Russian-Jewish table; just a *cluck* away. Not only was the chicken the prime ingredient for the fabled soup, but boiled, roasted, carried cold on journeys, it sustained the family, nourished the sick, and provided a flavoring fat, a frying medium free of the forbidden lards, and the butter in non-dairy dishes. The chicken's head was never chopped off in the brutal Gentile way, but it was eased to the pot by a swiftly slashed neck, after a prayer said for its soul and for its owner by a ritually directed chicken executioner. Chicken plucking was a scratchy trade. Market women knew how to grope a live chicken to see if it was prime with eggs. The poor enjoyed chicken dishes as an event, the rich elevated the fowl into a gourmet item with sauces, fillings, condiments.

BARBECUED CHICKEN WINGS

3 pounds chicken wings   ½ cup Chicken Soup
Salt, freshly ground pepper   2 cloves garlic, chopped
1 cup honey   2 tablespoons tomato sauce

Preheat oven to 350°. With sharp knife cut off small wing tips and discard. Cut the remaining pieces of wings in half and place in a baking pan. Combine all ingredients, pour over wings. Bake at 350° 1 hour. Serve on a bed of rice.
15 servings.

Fish

BAKED CHOPPED HERRING

In the Baltic and North Sea regions, to start a meal without some kind of a herring—fillet, baked dish, fried, pickled—was a sort of social sin. The Russian Jews found the herring, fresh or imported in brine in barrels, not only a tasty filling food at a low price, but also a business a man could enter without too much capital, as a herring merchant. And if he didn't stand himself in the market place by a barrel of herrings, his wife usually did, while he studied the splendid logic of the Talmud and Torah at the shul.

3 herrings	2 tablespoons butter
6 onions, sliced	3 tablespoons heavy cream

Preheat the oven to 350°. Having soaked the herrings in cold water overnight, changing water occasionally to remove the salt, proceed. Skin, bone, and chop herrings into serving pieces about 2 inches wide. In a saucepan put onions, cover with boiling water, bring to a boil, drain. Place herrings in buttered casserole, top with onion slices, and dot with butter. Place in oven. Bake 22 minutes; add the cream and bake 10 minutes more. Recipe should serve 6. *We* never could serve more than 3 people on this portion, once they tasted this dish.

BARON GÜNZBURG'S
MARINATED SALMON IN SOUR CREAM

A rich successful Jewish banker in Russia usually had a dish named after him.

1 pound cooked salmon	6 whole black peppercorns,
Juice of 1 lemon	crushed
2 teaspoons chopped chives	1/4 teaspoon ground cloves
1 cup onion rings	1/2 teaspoon salt
1/4 teaspoon dried rosemary leaves	1 cup sour cream

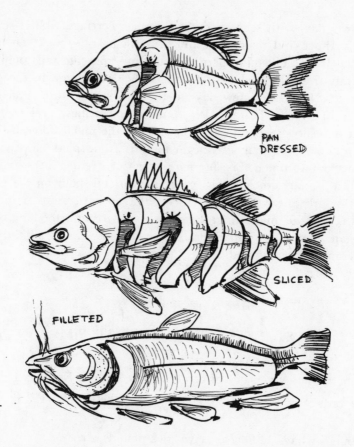

Take cooked salmon and cut into 2-inch chunks. Mix up the remaining ingredients; pour over fish; toss lightly with fork. Chill 2 hours before serving.

4 servings.

PICKLED HERRING WITH MILCH

6 schmaltz herrings	⅔ cup sugar
¾ cup white vinegar	1 tablespoon salt
3 cups water	Milch of 6 herrings
1 tablespoon pickling spices	3 large Spanish onions

First soak schmaltz herrings overnight in water in the refrigerator. Mix the vinegar, water, and pickling spices in saucepan. Bring to a boil. Stir in sugar. Add salt. Let mixture stand overnight at room temperature. Next day, with scissors, cut off fins of herrings. Split open with scissors, remove and reserve the milch. With a knife, make an incision down the backs. Fillet the herrings, starting from the tail, pulling the meat away from the backbone. Small bones that remain in the herring seem to dissolve after a few days in the pickling mixture. Pull off the skins, starting from the tails. Rinse and dry herrings. Peel the onions and cut into slices. Separate into rings. Take the milch, force it through a food mill or sieve. Pour off vinegar mixture from spices, discard spices. Stir vinegar into milch. Fix alternate layers of herring slices and onion rings in a 3-quart crock. When crock is near full, pour on the vinegar-milch mixture to cover. Cover crock, chill in refrigerator a month to 4 months. For the unknowing, the milch in a herring is the long banana-like organ, pinkish-gray in color. You can't miss it—as all the rest of the interior has been gutted.

10–12 servings.

ST. PETERSBURG GEFILTE FISH

There are many versions of gefilte fish in Eastern Europe. This is the basic recipe. Changes in shapes, sizes, seasoning, and types of fish are regional.

2 pounds whitefish, filleted (save head, skin, and bones)	2 pounds carp
	3 eggs
5 onions, sliced	1 cup ice water
2 quarts water	½ teaspoon sugar
4 teaspoons salt	½ cup matzo meal
1½ teaspoons pepper	3 carrots, sliced
2 pounds pike	

Mix head, skin, bones, and 3 onions with 1 quart of water and 1 teaspoon each salt and pepper. Cook on high heat 30 minutes; re-move head, skin, bones. Chop or grind the fish and 2 remaining onions. Set in a chopping bowl, add the eggs, water, sugar, meal, salt and pepper. Chop fine. Wet your hands; shape mix into balls and drop into fish stock. Add carrots. Cover loosely, cook on low heat 1½ hours. Take off cover last 30 minutes. Cool. Remove to a bowl. Strain stock over it, set carrots around fish. Chill well, overnight if you can. Serve with horseradish colored with beet juice.

8–10 servings.

BROILED FISH

The favorite of businessmen with delicate stomachs, *and* rich Jewish widows entertaining a prospect. Salmon, sea bass, and trout can serve as the main item.

2 pounds fish, filleted
Salt, pepper to taste
1 tablespoon lemon juice
1 onion, thinly sliced
2 tablespoons margarine

1 cup dry white dinner wine
1 tablespoon flour
3 tablespoons warm water
6 stuffed olives, sliced
1 teaspoon onion juice

Put fish fillets in greased shallow pan. Sprinkle with salt, pepper, and lemon juice; spread onion slices over whole surface. Dot with margarine and place under broiler. When margarine is melting, baste with wine. Broil, basting frequently until fish flakes, about 20 minutes. Remove to hot platter. Thicken pan liquid with flour mixed with warm water. Add olive slices and onion juice; pour over fish.
4 servings.

RABBI'S SALTED CODFISH

1 pound dried salted codfish
½ cup oil
6 onions, chopped
1 teaspoon chopped parsley
6 scallions

2 pounds cherry tomatoes, chopped
1 clove garlic
1 teaspoon ginger

Soak fish in hot water for 4 hours. Pour oil in pan, fry fish lightly. Remove fish. Add onions, parsley, scallions, and tomatoes. Cook until onions are soft. Strain onions, parsley, scallions, and tomatoes, add garlic and ginger, and simmer with fish another 10 minutes.
4 servings.

FRESH STURGEON IN MARINADE

Popular with unorthodox intellectual radical Jews of the Trotsky set.

1 cup dry white wine	4 sprigs parsley
½ cup water	1 stalk celery, with leaves
4 peppercorns	2 pounds boneless fresh sturgeon
Salt to taste	⅔ cup olive oil
1 small onion	½ cup chopped parsley

Mix wine, water, peppercorns, salt, onion, parsley, and celery in a saucepan. Bring to a boil and simmer for 15 minutes. Add sturgeon. Cover and simmer for 15 minutes. Remove fish from broth. Turn heat under broth up high, reduce till there is only ⅓ cup liquid in pot. Strain, reserve liquid. Slice sturgeon carefully. Mix liquid with olive oil. Pour over slices arranged in a serving dish. Chill overnight. Sprinkle with chopped parsley.
6 servings.

Soup

CHICKEN SOUP

This is the most joked about and notorious item in Jewish cooking. It has been the butt of much humor, and there is rumor of a Ph.D. writing a thesis on the myth and legends of the subject. Actually, the renowned soup takes many forms, and is eaten with noodles, matzo balls, egg drops, kasha, and dumplings. There is an old shtetl joke (that is now universal and blamed on other Eastern European ethnic groups) whose original version is: "If a Jewish farmer eats a chicken, *one* of them is sick."

The following is the basic chicken soup of Russian Jews.

1 (5-pound) chicken, cut in
  quarters, wings and legs
  disjointed, and giblets
1 beef knee bone, split open
Chopped fresh dill
4 stalks celery, with leaves, cut
  up
1 knob celery, pared, quartered

1 large root parsley, with leaves,
  pared
4 large carrots, cut in half
  lengthwise
2 large onions, quartered
Salt, white pepper to taste
1 small bunch fresh curly
  parsley

In a 6-quart pot place chicken, giblets, bone, dill, and all vegetables (except parsley). Cover meat and vegetables with boiling water, bring to a boil, skim, lower heat, simmer 1 hour, covered. Add salt and white pepper to taste. Add parsley to soup. Cover and cook until chicken is tender, 1 hour more. Water is added during cooking if necessary. Always served in large soup plates. *Never* in cups.
6–8 servings.

RIGA LIMA BEAN SOUP

1 pound dried large lima beans
1 soup bone with marrow
1 large onion, chopped
1 green pepper, minced

2 tablespoons olive oil
6 ounces stewed tomatoes, in bits
Salt, pepper to taste

Put lima beans in bowl, add water to cover by 3 inches. Soak overnight. Drain beans, remove skins. In a saucepan cook the beans with bone in salted water 30 minutes, until tender. Discard bone. Drain beans and put through the fine blade of food mill. In a saucepan sauté onion and green pepper in olive oil until golden. Add onion, green pepper, puréed beans, stewed tomatoes, with their liquid, pepper, and salt to taste. Simmer the soup (stir twice) 30 minutes.
4 servings.

GREEN BEAN SOUP

1½ pounds green beans
4 cups Chicken Soup
2 tablespoons cognac (optional)

Salt, pepper to taste
2 tablespoons chopped parsley
2 tablespoons chopped chives

In a saucepan cook green beans in boiling salted water for 10 minutes and drain. Add chicken soup and simmer beans 15 minutes, until beans are tender. Put mixture through a food mill. Heat just to boiling point. Add cognac, salt and pepper to taste. Bring soup to boil and serve with garnish of parsley and chives.

4 servings.

UKRAINIAN BRIS BORSCH

A bris is a ritual circumcision ceremony—and a time of drinking and eating for the male, who was king among the Jews *before* Women's Lib.

1 onion, finely chopped	¼ cup wine vinegar
1 clove garlic, finely chopped	1 teaspoon salt
¼ cup margarine	1 teaspoon sugar
2 cups shredded beets	2 cups shredded cabbage
1 cup shredded celery root	1 cup stewed tomatoes, drained
8 cups beef broth or soup	1 teaspoon chopped dill
½ cup chopped parsley	1 pint sour cream

In a saucepan sauté onion and garlic clove in margarine, until onion is *lightly* browned. Add shredded beets, celery root, 3 cups beef broth, chopped parsley, wine vinegar, salt, and sugar and cook mixture for 10 minutes. Add 3 more cups beef broth and cook soup for 20 minutes. Add shredded cabbage and cook another 20 minutes. Add remaining 2 cups beef broth and tomatoes, simmer soup for 20 minutes until the cabbage is tender. Garnish the borsch with chopped dill and serve it with sour cream.

6 servings.

TRAVELER'S BEEF NOODLE SOUP

Guaranteed to carry one on a wintery Siberian day.

½ pound beef bones
2 quarts water
1½ stalks celery, with leaves, cut up
½ onion, sliced

1 carrot
¼ green pepper
Salt, pepper to taste
½ pound egg noodles
½ cup chopped chives

Get half the beef bones as marrow bones, the remainder as plain beef bones, and ask the butcher to chop them into pieces. Combine bones, water, celery, onion, carrot, and green pepper in large kettle. Add salt and pepper. Bring to a boil, skim, reduce heat, cover, and simmer 6 hours. Strain stock through cheesecloth. Return to kettle, add noodles, and cook until tender. Garnish each serving with sprinkling of chopped chives.

8 servings.

FETTER'S (UNCLE'S) FILBERT SOUP

⅓ cup chopped onion
⅓ cup chopped celery
1 cup margarine
3 cups Chicken Soup
Peel of 1 lemon

1 cup ground or grated filberts
⅛ teaspoon pepper
Salt to taste
Chopped parsley

In pot cook onion and celery in margarine until crisp but not browned. Boil soup, add lemon peel. Discard peel. Stir chicken soup into filberts, pepper and salt to taste. Cover, bring to a boil, simmer 15 minutes. Cool. For an extra touch, whir soup a little at a time in blender. Serve hot or cold. Garnish with chopped parsley.

4 servings.

KIMPITOUREN (NEW MOTHER) EGG DROP SOUP

1 tablespoon cornstarch
4 cups Chicken Soup
¼ cup minced, cooked chicken

2 teaspoons, dry white wine
2 eggs, well beaten
2 cups dried noodles

Put the cornstarch with 1 cup of chicken soup in a pot, then add the rest of the soup with the minced chicken and wine. Bring to a fast boil, slowly add beaten eggs, stir constantly as the eggs cook to shreds. Remove from heat, serve with dried noodles.
4 servings.

Vegetables

PURIM BEAN CAKES

1 cup black-eyed peas
1 small ripe tomato
1 small onion, halved

Salt, pepper to taste
2 cups oil

First wash the peas; soak 2 hours until they are soft. Purée in a blender, add water until the mixture is smooth. Purée the tomato and onion. Add the tomato-onion mixture to the peas. Season with salt and pepper. Heat the oil very hot. Drop the dough by tablespoonfuls into hot oil. Fry until brown on both sides.
6 servings.

POTATOES WITH TOMATOES

This dish and the next are said to have been brought back by Jewish spice merchants who traded in Asia.

½ teaspoon mustard seeds
3 tablespoons oil
3 large potatoes, peeled, cooked, diced
2 tomatoes, sliced
2 teaspoons minced green pepper

1 teaspoon turmeric
Pinch of cayenne
1 teaspoon salt
½ teaspoon sugar
1 teaspoon chopped coriander leaves

Fry the mustard seeds in hot oil. Add diced potatoes, fry 5 minutes. Add tomatoes, green pepper, turmeric, cayenne, salt, sugar, and coriander leaves. Cook slowly until tomatoes are done. Remove from fire and serve hot.
6 servings.

"HOT" ONION RELISH

1 large onion
1 large green pepper
2 medium ripe tomatoes
1½ teaspoons salt
⅛ teaspoon ground hot red pepper

¼ teaspoon grated lemon rind
1 teaspoon fresh lemon juice
1 tablespoon cider vinegar
1 teaspoon turmeric

Chop onions, green pepper, and tomatoes very fine. Add remaining ingredients and mix well. Let stand at least 2 hours before serving.
Makes 4 cups.

PICKLED RED CABBAGE

2 pounds red cabbage
½ cup salt
1 tablespoon dry mustard
2 quarts wine vinegar
½ cup brown sugar

1 teaspoon ground cloves
1 teaspoon allspice
1 teaspoon mustard seeds
½ teaspoon ground cinnamon
½ teaspoon celery seeds

Cut cabbage into wedges, salt the pieces, working salt into the leaves. Let stand overnight. Shake wedges to remove the excess salt. Put them in a kettle, add water to cover. Cook cabbage gently until it is tender, drain and set in jars. In a saucepan add dry mustard to wine vinegar.

Blend it smoothly. Add brown sugar, cloves, allspice, mustard seeds, cinnamon, and celery seeds. Cook mixture over medium heat until it comes to a boil. Boil the mixture 5 minutes, stir constantly. Pour hot liquid over the cabbage and seal jars. Let cabbage stand 24 hours. Great with corned beef or other meats, even fish.

Makes about 2 quarts.

WILTED CUCUMBERS AND ONIONS

2 large cucumbers
1 large onion, sliced
2 cups vinegar
1 teaspoon celery seeds

1 teaspoon sugar
½ teaspoon salt
¼ teaspoon pepper
Touch of dill

Peel cucumbers; slice thin. Add the rest of the ingredients. Let stand in refrigerator 3 hours before serving.

Makes 1 quart.

BEETS WITH SOUR CREAM

9 medium-sized beets
½ cup margarine
1 tablespoon lemon juice

Pinch each, salt and pepper
½ cup sour cream
1 teaspoon chopped chives

Cook beets in boiling salted water for 25 minutes. Cool slightly and slip off skins, roots, and stems. In a pan reheat beets in margarine. Add lemon juice, salt, and pepper. Fold in sour cream and heat mixture—do *not* let it come to a boil. Serve with a sprinkling of chopped chives.
4–6 servings.

BROAD BEANS WITH SOUR CREAM

The fancy St. Petersburg Jews called sour cream by the French name of *crème fraîche*. Close, but not a bull's-eye.

3 pounds broad beans
½ cup butter
Salt and freshly ground pepper to
taste

½ cup sour cream
½ cup chopped parsley

Shell broad beans, cook in boiling salted water until they are tender, drain. Let them stand until they are cool. In a saucepan reheat the beans in butter. Season with salt and freshly ground pepper to taste. Before serving, stir in sour cream and heat mixture for 30 seconds. Do not let it come to a boil. Transfer the beans to a hot dish and sprinkle them with chopped parsley. Serve.
8 servings.

HOMEMADE SOUR CREAM

We are so used to deliveries of finished products, we forget how in St. Petersburg sour cream was made; a sour cream that can be kept in the refrigerator 4 to 6 weeks.

1 quart heavy cream
1 cup buttermilk

Mix cream and buttermilk in a large 2-quart screw-top Mason jar. Shake the jar with vigor for 1 minute. Stand jar at room temperature 2 days (48 hours). The mixture is then thick and the sour cream genuine. Refrigerate 2 to 3 days. With fresh fruit, on latkes, added to pickled herring, and as a spread instead of butter—sour cream!
Makes 1 quart.

SOUR CREAM DRESSING

1 medium onion   1 pint sour cream
1 tablespoon parsley   1 tablespoon salt

A dressing for baked potatoes is made by grinding onion and parsley together, using the fine blade of a food mill. Mix well with sour cream and salt.
For 4 potatoes.

HORSERADISH SAUCE ROTHSCHILD

To many Jews, horseradish, ground up and fiery, was the spice of life at the table. Even a Rothschild, the legend was, used it.

½ pound fresh horseradish root   2 tablespoons dry mustard
1 cup dampened bread crumbs   2 tablespoons vinegar
1 cup dry white wine   Pinch of salt, pepper to taste
½ teaspoon sugar

Grate fresh horseradish (peeled). Add bread crumbs moistened with wine. Add sugar, dry mustard, and vinegar. Season with salt and pepper to taste and chill.

The Kiev version skipped the bread crumbs, the wine, the mustard, and colored the sauce by adding ¼ cup of beet juice.

GREEN-TOMATO PICKLE

4 quarts thinly sliced green   1 tablespoon black pepper
   tomatoes   1 teaspoon celery seeds
1 quart sliced onions   1 tablespoon mustard seeds
⅓ cup salt   ⅛ teaspoon cayenne
3 cups vinegar   1 lemon, thinly sliced
1 teaspoon allspice   3 cups brown sugar

Place tomatoes and onions in large bowl and sprinkle on salt; cover, let stand overnight. Drain. Heat remaining ingredients to boiling. Add tomatoes and onions and bring to boil, simmer 10 minutes, stir several times. Pour into hot sterilized jars, seal.

Makes 5 pints.

CARROT AND APPLE TZIMMES

The tzimmes seems an ethnic invention, a mixture of fruits, vegetables, and, as here, often meat. Served either with the main course, or after, it seems to have no rational function but to remain tasty. The word tzimmes also means mixed up, or to raise trouble: "A regular tzimmes."

1½ pounds breast flanken
1 bunch carrots, scraped, diced
2 large apples, cored, quartered, not peeled
1 small onion, diced

1 cup apple cider
½ cup dark brown sugar
½ teaspoon salt
1 cup water

Put the flanken in a saucepan, add salted water to cover. Boil 5 minutes and drain—wash in cold water. Cut beef strip into 4 parts. Put meat and all ingredients in a 3-quart pot with a lid. Add 1 cup water, bring to boil, lower heat, simmer gently ¾ hour. While this is cooking, make the knaidlach, often added to this dish 10 minutes before serving. You will find a recipe for it in the book.

6 servings.

TOASTED PUMPKIN SEEDS

Russian Jews chewed on sunflower, squash, or pumpkin seeds, a habit they got from the peasants. Here is a shtetl recipe.

1 cup pumpkin seeds
2 tablespoons peanut oil
Kosher coarse salt to taste

First wipe the fibers from pumpkin seeds, but do *not* wash. Coat seeds with peanut oil and spread them out on a baking sheet. Sprinkle seeds with coarse salt to taste, toast in moderate oven (350°) for 30 minutes, until they are golden brown and crisp.

Doughs

CHALLAH (BRAIDED SABBATH BREAD)

No Friday night seemed complete unless the braided challah, shiny in a patina of egg and oil paint, was set on the table between the holy copper candlesticks and the grated horseradish colored with beet juice. This recipe came to us as "The Chazzen's Challah," a cantor's favorite we gathered. But as he practiced most likely only his cantorial art, the makings, we would think, are his wife's.

1 package dry yeast	2 teaspoons salt
¼ cup warm water	1 cup scalded milk
½ cup margarine	5 cups flour
3 tablespoons sugar	1 egg
2 eggs, beaten	2 tablespoons cooking oil

Mix dry yeast in warm water. In a large bowl combine margarine, sugar, beaten eggs, salt, and scalded milk. Cool to lukewarm, stir in yeast. Stir in flour to make a stiff dough. Turn the dough out onto a floured board, knead for 7 minutes until smooth and shiny. Put dough in a buttered bowl. Cover dough and let it rise in a warm draft-free room for 2 hours, until it is double in bulk. Cut the dough into 8 equal pieces, shape pieces into balls. Cover balls and let them stand for 15 minutes. Form each ball into a strip 1 inch wide, 12 inches long. Grease 2 cookie sheets. Put 4 of the dough strips on each sheet, side by side. Pinch together at one end, braid them, pinch other end together. Make another loaf in the same way. Cover loaves, let them rise in a warm place for 1 hour until they are double in bulk. Beat 1 egg with cooking oil and brush loaves thickly with the mixture. Bake loaves in a moderately hot oven (375°) 35 minutes until they are golden brown. Remove and let cool.

Makes 2 loaves.

BAGELS

The modern bagel, according to bagel historians, came to Russia from Austria. But some diehards claim it was recorded in Poland in the seventeenth century. However, here is the basic Odessa bagel as known all along the coasts of the Black Sea.

3 cups flour	½ cup warm water
1½ teaspoons salt	3 tablespoons oil
½ cup sugar	1 egg, slightly beaten
1 package dry yeast	4 quarts water

Mix flour, salt, and 2 tablespoons sugar together in deep bowl. Dissolve yeast in ½ cup warm water, stir. Make well in flour, stir in the oil, add egg. Stir up to form a ball of dough. Knead on a floured board 2 minutes. Return dough to bowl, smooth side up, and punch a few times. Cover, let rise to top of the bowl—about 40 minutes. Knead again till smooth, firm, elastic. Divide dough into 12 bits—form into lengths ¾ inch thick. Make circles of lengths. Put on floured cookie sheet and put under broiler for 3 minutes. In a deep pot bring water and remaining sugar to a boil. Drop bagels into water 3 at a time. Remove after 15 minutes, then bake at 400° for 10 minutes until bagel is browned, crust is crisp.

Makes 12 bagels.

NOTE: If bagel-making is your thing, you can buy a home bagel-shaping machine.

KIEV POTATO LATKES (PANCAKES)

Next to bread, the latke was once the staff of life, not just among the shtetlach, but in the big cities, and both poor and rich relished them, and still do. When Second Avenue in New York City was famous for its Jewish theater from *King Lear* in German-Yiddish to *Yaska-Kalb,* the uptowners would often have dinner first in an Old World eating place that featured the latke; *even* the proud Sephardic Jews came.

4 eggs, separated
6 large potatoes, peeled, grated,
    drained
1 large onion, grated

Salt, pepper to taste
Pinch of baking powder
1 cup oil

Beat egg whites stiff and dry. In a bowl mix potatoes, onion, egg yolks, salt, pepper, and baking powder. Add egg whites, fold in, mix well. Heat oil in a large frying pan and drop latkes from a tablespoon into hot fat. Fry golden brown on both sides; drain on paper. Can be served with meats, or with sugar, applesauce, sour cream.
Makes 1½ dozen latkes.

NOTE: You *can* grate the potatoes in a blender—*IF* you take care. Slice the potatoes into blender—turn switch on for a second, off for a second—on for a second, off for a second. Three times should do it. If longer, you'll get mush.

POTATO KUGEL (BAKED POTATO PUDDING)

This was a favorite of the Khevreh Keddisha (burial society) and bar mitzvahs around Moscow. Served steaming hot and often eaten with scalded fingers, it was also enjoyed cold by some as a nosh (a hasty tidbit). It usually accompanied boiled or roasted meat.

3 eggs, separated
8 large potatoes, peeled, grated,
    drained
2 large onions, well grated
Salt, pepper to taste

1 cup fine bread crumbs or matzo
    meal
Pinch of baking powder
⅓ cup chicken fat

Preheat oven to 350°. Beat egg whites stiff. In large bowl mix all ingredients but egg whites and fat. Beat well. Fold in egg whites and mix again. Grease a pan with chicken fat, pour in mixture. Bake in oven 1 hour. When edges and top are brown and crisp, it is done. Slice in pan. 10 servings.

LOKSHEN (SOUP NOODLES)

While most cooks today buy the already prepared boxed noddles, here is the original recipe.

3 eggs   Pinch of pepper
½ teaspoon salt   2 cups flour

In a bowl beat eggs and salt and pepper. Add flour to make a soft dough. Put dough onto a well-floured board. Knead 5 minutes till smooth, elastic. Roll dough out into the shape of a circle, thin, without tearing. Set dough to dry on a cloth over the back of a chair. If dough feels stiff to touch, it is ready to cut. Put dry dough on board and roll up. like a jelly roll. With a sharp knife, cut fine or broad noodles. *Watch* your fingers. Shake noodles loose, cook in boiling salted water 5 minutes. Add to soup. If lightly covered in a jar, uncooked noodles will keep in the refrigerator for 4 months.
4 servings.

MINSK SWEET POTATO BISCUITS

1½ cups flour   ¼ teaspoon ground cloves
2 tablespoons light brown sugar   ½ cup butter
4 teaspoons baking powder   1 cup cooked sweet potato purée
1 teaspoon salt   ½ cup milk
½ teaspoon ground cinnamon

Preheat oven to 425°. Mix together in a bowl flour, light brown sugar, baking powder, salt, cinnamon, and ground cloves. Add butter diced, stir until it resembles meal. Stir in sweet potato and milk. Drop the batter by tablespoons on a greased baking sheet and bake in pre-heated hot oven 15 minutes until they are golden. Butter or honey on a biscuit is fine eating.
Makes 24 biscuits.

GOLDEN CORN CAKE

Corn meal was often a basic food in hard times, but even in good times there was a demand for the corn cake, crisp, nutty, and filling.

1 cup corn meal	1 cup milk
1 cup flour	1 egg, well beaten
3 teaspoons baking powder	2 tablespoons melted shortening
½ teaspoon salt	
½ cup small onion bits, slightly browned	

Heat oven to 350°. Mix and sift dry ingredients; add onion bits, milk, egg, and shortening. Bake in 8-inch-square greased pan at 350° for 20 minutes. Serve with a dab of butter on hot cakes.
4 servings.

BREAD-GARLIC NOSH

A use for hard overaged rye bread crusts—and a taste for garlic that *needs* to be developed.

2 teaspoons salt
2 dry rye bread crusts
2 whole cloves garlic, peeled

Preheat oven to 400°. Salt top of bread crusts. Rub a garlic clove back and forth on each crust a few times. Toast in hot 400° oven 5½ minutes till browned.
2 servings.

KASHA (BUCKWHEAT GROATS)

This can be bought in any market now in dry uncooked form, and has long delighted those who could afford to eat it with the best cuts of meat. *And* those who ate it with a little meat fat dripping as a main course. It has also become popular as stuffing for fowl.

1 egg
1 cup kasha
2 cups hot Chicken Soup

Beat the egg and pour it over the kasha. Mix well. Preheat a heavy skillet with no fat, and pour in kasha. Stir constantly so kasha will not stick to the bottom of pan—until the grain is separated and dry. Heat the chicken soup. Put kasha into a saucepan, pour the chicken soup in. Cover, bring to boil. Reduce heat, simmer on a very low flame for ½ hour. Serve in a preheated vegetable dish.
4 servings.

MANDLEN

These small, nutlike bits of dough for putting in soup, like that famous auto-renting firm, are Number Two in the soup derby, and so they try harder. (The matzo ball is Number One in popularity, the noodle a good third.)

1 cup flour
½ teaspoon baking powder
½ teaspoon salt

2 tablespoons cooking oil
2 eggs, slightly beaten

Sift flour, baking powder, and salt together and add to mixture of oil and eggs. Knead until smooth. Roll pieces of dough into ½ inch thick strips. Cut strips in 1-inch pieces. Set out on a greased baking sheet and bake at 375°, 15 minutes. Move pan occasionally to brown evenly. Add ½ dozen to each plate of hot soup. Store leftover mandlen in a covered jar.
Makes about 150.

KNAIDLACH (FARINA SOUP BALLS)

A farina dough ball for soup as a change from mandlen or noodles.

½ cup flour
½ cup farina
Salt, ground pepper to taste

1 onion, diced
½ cup ground beef fat
¼ teaspoon baking powder

Mix all ingredients well. Dough should be sticky but firm. When the soup has cooked ¾ hour, remove lid and, with a tablespoon, drop walnut-sized lumps of dough into soup. Replace lid, return to boil, lower heat, and simmer ½ hour. Also a delightful side dish.
4 servings.

LAKACH (HONEY BREAD)

Many people kept their own hives of bees, and if sugar prices rose, they could always sweeten with honey. And as they baked their own bread, the combination came naturally.

1 cup honey	1 teaspoon salt
1 cup packed brown sugar	1 teaspoon ground cardamom
¼ cup butter	1 teaspoon ground cinnamon
1 cup orange marmalade	1 teaspoon ground cloves
4 cups sifted flour	½ cup milk
3 teaspoons baking powder	Blanched almonds, split

Mix the honey, sugar, and butter in a saucepan. Bring to a boil, stirring. Remove from heat and add orange marmalade. Mix together in a bowl flour, baking powder, salt, cardamom, cinnamon, and cloves. Add the honey mixture, milk, mix smooth. Turn batter into 2 greased 9×5-

inch cake pans. Set almonds on top of loaves in design, press into batter slightly. Bake at 370° for 40 minutes, until cake tester pushed into center comes out clean. Remove from pans and cool.
Makes 2 loaves.

Salads

HOT CHERAIGOV CHICKEN SALAD

Middle and upper class Russian Jews were fond of special salads and developed several that still survive in other countries. As they ate these salads often with meat and fowl dishes, creams and butters were usually avoided in Orthodox homes, yet the following contains mayonnaise.

2 cups diced, cooked chicken
2 tablespoons finely chopped
  green onions
¼ cup chopped celery
2 tablespoons chopped pimento
¾ cup chopped pitted ripe olives

¾ cup mayonnaise
½ teaspoon salt
2 cups crushed cornflakes
1 cup bread crumbs
1 tablespoon oil

Preheat oven to 400°. Mix all ingredients except crumbs and oil; put in a casserole. Combine crumbs with oil and sprinkle over chicken. Bake at 400°, just 15 minutes.
4 servings.

CABBAGE SALAD

4 cups shredded cabbage
1 small onion, finely chopped
1 tablespoon chopped fresh green
  chili pepper
1 teaspoon salt

3 tablespoons chopped coriander
  leaves
2 tablespoons vegetable oil
Juice of 2 limes

In a large bowl combine all ingredients and mix well. Be sure cabbage is well chilled, and the chili pepper is *not* the real hot one.
6 servings.

CHICK-PEA SALAD

1 quart chick-peas, cooked
1 cup vinegar
½ cup oil
1 medium onion, chopped
½ cup chopped celery
¼ cup chopped pimento

¼ cup chopped green pepper
½ teaspoon oregano
½ teaspoon salt
¼ teaspoon pepper
¼ teaspoon crushed garlic

Drain chick-peas, and mix remaining ingredients into a well-combined dressing. Add to chick-peas and keep chilled until served.
12 servings.

BEET SALAD WITH HORSERADISH

"Horseradish that doesn't bring a pious tear to the eye is not God's horseradish."

Tevya, the milkman

1 cup diced cooked beets
1¼ cups sour cream
2 tablespoons white horseradish
1 tablespoon sugar

Salt to taste
½ cup diced celery
½ cup sliced raw onion rings
Crisp dry lettuce

Chill beets. Mix with ¼ cup sour cream, horseradish, sugar, and salt to taste and chill overnight in refrigerator. Drain beets and mix with celery, onion rings. Serve on lettuce topped with remaining sour cream.
4 servings.

KRAUT SALAD

1 cup vinegar
1 cup sugar
1 pound sauerkraut, well
   drained
1 onion, finely chopped

1 small (2-ounce) jar pimento,
   chopped, drained
2 cups finely chopped celery
1 green pepper, finely chopped

Bring vinegar and sugar to a boil and pour over the vegetables. Chill, covered, for 24 hours. This dish combines a salad with a kind of relish and serves two purposes with its special tang.
6–8 servings.

HERBED KALE

4 bunches kale
½ cup boiling water
1 onion, chopped
¾ teaspoon salt

Sugar to taste
Pinch of pepper
2 tablespoons margarine

Wash kale, pinch leaves off stems. Place leaves in saucepan with boiling water, onion, salt, sugar, pepper. Cover and cook 20 minutes, until kale is tender. Drain. Add margarine. Mix and serve.
6 servings.

Dessert

JEWISH-RUSSIAN STRUDEL

The *best* strudel, according to Austrians, is theirs. The *only* true inventors of it, the Romanians claim, were Romanians. The Germans have their *own* ideas on the subject. *All* strudels, if well made, are good, filling, and rich. In stretching the dough paper thin, it is a disgrace for a housewife to tear a hole in it (which can be patched). Today you can buy the dough leaves ready for filling, if so you desire.

2½ cups flour	1 large egg or 2 small eggs
½ teaspoon baking powder	5 tablespoons cooking oil
⅛ teaspoon salt	1 cup strained cold orange juice

Preheat oven to 375°, and in a large bowl mix flour, baking powder, salt. Beat egg with oil, orange juice, add flour mixture. Mix into a dough that is solid enough to handle. Place dough on a well-floured board and cover with a bowl rinsed in hot water and dried. Allow dough to remain under bowl for ½ hour. While the dough is under the bowl, make the following filling:

6 cups peeled, chopped apples	½ teaspoon nutmeg
1 whole lemon, grated, leave in rind, pulp, juice, pits removed	1 cup bread crumbs
	1 cup oil
½ cup white raisins	Powdered sugar
½ cup chopped baking cherries	
1 cup chopped almonds, blanched	

Mix together all ingredients except bread crumbs, oil, and powdered sugar. Place dough in the center of a well-floured cloth-topped table. Start from the center, roll dough in a circle, as thin as possible *without* tearing. Oil dough surface with a pastry brush and spread with half of the bread crumbs. Put on apple filling and sprinkle remaining crumbs over top of filling. With both hands, *carefully* roll up the strudel. Seal ends by folding over; place, flap end down, on oil rimmed cookie sheet.

Brush top of strudel with oil and bake 50 minutes, until strudel is brown. Allow to cool. Cut into 2-inch slices, sprinkle with powdered sugar.

12 servings.

PIROGEN

Another dish to bring sighs to the Russian-Jewish exiles—yet the pirogen are simple things—and tasty—much aided by the liberal use of sour cream.

1 cup sifted flour	1 egg
Salt to taste	2 tablespoons water
1 cup cooked, peeled, grated	1 quart water
potatoes	½ cup butter

Mix flour and salt together, add this to grated potatoes. Now beat egg and 2 tablespoons water. Make a well in dry mixture, pour in egg. Mix to make dough, knead it well, roll it out on floured board to ¼ inch thickness. Cut into 2½-inch circles, then roll out to 3½ inches. Add a teaspoonful of filling, fold to form half-moons, pressure edges to seal. Drop into 1 quart of boiling salted water. Boil 5 minutes, drain. Melt butter in pan, fry pirogen until golden brown on each side. Serve with sour cream, lots of it.

10 servings.

NOTE ON FILLING: The Jews usually filled with chopped nuts, cottage cheese, and the bolder ones with chopped meat.

TEIGLACH (DOUGH COOKIES)

"Something sticky and sweet, crunchy to bite into while sipping a glass of tea, or arguing a point in the Pentateuch with a Talmud scholar."

Old letter—1880

4 cups flour	1 cup sugar
2 teaspoons baking powder	1 teaspoon crushed gingerroot
8 eggs	½ cup chopped walnuts
1 pound light honey	½ cup chopped cherries

Mix flour, baking powder, and eggs to a stiff dough. Knead it firmly. On lightly floured board, roll pieces of dough into lengths ½ inch thick. Slice into 1-inch lengths. Put the honey in wide saucepan, add sugar, gingerroot, bring to a boil. Put pieces of dough into syrup, stir frequently. Cookies are ready cooked when they rise to the top, light brown. Remove cookies to platter, top with the walnuts and cherries.
Makes about 30 teiglach.

TEATIME ROGELACH (BAKED COOKIES)

A hostess with a desire for social gossip tried to establish an afternoon tea for a few close women friends and served these as a snack.

½ cup butter	1 teaspoon water
½ cup cream cheese	1 egg white
½ cup sour cream	Kosher coarse salt
1¼ cups flour	Caraway seeds

Cream butter and cream cheese, mix with sour cream, and add the flour. Separate dough into 3 balls, chill overnight. Roll out dough into 8-inch circles and cut up in wedges. Roll up toward center. Mix water and egg white and brush over wedges. Sprinkle lightly with salt, caraway seeds. Bake on a greased cookie sheet 20 minutes at 350°.
Makes 35 cookies.

FESTIVE CHEESE CAKE (SOUR CREAM TOP)

1½ pounds cream cheese
4 eggs
1½ cups sugar
¼ teaspoon salt

¾ teaspoon almond extract
1½ cups sour cream
½ teaspoon vanilla

Beat cream cheese in a mixer bowl with wooden spoon until soft. Add eggs, 1 cup sugar, salt, and almond extract. Beat smooth and thick. Pour into buttered 9-inch spring-form cake pan. Bake in moderate oven, 325°, 50 minutes, until set. Remove and cool on cake rack 20 minutes. Mix rest of sugar, sour cream, vanilla. Pour over cake. Return to oven, and bake 10 minutes at 325°.
8 servings.

SEEDCAKE

1 cup butter
1 cup sugar
5 eggs
2 cups all-purpose flour

½ teaspoon salt
1 teaspoon baking powder
1 teaspoon vanilla
1 tablespoon caraway seeds

Preheat oven to 350°. Mix butter and sugar together. Add eggs, one at a time, beating after each addition. Add other ingredients, beat for 5 minutes by hand, or with electric mixer beat for 2 minutes at low speed. Butter and flour a 9-inch pan, pour the batter in. Bake in oven 45 minutes, or until cake tests done (a toothpick will come out not sticky when cake is pricked).
6 servings.

BAKED PRUNES IN PORT WINE

With stuffed derma or cholent, some claimed *this* dish was a necessity.

1 pound large luxury prunes
1 quart port
½ cup sugar

1 cinnamon stick
Grated rind and juice of 1 lemon
2 cloves

First soak prunes overnight in port wine. Next day place in a baking dish, add more port to cover prunes. Add remaining ingredients. Cover baking dish, and bake in a 325° oven 1 hour, until the prunes are tender. Cool the prunes. Serve with thick sour cream.
6 servings.

SUCCOTH DATE AND NUT PUDDING

2 cups chopped pitted dates
1 cup walnut halves
¾ cup all-purpose flour
1½ teaspoons baking powder

½ teaspoon salt
3 eggs
1 tablespoon sugar
1 pint whipping cream

Preheat oven to 325°. Mix dates and nuts with sifted flour, baking powder, salt. Beat the eggs lightly, add sugar, and mix with dry ingredients. Turn into greased deep 9-inch square pan. Bake 40 minutes. Cut in wedges while warm—serve with whipped cream.
8 servings.

PRUNE-HONEY PUDDING

1 cup chopped cooked prunes
½ cup honey
½ cup chopped almonds
½ cup milk
Grated rind of 1 lemon

1 tablespoon margarine
½ cup bread crumbs
1 teaspoon baking powder
1 pint heavy cream, whipped

Preheat oven to 350°. Combine all ingredients but cream and pour into buttered baking dish. Place dish in shallow pan of hot water. Bake in moderate oven, 350° for 35 minutes. Serve cold, with whipped cream on top.

6 servings.

POLAND

The nearer the bone, the sweeter the meat.
Native Proverb, 1559

Poland, mostly under Russian control, shared with its masters an interest in certain foods, and the Polish Jews were residents of that country in many vicinities as long, if not longer, than the nation's nobles, who seemed to be as plentiful as Mexican generals.

While the Jews were often confined to their villages, many were active in the big cities of Warsaw, Lvov, Vilna, Posen, Krakow, Kolomyja. In periods of relative freedom, they were merchants, textile manufacturers, teachers, contractors, literary figures, shopkeepers, radicals and bankers, cattle drovers; fitting their lives to the conditions of a Polish nation unhappy with its Russian overlords, and needing someone to victimize. The novels of the Singer brothers, the short stories of Sholem Aleichem, give us a rounded picture of Polish-Jewish life, what was cooked, what was dreamed about in the bounded life in the Pale and the crowded competition of the cities. How to believe the Talmud's orders? "Take thine ease, eat, drink, be merry."

Mixing their own ritual preparation of Jewish food with the best in Polish cooking, the Jews created a splendid tasty cuisine. They even named dishes or food after certain Polish towns in which they were forced to live. There was, and *is,* the bialy, a flat roll, baked after being topped with strips of onion. It was named in honor of its first appearance in the Jewish section of the shtetl of Bialystok. As for the primitive bagel, something is mentioned by that name—but not described—in Krakow, Poland, in a document dated the year 1610, as "a gift for women in childbirth." However, the modern bagel did not come along until after the middle of the nineteenth century. As for lox, the salted salmon, a name which came from the Scandinavian word *lax,* not only did no Jew in Poland ever hear of it, the tasty item was unknown to Eastern European Jews. Bagel and lox (with cream cheese added) had to wait for its first appearance in food history on the tables of American Jews in New York City *after* the turn of the century.

The Polish Jews had their own version of gefilte fish, with chrayn (ground horseradish colored with red beet juice). They also adopted their version of the barszaza, beet soup made with or without meat, but with some kvas added (a beverage of fermented cereals), which kvas gave the dish its sharp fiesty flavor. The Jewish mishpocheh stew (family stew) is a direct descendant of the Polish foresters' bigos, or hunter's stew. The Jewish wife used beef flanken instead of venison, but kept the key ingredient—a head of pickled cabbage, or a big portion of sauerkraut. For special events, there was the Pale's version of pieczen huzarska, or hussar's roast, a pot made with scalding hot vinegar.

Primary Jewish dishes were stuffed yontif kishka, or derma, a section of steer gut stuffed with flour, fat, and spices, and baked. The gut was usually from a cow that the ritual slaughterer (the village shochet) had passed as fit for religious Jews to eat. Since the Diaspora, the great Exile from Judea in Roman times, the Jews had remembered their tzimmes of fruit and vegetables. The blintz was popular in Poland as a kind of Jewish crêpe filled with cheese. And on the feast of Purim, to celebrate when the Asian king Haman, a tyrant, met his end, there was eaten the hamantasch, a three-cornered pasty filled with prunes and poppy seeds. Some items of food that could be eaten hot or cold, with the fingers, were called noshen (snacks), such as chopped chicken liver on a slab of matzo, spiced herring, pickled herring on corn-rye bread or black bread, or an aspic fish sauce dipped up with a section of Friday night's challah by the Landsleit (people who came from one's own village) and helped out with buraki (grated beets).

Jews who traveled for business, who had flats or houses in Warsaw or Vilna, adapted a great deal of the Polish cuisine to their own needs, purifying it for ritual reasons, eliminating those items of pork or shellfish or meat prepared with butter or cream that their creed forbade. In such a process, an actual new dish would often come about.

The Jewish cooks delighted in their versions of pike, perch, or trout in a fish Polonaise with raisin sauce, dishes made with sour clabbered milk, the dough pockets called piroshki, filled with various items one had on hand: cheese, meat, kasha, even sauerkraut or jam, berries. To impress, a Jewish merchant could open the meal, besides the expected chopped chicken liver, or fillets of pickled herring, by adding the Jewish version of the native appetizers called zakonski, which included canapés of caviar, jellied carp, pickled mushrooms, anchovies. To keep it kosher, however, he never mixed these with a meat version that could include calf's foot jelly, jellied turkey, and non-pork cold cuts called wendlina. ("God gave us teeth, let us trust him to supply the right food." A Vilna Talmud student.)

Jewish drinking was simple and frugal; a small tot of plum brandy, a glass of krupnik (a punch of wine and brandy and honey), served after a wedding or male birth rite, with honey and cake. The guests toasted each other, as always, with the Hebrew words "L'chayim! To life!"

Appetizers

KASHA AND MUSHROOMS

1 cup kasha (buckwheat groats)
1 onion, chopped
½ pound fresh mushrooms, sliced

3 tablespoons chicken fat
Salt, ground pepper to taste

Cook kasha according to directions. Then sauté onion and mushrooms in chicken fat until soft, but do not brown. Mix sautéed onion, mushrooms, salt, pepper, and kasha. Use gravy from a roast for added flavor, if served with meat.
6 servings.

WEDDING BUFFET MEATBALLS

1½ pounds ground beef
2 cups Chicken Soup
½ cup catsup
1¼ teaspoons salt
⅛ teaspoon pepper
½ teaspoon garlic salt

½ teaspoon oregano
1 cup oil
1 teaspoon water
1 teaspoon dillweed
Paprika

Mix beef, ¼ cup chicken soup, catsup, salt, pepper, garlic salt, and oregano. Shape into meatballs the size of a golf ball. Brown balls in hot oil, pour off excess fat. Remove meatballs. Add water, cover, simmer 15 minutes. Combine remaining soup and dill in skillet in which meatballs cooked. Heat and pour over meatballs. Sprinkle with paprika.
6 servings.

HOLIDAY CHEESE LATKES

3 eggs
1 cup milk
1 cup cottage cheese
1 cup matzo meal

¾ teaspoon salt
½ teaspoon ground cinnamon
1 tablespoon sugar

Beat eggs and add milk and cheese. Mix matzo meal with other ingredients. Add to egg mixture and beat. Drop from tablespoon onto hot, greased frying pan. Brown on one side, turn, brown on the other side. Serve hot with sour cream or applesauce.
4 servings.

Meat

DOLINA (MARINATED RAW BEEF)

1½ pounds fillet of beef, sliced
    paper thin
½ cup olive oil
3 tablespoons wine vinegar
3 tablespoons slivowitz (plum
    brandy)
1 tablespoon salt

1 teaspoon each, ground pepper,
    thyme
2 onions, chopped
2 cloves garlic, finely chopped
½ sliced lemon
2 tablespoons chopped parsley

On a serving dish, pat down slices of fillet of beef. Mix olive oil in a dish with wine vinegar and slivowitz, salt, ground pepper, thyme, onions, and garlic cloves. Pour this marinade over beef, let it stand, refrigerated, turning the beef a few times, for 6 hours. Garnish with slices of lemon, chopped parsley.
10 servings.

LIVER PUDDING

1 cup rice	1 tablespoon ground ginger
1½ cups water	½ cup raisins
2 tablespoons margarine	¼ teaspoon white pepper
1 small onion, chopped	1 teaspoon marjoram
2 cups Chicken Soup	1 egg, beaten
1 pound liver, chopped	Dry bread crumbs
4 tablespoons dark corn syrup	Strawberry, or any berry jam

Preheat oven to 375°. First cook rice in boiling water until water is absorbed, rice is tender. Melt 1 tablespoon margarine, add onion. Cook till lightly browned. Mix onion, soup, liver, corn syrup, ginger, raisins, white pepper, marjoram, and rice. Stir in beaten egg and turn into a greased baking dish. Sprinkle with bread crumbs, dot with remaining margarine. Bake at 375° for 45 minutes. Serve with berry jam.
4 servings.

JEWISH-POLISH PIROSHKI (LITTLE MEAT PIES)

1½ cups flour	½ teaspoon salt
½ teaspoon baking powder	½ cup chicken fat

Preheat oven to 400°. Mix all dry ingredients in a bowl; add chicken fat. Add enough water to mix to form a ball of dough. Wrap dough in waxed paper and set in refrigerator while you fix filling.

FOR THE FILLING:

1 onion, minced	1 pound chopped beef chuck,
1 tablespoon chicken fat	twice ground
1 egg	Salt, pepper to taste

Brown onion in fat. Add egg to meat, salt, pepper, onion. Fry 5 minutes, stir constantly. Place dough on floured board, roll out thin. Cut dough into 3-inch squares. Put 1 tablespoon of meat filling on half of

each square—fold over to make a triangle. Press edges firmly to seal.
Bake on greased cookie sheet 15 minutes until pies are browned.
Makes 2 dozen piroshki.

BRAISED CALVES' SWEETBREADS

2 pounds sweetbreads and	Flour
Chicken Soup to cover	12 mushroom caps
1 bay leaf	4 tablespoons shortening
4 peppercorns	1 quart thick Chicken Soup
1 onion, chopped	½ cup dry sherry
½ cup chopped celery tops	

First parboil sweetbreads 15 minutes in chicken soup to cover with bay
leaf, peppercorns, onion, and celery. Let cool. Remove, trim, dry, season,
flour lightly. Sauté with mushrooms in shortening until golden brown.
Drain. Add chicken soup (1 quart), let simmer 5 minutes. Add sherry
5 minutes before serving. Use as sauce.
6 servings.

SWEETBREADS À LA ROTHSCHILD

The name on a dish gave tam (savory taste) to the upper class
Jewish families who served it.

2 pounds sweetbreads	1 pound fresh mushrooms,
Salt	sliced
1 onion, sliced in rings	4 teaspoons flour
1 green pepper, cut in rings	1 cup chicken or beef broth
2 tablespoons margarine or	1 cup dry sherry
chicken fat	Toast
1 pimento, cut in rings	Green pepper to garnish

Always wash sweetbreads in cold water. Cover with salted water in
saucepan; bring to boil. Reduce heat, simmer 5 minutes. Cool in broth.
In a pan sauté onion and green pepper in half of margarine 4 minutes
and add pimento. Remove sweetbreads, reserve broth. Cut in strips 2
inches long and ½ inch thick. Add sweetbreads and mushrooms to
onion mix. Stir gently over low heat until hot. Remove from heat, and

with remaining margarine in pan, blend in flour. Stir in hot broth and 1 cup sweetbread broth. Cook, stir until smooth, slightly thick. Add sherry, pour on sweetbreads. Serve on toast, garnish with green pepper, sliced. 6 servings.

FRESH CALF'S TONGUE WITH CHICKEN FAT

Fresh smoked or pickled, the Russian Jews delighted in tongue dishes. They always sliced it crossways at a slight angle, ate it with a strong horseradish sauce.

1 (2-pound) fresh calf's tongue   1 clove garlic, chopped
1 medium onion, sliced   5 peppercorns
1 bay leaf

Put all ingredients in a pot and cover with cold water. Bring to a boil, simmer 1 hour until the tongue is tender. Remove tongue with large fork and wash for 1/2 minute under cold water. Peel off skin, remove roots.

FOR THE SAUCE:

1/4 cup chicken fat   2 tablespoons ground horseradish
3 tablespoons capers   Salt, pepper to taste
1 tablespoon vinegar

Heat fat in small skillet. Remove from heat and add capers. Slowly stir in vinegar, horseradish, season to taste with salt and pepper.
5 servings.

BOILED BEEF TONGUE

1 (4-pound) beef tongue, corned or smoked
1 tablespoon dill

Cover tongue with cold water in a kettle. Bring to boil, drain. Use fresh water; boil and drain again. Refresh water a third time, bring to a boil, add dill, and simmer an hour or until tongue is tender when pierced with fork. Remove from heat and cool in liquid. When cool, remove skin and membranes at back of tongue. Slice into thin pieces. Serve with potato latkes, sauerkraut.
10 servings.

JEWISH STEAK TARTARE

This differs from the Russian-Tartar version but it's *still* raw ground meat. They may have brought it up from the Middle East.

1 teaspoon whole black peppercorns
1 teaspoon salt
1/4 teaspoon ground cinnamon
1 small onion, cubed
1 pound ground beef or lamb
1 cup cracked wheat, soaked
1/2 cup olive oil
Parsley to garnish

Crush together peppercorns, salt, cinnamon, and cubed onion. Knead mixture into the ground meat, run twice through the grinder. Add the cracked wheat and run through grinder again. Knead half the oil into mixture and use a little water if mixture is too dry. Run through grinder once again. Mold on serving dish and garnish with olive oil and parsley.
4 servings.

STEAK TARTARE CHALIAPIN

This is the authentic steak Tartare prepared by the Jewish cook of the great Russian operatic bass, Feodor Chaliapin.

4 pounds ground lean round steak	Salt
4 egg yolks	Pepper
1 cup capers	1 cup chopped onions
4 anchovy fillets	Rye bread, sliced, buttered
Mustard	

On plates arrange each serving in a mound. Make an indentation in each; drop in 1 raw egg yolk. Garnish with capers, anchovy fillets. Set out mustard, salt, pepper mill, chopped onions. Each guest seasons to taste and eats his steak on sliced buttered rye bread.
4 servings.

JEWISH-POLISH KIELBASA AND SAUERKRAUT

This national dish depends in its Jewish version on a kielbasa sausage made with beef or veal—*not* the usual pork.

2 pounds sauerkraut	2 tablespoons light brown sugar
½ cup chopped onion	1 tablespoon juniper berries
2 tablespoons salad oil	1 medium potato, peeled, grated
2 cups Chicken Soup	1 (2-pound) Polish kielbasa
1½ cups apple juice	1 medium apple, peeled
¼ cup cider vinegar	½ cup margarine

First drain sauerkraut in colander and wash under cold water. Drain, squeeze dry. In a large saucepan sauté onion in oil 5 minutes until golden. Add sauerkraut, chicken soup, apple juice, cider vinegar, brown sugar, juniper berries. Mix well. Bring to a boil over medium heat. Reduce heat, simmer 1½ hours covered, stir from time to time. Put in potato, cook 30 minutes until liquid thickens. Cut 3 slashes in kielbasa. Put in large saucepan, add water to cover. Bring to a boil, reduce heat, simmer 45 minutes. Slice apple, sauté in margarine until light brown. Set sauerkraut and apple on platter. Slice kielbasa and pattern in ring on top. Serve with pickled beets.
6 servings.

JEWISH-POLISH CASSOULET

Upper middle class Jewish life in the big cities of Poland, before 1939, had a Continental touch. It was living well while one still could. One of its best dishes was a version of the popular French cassoulet.

6 cups dried white Great
   Northern beans
4 pounds breast of lamb pieces
1 clove garlic, minced
Salt, pepper to taste

1 cup cooking oil
½ pound diced chicken breast
1 Polish beef sausage, cut in 1-
   inch pieces
1 cup dry red wine

Soak beans for 6 hours, drain, cover with water, cook slowly for 1 hour. While waiting, rub lamb with garlic, season with salt and pepper. Brown in skillet in oil. Remove and add the diced chicken. Cook until light brown. Return lamb to pan, cover meat with water and cook meat at a simmer ½ hour. Place beans in a thin layer in a large casserole. Add a layer of sausage, one of beans, a layer of lamb and chicken, another of beans, repeat, ending with a layer of beans. Add wine and meat broth to bean liquid, pour over beans. Put uncovered casserole in a 350° oven 1½ hours. When top is light brown and bubbly it's ready.
8 servings.

STEWED LAMB WITH TOMATOES

2 pounds stew lamb
2 tablespoons vegetable oil
1 large onion, sliced
4 cloves
1 teaspoon cumin
½ teaspoon crushed aniseed
¼ teaspoon crushed black
   peppercorns
⅛ teaspoon ground cardamom

1 teaspoon chopped mint leaves
1 teaspoon chopped coriander and
   leaves
1½ teaspoons salt
2 large tomatoes, peeled, chopped
2 large potatoes, peeled,
   quartered
Juice of ½ lemon

Cut meat into 2-inch cubes. Simmer lamb in water to cover for 1 hour. Skim off excess fat. Heat oil, brown the onion. Add cloves, cumin, aniseed, black peppercorns, cardamom. Fry 3 minutes. Add to lamb and put in mint leaves, coriander and leaves, salt, and tomatoes. Simmer 20 minutes. Add potatoes, cook until meat is tender. Stir in lemon juice before serving.

6 servings.

KAROBKI POT ROAST

The karobki was the Czar's official tax on kosher meat. The title of this dish is *meant* to be ironic—for it survived after the Revolution of 1917.

3 large onions, sliced	Pinch of oregano
1 clove garlic, mashed or finely diced	Pinch of sugar
	Salt, ground pepper to taste
1 pound stewed tomatoes	4 pounds beef brisket
4 carrots, scraped, quartered	½ pound fresh mushrooms
	½ cup dry red wine

In a 5-quart pot with a lid put the sliced onions, garlic, tomatoes, carrots, a pinch of oregano, a dash of sugar, and salt and pepper. Put meat on top, cover pot tightly, bring to a boil. Lower heat, simmer for 1 hour. Slice the mushrooms and mix with wine. Remove meat and slice against the grain. Add mushrooms and wine to gravy. Put sliced meat in pot, cover tightly, return to boil, lower heat, simmer ½ hour until meat is tender. Serve with potato latkes.

6 servings.

Fowl

PEACH-BAKED CHICKEN

¼ cup prepared yellow mustard	6 peach halves
¼ cup peach preserves	1 teaspoon dried parsley
1 (3-pound) broiler-fryer, cut in sections	(optional)

Preheat oven to 350°. Mix mustard with peach preserves. Arrange chicken skin side down in greased shallow baking dish. Bake at 350° 20 minutes. Spoon half the sauce over chicken and bake 30 minutes more until golden brown and tender. Garnish with rest of sauce, with peach halves, and parsley, if wished.
6 servings.

FIDDLER'S CHICKEN-IN-THE-POT

The story was that Jewish fiddlers at weddings and parties demanded a pot of this chicken as their fee—with free brandy. There is no record that any Jewish fiddler ever played on a roof except in a Chagall painting.

1 (4-pound) chicken and
  giblets
1 veal knuckle, chopped
2 carrots, sliced
2 leeks, sliced
2 celery stalks, sliced
1 onion
1 clove
3 sprigs parsley

1 bay leaf
5 peppercorns
1 teaspoon salt
6 cups water
2 cups Chicken Soup
½ pound peas
1 cup wide noodles, cooked
1 teaspoon chopped parsley

Place chicken and giblets in a kettle with veal knuckle, carrots, leeks, celery, onion, clove, parsley, bay leaf, peppercorns, salt, water, chicken soup. Bring to a boil. Reduce heat, simmer 2 hours. Discard veal knuckle, parsley, and bay leaf. Add peas. Simmer 5 minutes. Add noodles and heat well. Remove chicken, cut into serving sections. Place chicken pieces in a large casserole, pour the contents of kettle on them. Sprinkle with parsley.
6 servings.

CHICKEN GIZZARDS AND HEARTS

Delicious. Don't make a face *until* you've tried it.

2 pounds chicken gizzards and
   hearts
4 tablespoons olive oil
2 onions, sliced
4 cloves garlic, minced
1 cup dry white wine
1 cup tomato sauce

1 tomato, peeled, chopped
½ teaspoon salt
Pinch each, oregano, sage, thyme,
   rosemary
Pepper to taste
½ cup Chicken Soup

In a skillet lightly brown chicken gizzards and hearts, trimmed, in olive oil; add more oil if necessary. Add onions and garlic cloves, brown them. Add white wine, tomato sauce; cook mixture, stirring, 2 minutes. Add tomato, salt, oregano, sage, thyme, and rosemary, and pepper to taste. Simmer mixture covered for 1½ hours. Add ½ cup chicken soup and simmer for 1½ hours more until the gizzards and hearts are tender.
4 servings.

CHOPPED CHICKEN LIVER WITH GRIEBEN

The poor called it chopped liver, the rich, Jewish pâté. Scotland Yard in 1888 maintained Jack the Ripper was "a low class Polish Jew," a butcher who sold chicken livers for chopping. A letter from Jack said, "I'm not a butcher. I'm not a Yid. Nor yet a foreign skipper . . . Yours truly, Jack the Ripper." Today, most think Jack was one of Queen Victoria's grandsons, Prince Albert Edward. None of this decreased any production of the popular chopped chicken liver.

3 large onions, chopped
¼ cup chicken fat
12 chicken livers, sliced into cubes
¼ cup grieben (skin from
   rendered chicken fat)

3 large hard-boiled eggs, shelled
Salt, ground pepper to taste

First sauté chopped onions in chicken fat until transparent. Add livers and fry, stirring constantly, 10 minutes. Cool. Mix livers and onions with grieben, 2 hard-boiled eggs, salt and pepper to taste. Put through grinder twice. Be sure mixture is thoroughly blended and smooth. Press third hard-boiled egg through a sieve, sprinkle over top of liver. Serve on a bed of lettuce.

12 servings.

SWEET-SOUR CHICKEN WINGS

2 pounds chicken wings
1/2 cup oil
1/2 cup vinegar
1/2 cup water
1/2 cup catsup

1/2 cup sugar
Salt to taste
1 teaspoon dry mustard
1 tablespoon cornstarch
1/2 cup water

Clip and trim tips of wings. Fry chicken wings in oil until brown and tender. Remove. Drain on paper towels. In a pan combine vinegar, water, catsup, sugar, salt to taste and mustard, and heat. Mix cornstarch with 1/2 cup of water to make a paste and stir into sweet-sour sauce. Cook and stir until smooth and thickened. Serve hot as dip sauce for chicken wings.

Makes 6 entrées.

ROAST GOOSE

It was the duty of the housewife to keep a goose in a pen and to force feed it 3 times a day, holding its beak open and pushing corn down its throat by the pound. An overweight goose was a sign of a hard-working wife.

1 (10-pound) goose
1/2 cup brandy
Salt
2 cups chopped-up white toast
1 medium onion, diced
2 stalks celery with leaves, finely cut

1 cup each, dried prunes, dried apricots
1/2 cup chicken fat or margarine
Pinch each of salt, pepper, thyme, oregano
2 cups dry red dinner wine
2 cups beef or Chicken Soup

Preheat oven to 300°. Be sure plucking is well done. Rub goose with brandy, sprinkle with salt. Combine toast, onion, celery, prunes, apricots,

margarine, salt, pepper, thyme, and oregano. Moisten with water. Stuff goose, reserving some of dressing for use in gravy. Prick skin all over with fork. Roast uncovered on rack in oven at 300°, allowing 30 minutes per pound. Combine wine and soup to baste bird. When liquid accumulates in bottom of pan, skim off and discard fat. For gravy, combine pan liquid with reserved dressing.
12 servings.

RAISIN GOOSE STUFFING

While a goose was roasted in the usual way—Jewish stuffing could be different for an 8 to 10 pound goose.

½ cup chopped onion
2 cups chopped celery
1½ cups margarine (chicken fat may be used)
4 quarts 3-day-old bread crumbs
2 cups seedless raisins (in boiling water)

½ cup chopped parsley
1 tablespoon salt
2 teaspoons poultry seasoning
1 cup burgundy wine

In a pan sauté onion and celery gently in melted margarine, stirring occasionally, until onion is soft. Add to bread crumbs, raisins, parsley, and seasonings. Mix well, lightly. Add enough wine to moisten stuffing. Stuff goose and roast in usual way (see Index), basted with a mixture of burgundy and melted margarine.

ROAST DUCK ROTHSCHILD

1 (5-pound) duck
Salt, pepper to taste
½ orange, cut in half
2 stalks celery, with leaves
2 onions, sliced
3 sprigs parsley
1 tablespoon flour
2 carrots, chopped

1 bay leaf
5 peppercorns
2 cups water
1 cup dry red table wine
Duck neck and giblets
1 tablespoon flour
1 tablespoon margarine
1 tablespoon dry red wine

Preheat oven to 450°. Rub the duck inside and out with salt and pepper. Stuff with orange, sliced celery stalks, onions, and parsley sprigs. Close opening with a skewer. In oven place duck on its back in a roasting pan. Roast for ¾ hour, turn duck, remove drippings, and roast another ¾ hour. Remove duck from oven, discard extra drippings. While duck is roasting, put into a large pot the flour, carrots, bay leaf, peppercorns, water, 1 cup red wine, neck and giblets. Bring to boil, simmer for 1 hour. Strain, reserve the broth. Reduce oven temperature to 400°. Return duck to oven, continue to cook for 40 minutes, baste every 10 minutes with the reserved broth. Place duck on serving plate.

Thicken drippings with 1 tablespoon each of flour, margarine, and red wine. Serve gravy on the side.
4 servings.

Fish

JEWISH-POLISH GEFILTE FISH BALLS

The word is that this is the original traditional gefilte fish—*not* in slices, but in ball form. The *slice* and *ball* schools have been debating for years, while the wives chopped and chopped. As for fish, carp and pike are usually favored, but this is a pure whitefish recipe.

2 large onions, sliced

4 carrots, sliced thin

3 celery stalks, with leaves, chopped

Head, bones, and skin of fish (no eyes), tied in cheesecloth

Salt, white pepper to taste

3 pounds whitefish fillet, chopped or ground twice

2 large onions, grated

3 egg yolks

1 cup bread crumbs

Salt and pepper to taste

3 tablespoons sugar

1 cup water

3 egg whites, beaten stiff

Cooked carrot slices and parsley to garnish

Place in 6-quart pot with tight lid sliced onions, carrots, celery, and cheesecloth bag with fish head, bones, skin inside. Add salt and white pepper to taste. Cover with water, bring to a boil; put lid on, lower heat, simmer ½ hour. While soup is simmering, in a large bowl mix ground fish, grated onions, egg yolks, bread crumbs, salt, pepper, sugar, and 1 cup cold water. Combine ingredients thoroughly. Add beaten egg whites and mix. Wet hands, scoop up fish, mold into round balls—large walnut size—and drop into simmering broth. Add enough boiling water to cover fish. Cover pot, simmer 2 hours. When fish has cooked 1 hour, check seasonings, re-cover, continue to cook. Cool fish in pot. Remove with spoon and arrange on platter. Garnish each piece with a carrot slice and parsley. Discard cheesecloth bag, strain fish soup, place in refrigerator to jell. Cover platter of fish and refrigerate until served with chrayn (horseradish) mixed with beet juice.

Makes 2 dozen fish balls.

ROSH HASHONAH (NEW YEAR) HERRING SALAD

1 cup cooked diced beets

1 cup cooked diced potato

1 large red apple, peeled, cored, sliced

1 matjes herring, sliced

½ cup diced dill pickle

1 medium onion, minced

½ cup red wine vinegar

Salt, pepper to taste

½ cup sour cream

In a bowl mix beets, potatoes, apple, matjes herring, dill pickle, minced onion, wine vinegar, salt and pepper to taste. Fold in sour cream. Cover bowl and chill for 3 hours. Toss salad to serve.

2 servings.

STEWED HERRING

2 herrings, soaked overnight
Juice of 1 lemon
1/2 cup chopped onion

2 tablespoons cooking oil
1/2 cup peeled, sliced tomatoes
1 tablespoon curry powder

Cut herrings into 4 pieces. Put in a saucepan. Squeeze lemon over fish. Cook over medium flame 3 minutes. In another pan, fry onion in oil. Add tomatoes and curry powder. Stir. Pour mixture over fried herrings, cover pan. Cook for 30 minutes.
4 servings.

HERRING PIE

2 herrings, filleted
1 cup milk
1 cup water
6 tablespoons butter
1 tablespoon flour
Salt, pepper to taste

1 tablespoon chopped parsley
3 hard-boiled eggs, sliced
3 tomatoes
1 1/2 pounds potatoes, boiled
1/2 cup milk

Simmer fish in milk, or mixture of milk and water, until very soft. Drain, flake the fish, reserve the liquid. Mix 1 tablespoon butter, flour, and 1/2 cup of the strained fish liquor. Season and add flaked fish and chopped parsley. Spread in the bottom of a soufflé dish. Put hard-boiled eggs over the fish. Skin tomatoes, slice, and lay on top of the eggs. Mix potatoes with remaining butter and 1/2 cup of milk; mash; season, spread over tomatoes. Bake 30 minutes at 325°.
4 servings.

WINTER PICKLED HERRING

2 Iceland salt herrings
1/2 cup sugar
1 cup white vinegar

2 teaspoons mixed pickling spices
10 crushed cardamom seeds
2 medium onions, sliced thin

Skin and split herrings, cover with cold water, and let stand overnight. Drain herrings on paper. In a bowl combine sugar with white vinegar. Pour mixture into a saucepan and stir in most of mixed pickling spices and cardamom seeds. Bring mixture to a boil, stir constantly, dissolve the sugar. Let cool. Cut herrings into 2-inch pieces. Add some of sliced onions. Put a layer of fish in a 1-quart crock, top it with layer of onion slices, add a little pickling mixture. Repeat layers until all ingredients are used. If more liquid is needed, heat equal amounts of sugar and vinegar, add to crock. Cover crock, let stand in a cold place for a week. 10 servings.

BAKED FISH, OLIVE SAUCE

1 cup chopped shallots	1 teaspoon chopped coriander
2 green peppers, diced	2 cups orange juice
⅓ cup oil	½ cup lemon juice
2 cups stuffed olives	1 (4-pound) pike or other whole
1 teaspoon salt	fish
Pepper	1 cup shredded lettuce

Preheat oven to 400°. Fry shallots and green peppers in oil 2 minutes. Add 1½ cups olives, salt, pepper, coriander, and juices. Place fish in oiled roasting pan. Pour olive sauce over fish. Bake uncovered at 400° for 45 minutes until fish flakes with a fork. Baste often. Place fish on a platter, pour sauce on top. Garnish with shredded lettuce and remaining olives.
6 servings.

SHTETL (VILLAGE) SCHARFE FISH

3 onions, sliced

3 carrots, sliced

1 stalk celery, sliced

3 cups water

Salt, ground pepper to taste

4 pounds sliced pike or whitefish

2 tablespoons lemon juice

2 egg yolks, beaten

3 sprigs parsley to garnish

In a saucepan mix onions, carrots, celery, 3 cups water, and salt and pepper to taste. Bring to boil, add fish slices. Reduce heat, cover, simmer 30 minutes. Remove fish to platter, strain cooking liquid. Add lemon juice to beaten egg yolks in pan. Add strained liquid, cook until thickened but do *not* boil. Pour sauce over fish. Garnish with parsley. Good hot or cold.

6 servings.

Soup

COLD KRAKOW BORSCH

2 pounds fresh beets, cubed

2 onions, chopped

1 quart water

1 tablespoon each, salt, sugar,
    lemon juice

3 eggs

4 hot boiled potatoes

1 pint sour cream

Cook the beets and onions in saucepan with 1 quart of water for 1 hour. Drain, reserving liquid; put through a food mill (or blender), using some of the liquid. Mix in salt, sugar, and lemon juice. Beat the eggs, add gradually into reserved hot liquid, and beat 1 minute. Mix egg mixture with the puréed mixture. Chill soup for serving. Serve with hot potatoes and sour cream.

8 servings.

HOT BEET BORSCH

6 beets with tops
Juice of 2 lemons
¼ teaspoon salt
1 cup sugar

2 quarts water
1 cup sour cream
6 cold boiled potatoes
3 sprigs fresh mint to garnish

Peel beets, wash with beet tops. Slice beets into a large saucepan; chop up beet tops, place in pot. Add lemon juice, salt, sugar, and 2 quarts hot water. Boil 10 minutes, skim liquid, lower heat, simmer ½ hour until beets are tender. Serve hot in soup plates with dollop of sour cream and a *cold* potato. Garnish with fresh mint.
4 servings.

TANTE'S (AUNT'S) CHICKEN SOUP

The Polish-Jewish chicken soup is as famous as the Russian version. There is a canard; Polish hens eat better, taste better. Also a Hasidic story that the Lubavitcher Rabbi Menachem Schneerson told his disciples that Lazarus actually rose from the dead because he was smelling the chicken soup his mother was cooking for his burial feast.

4 chicken feet
1 (5-pound) chicken, cut in
  sections, gizzard and heart
2 whole onions
1 tablespoon salt
2 carrots, diced

3 stalks celery, with leaves,
  chopped, sliced
1 parsnip
3 sprigs parsley
1 sprig dill
Salt, white pepper to taste

The feet add flavor, so ask butcher for 2 extra.

Scald chicken feet in boiling water for 2 minutes. With knife, scrape off outer skin. Chop off claws. In large soup pot, cover chicken, gizzard, heart (no liver). Add onions and salt, bring to boil. Skim off top. Simmer for 1½ hours. Add carrots, celery, parsnip, parsley, and dill, and season to taste with salt and white pepper. Simmer for 1½ hours more. Remove chicken when tender, set aside. Add water if needed. Strain. Serve with noodles (lokshen—see Index) cooked separately in salted water—or with mandlen—hard soup doughs (see Index).
8 servings.

GARLIC SOUP WITH TAM (SAVORY TASTE)

2 cups minced peeled cloves garlic	1 quart Chicken Soup
2 tablespoons chopped onion	Salt, pepper to taste
2 tablespoons olive oil	1 egg, beaten
1 cup drained tomatoes	2 cups rye croutons

Combine garlic with chopped onion. Heat oil in a deep saucepan. Add garlic and onion, sauté slowly until soft but not brown. Mix in tomatoes, add soup. Season with salt, pepper, simmer, covered, for 15 minutes. Reduce heat. Stir in beaten egg, slowly. Serve with rye croutons.
6 servings.

BIALYSTOK CABBAGE BORSCH

Of the making of borschs, there is no end. And champions defend their favorites. In our poll, the Polish cabbage borsch won out over the Russian but it was close.

2½ pounds beef flanken
1 marrow bone
6 cups cold water
1 onion, quartered
1 cup cut-up celery
1 (1-pound) can stewed tomatoes

½ head cabbage, shredded
2 teaspoons salt
Pepper to taste
Juice of 2 lemons
2 teaspoons sugar
½ cup white raisins

Put meat and marrow bone in cold water in large kettle and bring to a boil. Add onion, celery, tomatoes. Again bring back to a boil. Reduce heat, cover, and simmer 2 hours until meat is tender. Add cabbage, salt, pepper to taste. Cook 30 minutes until cabbage is tender. Add lemon juice, sugar, and raisins and cook 10 minutes longer.
6 servings.

WARSAW KNAYDLACH (MATZO BALLS)

2 large eggs, separated
3 tablespoons chicken fat
1 cup matzo meal
½ teaspoon salt

½ teaspoon ground ginger
½ cup hot Chicken Soup
2½ quarts salted water

Beat egg whites stiff and dry. Then, in a separate bowl, beat yolks and chicken fat to blend. Mix matzo meal, salt, and ginger in bowl and add hot soup and egg yolks. Beat well. Fold in egg whites and put in refrigerator for 1 hour. Boil 2½ quarts salted water in 3-quart pot with a lid. Take matzo dough from refrigerator. Wet your hands, form walnut-size balls, drop into boiling water. Cover, boil 25 minutes. Drain and serve in hot chicken soup, where else?
3 servings.

POTATO-BEEF SOUP

½ pound ground chuck
2 tablespoons margarine
1 onion, sliced
2 cups Chicken Soup
2 cups water

2 medium potatoes, peeled, diced
1 cup tomatoes, stewed
Pinch each, paprika, seasoning
   salt, salt

Sauté ground beef in margarine until it loses its red inside color. Move to soup pot. Add sliced onion, soup, water, potatoes, tomatoes, paprika, seasoning salt, salt. Cover, simmer 30 minutes.
4 servings.

BAAL SHEM TOV BLACK BEAN SOUP

Baal Shem Tov was really Israel ben Eliezer, a wandering mystic who inspired the Hasidim to dance and sing, to require no synagogue, to show their joy in God. He is said to have been addicted to the black bean soup named for him.

2 cups black turtle beans
3 tablespoons margarine or
chicken fat
2 onions, chopped
1 cup chopped celery
1 *bouquet garni* of parsley,
thyme, bay leaf
1 beef bone, with some meat on
it
6 cups beef or Chicken Soup

4 cups water
Salt, pepper to taste
4 tablespoons slivowitz (plum
brandy)
2 tablespoons lemon juice
2 hard-boiled eggs, chopped
1 tablespoon chopped parsley to
garnish
½ lemon, sliced thin, to garnish

First put beans in water to cover for 6 hours and drain. In a kettle, melt 3 tablespoons margarine. Add chopped onions, celery, and *bouquet garni.* Cook over low heat 10 minutes. Add beef bone, beans, soup, water, salt, pepper. Bring soup to boil, reduce heat, simmer (adding more liquid if necessary) 4 hours. Discard the beef bone and *bouquet garni,* and add slivowitz. Reheat soup, season with lemon juice. Thin soup, if necessary. Garnish with chopped hard-boiled eggs, chopped parsley, lemon slices.
8 servings.

ZAYDE (GRANDFATHER) VEGETABLE BROTH

For a bland diet and no meat—favored it is said by the great Gaon of Vilna, Elijah ben Solomon in his old age.

3 carrots, chopped   1 tablespoon salt
3 onions, chopped   1 bay leaf
3 cups chopped celery   3 quarts water
3 leeks, cut up

In a soup kettle combine carrots, onions, celery, leeks, salt, bay leaf, and water. Bring to a boil, reduce heat, and simmer the mixture, covered, for 3 hours. Strain the broth.
6 servings.

JEWISH-POLISH ZOLUVIKA SAUERKRAUT SOUP

This was a favorite of the Jewish-Polish raconteurs, bons vivants; rich men, or acting rich on the Warsaw stock exchange.

2 strips breast flanken   1 large onion, diced
2 beef bones, split   1 tablespoon oil
1–2 pounds sauerkraut   1 teaspoon sugar
1½ quarts water   6 hot boiled potatoes
Salt, freshly ground black pepper   1 teaspoon caraway seeds

In a saucepan of water bring flanken and bones to a boil for 10 minutes. Drain and wash well under running water. In a 4-quart pot mix meat, bones, sauerkraut, 1½ quarts water, salt and pepper to taste. Bring to a boil, lower heat, simmer, covered, 45 minutes. Sauté onion in oil until golden brown. Add onion, sugar, to pot. Replace lid, cook until meat is tender. Pour into soup plates, serve with hot boiled potatoes. For a garnish, add a few caraway seeds to each serving or add them to the pot while cooking.
6 servings.

BALEBOOSTEH'S (FINE HOUSEWIFE'S) VEGETABLE SOUP

1 (2-pound) beef soup bone,
with meat
1 (1-pound) veal bone
2 quarts water
1 clove garlic, crushed
2 bay leaves
1 tablespoon salt
2 sprigs parsley
2 stalks celery, with tops

1 onion, chopped
6 carrots, diced
3 turnips, diced
2 potatoes, peeled, sliced in
cubes
1 cup canned stewed tomatoes
1/2 cup green beans
Salt, pepper to taste

Put soup bone, water, garlic, bay leaves, salt, parsley, celery, onion in deep kettle. Cover and heat to a boil. Skim off scum, cover, reduce heat, simmer 4 hours. Discard bay leaves and bone, but keep any meat. Skim most of fat from soup, strain stock. Mix stock with meat, carrots, turnips, potatoes, tomatoes, beans. Cover, simmer 30 minutes. Season to taste with salt and pepper.
4 servings.

Vegetables

APPLES STUFFED WITH RED CABBAGE

1 1/2 heads red cabbage
2 cups boiling water
2/3 cup white vinegar
2 apples, peeled, cored, sliced
2 cups dry red wine
1/2 cup any berry preserves
1/2 cup lemon juice

1/2 teaspoon each sugar, ground
cinnamon
Salt, pepper to taste
1 onion, chopped
1 tablespoon margarine
1 cup beef soup
6 large green apples

Shred red cabbage. In a kettle scald cabbage in boiling water and white vinegar for 2 minutes. Drain. Set cabbage in a bowl and mix with 2 apples, red wine, preserves, lemon juice, sugar, cinnamon, and salt and pepper to taste. Cover bowl, chill mixture overnight. In a saucepan, sauté onion in margarine until tender, but *not* browned. Add cabbage, beef soup, and simmer mixture, covered, 1 hour, until cabbage is tender. Drain mixture. Peel, core, and hollow out the 6 green apples. Put on a rack in a saucepan; steam in ½ inch boiling water in a moderate oven (350°) 15 minutes, until barely tender. Move the apples with care to a platter and fill with the cabbage mixture. Goes fine with roast goose.
6 servings.

PICKLED BEETS

1 pound beets, cooked, sliced (reserve cooking liquid)
1 tablespoon mixed pickling spices
1 tablespoon cider vinegar

Drain liquid from beets into a saucepan; to this add pickling spices and vinegar. Heat to boil, lower heat; simmer 5 minutes. Place beets in a bowl. Strain beet liquid over and chill 4 hours.
6 servings.

GIANT LATKE (POTATO PANCAKE) AND APPLESAUCE

4 medium potatoes	⅛ teaspoon pepper
1 onion	3 tablespoons flour
2 eggs, beaten	½ cup oil or chicken fat
1 teaspoon salt	1 quart applesauce

Peel, grate potatoes and onion into a bowl. Stir in eggs. Add salt, pepper, and flour to thicken batter slightly. Heat 2 tablespoons oil in a medium shallow skillet. Pour in half the batter, and spread. Cook over moderate heat until well browned on one side. Slide out of pan onto large plate. Cover with another plate and flip over. Slide back into pan, brown other side. Repeat as long as batter holds out, adding more oil when needed. Cut pancakes into wedges. Serve with applesauce. For the traditional latke, just drop mixture by tablespoonfuls into oil, fry until brown and crisp, turning once.

6 servings.

TALMUDIC LEEKS

An idea that leeks were a brain food for scholars of holy rite inspired the title.

12 leeks	⅛ teaspoon pepper
¼ cup margarine	4 egg yolks, lightly beaten
3 tablespoons flour	½ cup grated Swiss cheese
¾ teaspoon salt	Bread crumbs

Preheat oven to 350°. Cut leeks in 1-inch lengths, include part of green tops. Cook until tender in water; drain, saving cooking liquid. Melt margarine in small saucepan, add flour, 1 cup of the cooking liquid; cook, stir constantly until thick. Add salt and pepper, beaten egg yolks gradually, stirring, and cheese. Stir until melted. Place leeks in casserole with cheese sauce. Cover lightly with bread crumbs. Bake in moderate oven 15 minutes. Serve with entrée.

6 servings.

BRAISED TURNIPS

2 pounds turnips
4 tablespoons margarine
¼ teaspoon sugar

1 cup beef soup
Salt, pepper to taste

Wash, peel, and quarter turnips. Set them in an enamel saucepan with 2 tablespoons of the margarine, sugar, and beef soup. Add salt, pepper to taste. Cover, cook until tender, 20 minutes. Discard liquid, if any. On serving, use remainder of margarine on turnips, or use garlic dressing below.

GARLIC DRESSING

1 cup salad oil
1 teaspoon each, dry mustard,
   sugar, lemon juice
1 tablespoon red wine vinegar
1 tablespoon coarsely ground
   pepper

1 garlic clove, crushed
1 egg yolk
Salt to taste

Mix all ingredients and whip. Chill thoroughly in covered dish. Makes 2 cups.

Doughs

FARM SWEET BREAD

½ cup yellow corn meal
½ cup margarine
¼ cup molasses
2 teaspoons salt
¾ cup boiling water
1 envelope dry yeast

¼ cup warm water
1 egg, beaten
3 cups flour
1 tablespoon corn meal mixed
  with pinch of salt

Mix corn meal, margarine, molasses, salt, and boiling water in bowl. Let stand 3 minutes, then mix well. Soften yeast in ¼ cup warm water in cup. Let stand 4 minutes, stir to dissolve. Add yeast, egg, 2 cups flour to corn meal mixture for a soft dough. Stir in remaining flour, working to form smooth dough. Place dough in a medium-size greased loaf pan. Cover and let rise in a warm place till dough reaches top of pan. Dust top with corn meal-salt mix. Preheat oven. Bake at 375°, 35 minutes, until solidly browned. Turn out onto wire rack. Cool before slicing.
Makes 1 loaf.

JEWISH-POLISH PANCAKES

½ cup water
½ cup milk
3 eggs
1 cup flour
½ teaspoon salt
½ cup butter
2 cups small curd cottage
  cheese

2 tablespoons sour cream
1 tablespoon grated orange peel
½ cup roasted slivered almonds
¼ cup white raisins
¼ cup sugar

Mix water, milk, 1 egg, flour, and salt in a bowl. Beat until smooth. Melt 1 tablespoon butter in a skillet, blend into batter. Heat skillet 1 minute, pour in ¼ cup batter. Tip pan to coat with the batter. Cook light brown, turn, brown other side. Repeat with remaining batter, for 8 pancakes. Add butter as needed. Spread baked cakes on table. Mix cottage cheese, sour cream, remaining 2 eggs, orange peel, almonds, raisins, and sugar. Spoon ⅓ cup filling on each pancake. Fold in 2 sides, roll up, enclosing filling. Melt 2 tablespoons butter in skillet, add pancakes, brown, turning once or twice. Serve hot with sour cream and cinnamon sugar.

8 servings.

KRAKOW SABBATH CHALLAH

The baking of the Friday challah took on a kind of regional challenge, and there were reports that the farther east of the Urals it was made, the *better* it tasted, the whiter the flour, the shinier the egg-varnished surface. The Polish Jews claimed *their* challah was better than the Russian, and the German Jews that their braided bread was better than the Polish, Litvak, and Galitzianer challah. It was said that Rabbi Isaac Eihanon Spektor of Kovno, annoyed at all this, commented, "According to this narrish talk of the farthest east it's baked, the *best* challah in the west is in Nippon [Japan]."

3 envelopes dry yeast	3 large eggs
2 cups warm water	½ cup cooking oil
1½ cups sugar	1 cup white raisins
8 cups unbleached flour	1 medium egg, beaten
3 tablespoons salt	Poppy seeds

In a small bowl put the dry yeast, 1 cup of warm water, and ½ cup sugar. Stir until yeast is dissolved. Let stand until mixture bubbles and rises almost to the top of the bowl. In a large bowl put flour, salt, 1 cup sugar and mix. Make a well in the center of flour, add the yeast mass, eggs, oil, 1 cup warm water, raisins, and knead thoroughly into a dough. Place dough on a well-floured board, knead 20 minutes, beating hard.

Push down with your hands away from you. Lift, push down, knead. Keep turning the dough. Place dough in a large bowl, greased with oil. Cover with a cloth and put in a warm place to allow to rise until doubled in size. Punch dough down, knead 10 minutes. Preheat oven to 375°. Divide dough in half. To braid, cut each loaf into 3 to 4 pieces, roll each into a rope that is wide in the middle and tapered at the ends. Braid ropes, tuck ends under. Roll to shape and put in medium-size oiled pans. Cover, allow dough to rise until pans are full and middle is above each pan. Brush tops of challahs with beaten egg. Sprinkle with poppy seeds. Bake 45 minutes. Remove challahs from pans. Put upside down on stove rack and bake 15 minutes.

Makes 2 challahs.

MILCHEDIG (DAIRY) ONION ROLLS

¼ cup warm water
1 package dry yeast
⅛ teaspoon ground ginger
½ cup butter
¼ cup sugar
2 teaspoons salt
¾ cup milk, boiled

4 cups flour
4 eggs, beaten
1 tablespoon grated orange
  rind
1 cup finely chopped onion
1 egg, beaten
½ cup poppy seeds

In the warm water dissolve the yeast, stir in the ginger. Add butter, sugar, salt to the milk, stir until butter melts. Cool to lukewarm and beat in 1 cup flour, eggs, yeast mixture, and orange rind. Beat ingredients well. Stir in remaining flour to produce a soft dough. Turn out on floured board and knead smooth. Put in a greased bowl, cover with damp cloth, and let rise 2 hours until doubled in bulk. Punch down and set in refrigerator overnight. Shape the dough flat, round rolls 3 inches across, and set on oiled baking sheet. Press in the center of each. Fill with ½ teaspoon onion. Cover rolls to let them rise for 1 hour until they have doubled in bulk. Brush rolls with beaten egg, sprinkle with poppy seeds. Preheat oven, bake at 375°, 20 minutes, until golden brown.

Makes about 24 rolls.

CHEESE PANCAKES

3 eggs
Salt to taste
½ teaspoon sugar
1 cup water

½ pound cottage cheese
1½ cups flour
1 teaspoon baking powder

Beat eggs, add salt, sugar, water, cheese, flour, and baking powder. If batter is too thick, add a little liquid. Drop enough batter in pan for cakes 3 inches across. Fry in butter or margarine. Serve with syrup or jam.
6 servings.

ONION PIE

40 soda crackers, crushed into
    crumbs
1 cup melted margarine
2½ cups thinly sliced onions
1½ cups milk, scalded

3 eggs, beaten
1 tablespoon salt
¼ teaspoon pepper
½ pound Cheddar cheese,
    shredded

Preheat oven to 350°. Combine cracker crumbs with ½ cup margarine and line the bottom of a 9-inch pie plate with it. Brown onions in remaining margarine. Place in pie. Scald milk and add to eggs, stir constantly. Add salt, pepper, cheese. Pour over onions and bake in 350° oven 45 minutes, until knife inserted in center of pie comes out clean.
6 servings.

Dessert

PRUNE COMPOTE

¾ cup dry white wine
1 tablespoon lemon juice

2 cups prunes, presoaked
2 pears, sliced

In a saucepan mix wine and lemon juice, bring to a boil. Continue boiling for 5 minutes. Cool, chill. Cook and drain prunes. Chill pears and prunes. Combine fruits when cold. Serve covered with cooked liquid. 6 servings.

BLUEBERRY KUCHEN

1½ cups flour
Pinch of salt
½ cup butter
1 tablespoon white vinegar

1 cup granulated sugar
Pinch of ground cinnamon
3 cups blueberries
Confectioners' sugar

Mix 1 cup flour, salt, and butter with pastry blender, or by hand. Add vinegar. In a loose-bottom layer cake pan, spread crust mixture on bottom ¼ inch deep, and around sides 1 inch thick. Mix 1 cup granulated sugar, 2 tablespoons flour, cinnamon, 2 cups blueberries. Pour onto crust. Bake in preheated oven at 400° for 1 hour. Remove. Add 1 cup blueberries on top. Cool; remove rim. Sprinkle with confectioners' sugar. 6 servings.

SIMCHA (JOY) CARROT CAKE

2 cups flour
2 cups sugar
2 teaspoons baking soda
2 teaspoons ground cinnamon

1½ cups cooking oil
4 eggs
3 carrots, grated
1 teaspoon salt

Preheat oven to 325°. Take all ingredients and beat together. Grease
2 medium square cake pans. Bake at 325° for 35 minutes. Can be
served with either whipped cream or sour cream.
6 servings.

PURIM HAMANTASCHEN POLISH STYLE

Made to celebrate the death of a tyrant who was cruel to the Jews—
one Haman, minister to King Ahasuerus of ancient Persia. The Polish
Jews had natives all around them acting out the Haman ideas—so the
eating of Hamantaschen was a reminder that at times man is still wolf
to man.

1 pound jumbo prunes
1 cup honey
Juice of 1 lemon

1½ cups chopped almonds or
other nuts
1 quart pie dough, well kneaded

Preheat oven to 370°. Put prunes in boiling water and soak overnight. Bring prunes to boil in the water in which they were soaked. Lower heat to simmer, add honey and half of lemon juice. Cover, simmer 1 hour. Allow to stand, remove prune pits. Mash prunes to a paste, add chopped nuts. Roll dough to ⅛ inch thick on floured board, cut into 3-inch squares. Put 1 teaspoon filling on each, bring edges together to form a triangle. Make small opening in center of each. Pinch edges together to seal. Bake on tray in oven at 370°, 20 minutes.

For some hamantaschen—instead of prunes use following:

POPPY SEED FILLING

2 cups ground poppy seeds
½ cup honey
¼ cup sugar
½ cup raisins chopped

⅛ teaspoon salt
½ cup chopped blanched almonds
Grated rind of 1 lemon
1 egg, beaten

Bake as above.
Makes about 4 dozen.

MANDELBROT (ALMOND FRUIT BARS) CAKES

3 large eggs
1¼ cups sugar
1 cup peanut oil
3 tablespoons orange juice
4 cups flour
4 teaspoons baking powder

¼ teaspoon salt
1 (3-ounce) jar Dromedary
mixed baking fruit
1 cup chopped blanched
almonds

Preheat oven to 350°. Beat eggs thick and add sugar first, half of oil, orange juice, and mix. Combine dry ingredients with fruit and almonds and add to mixture to make a soft dough. Grease a cookie sheet and sides with oil. Also your hands. Take up dough, form into bars the length of the sheet. Shape with fingers straight bars flattened on top, 3

to the sheet. Bake 40 minutes, till the bars are pale brown on top. Remove from oven and move onto a board. Cut into diagonal slices 1 inch wide. Allow to cool. Put into covered container.
Makes 3½ dozen slices.

LVOW CHEESE BLINTZES

There was a rich Jew of Lvow who had three blintz chefs—one for cheese, one for jam, and one for nuts in his blintzes. Everybody had heard of him—but we never found anyone who knew his name or when he lived. That's how myths are born.

1 pound cottage cheese	1 tablespoon sugar
½ pound pot cheese	2 teaspoons salt
½ pound cream cheese	1½ cups sifted flour
1 cup sweet butter	1½ cups milk
8 eggs	1 pint sour cream

FOR THE FILLING: beat the cheeses, 1 tablespoon soft butter, 2 eggs, sugar, and ½ teaspoon salt together well. As for the batter: beat 6 eggs with wire whip, frothy; add remaining salt, flour, stir to make a smooth paste. Add milk, stir constantly. Heat 6-inch skillet. Grease well with butter. Pour in batter (3 tablespoons). Batter is rolled around to cover bottom. Cook until firm and brown on one side. Put on a plate, brown side up. Grease skillet. Fry another pancake. To fill, use 1 tablespoon filling placed by one edge of pancake. Fold up once, fold over two sides, add one more turn. Continue frying until batter and filling are all gone. To serve, heat a tablespoon butter in a skillet. Fry blintzes golden brown on both sides. Serve with sour cream.
6 servings.

NOODLE PUDDING

½ cup sugar	8 ounces cooked, drained
4 eggs	noodles
1 cup cream cheese	1 cup bread crumbs
1 cup milk	1 teaspoon ground cinnamon
1 stick butter, melted	2 tablespoons sugar

Preheat oven to 375°. Whip together sugar, eggs, cream cheese, milk, and butter. Add to noodles, place in baking pan. Top with crumbs and sprinkle cinnamon and sugar on mixture. Bake in 375° oven, 1½ hours. 4 servings.

SUCCOTH RAISIN RELISH

1 cup white raisins
1 piece gingerroot
2 cloves garlic
1½ teaspoons sugar

¼ teaspoon mustard seeds
¼ teaspoon cayenne
¼ teaspoon salt
¼ cup vinegar

Grind all ingredients together until smooth, and mix well. Goes well with meat and fish.

SHEVUOTH PICKLED WALNUTS

50 walnuts, shelled
1 pound salt
1 gallon water
2 quarts malt vinegar

2 tablespoons whole black
   peppercorns
2 tablespoons allspice
2 tablespoons crushed gingerroot

Place walnuts in large kettle, cover them with salted water. Keep walnuts in brine 9 days, changing brine every 3 days. Drain walnuts, spread in a pan, and let dry for 5 days. In a large saucepan mix enough malt vinegar to cover walnuts, add peppercorns, allspice, and ginger. Boil mixture 10 minutes, pour over walnuts, seal in jars. Store in a cool place for 30 days before using.
Makes about 1 quart.

GERMANY

If thy enemy be hungry give him bread to eat . . .
Proverbs 25:21

When the great German-Jewish poet and wit Heinrich Heine (1797–1856), was asked why he became a Christian convert, he replied, "So I would be sure to be invited to eat at the homes of the rich Jews." The reputation of the upper class German-Jewish tables as a gourmet's delight was of long standing. The early Rothschilds, after they no longer hid their wealth and power behind simple façades, gave their name to certain recipes as "Amschel and Baron Nathan Meyer de Rothschild dishes," even if in many cases there was no proof the original Frankfurt house actually prepared or served them.

Jewish-German cooking entranced many, not only those impressed by the names of the Rothschilds. There was Baron Maurice de Hirsch, who planned colonies of Jews in South America; Chaim Weizmann; Jakob Wassermann, the novelist; the Ullsteins, with an empire of publishing. All helped, by fine cooking, to produce interest in the merging of the two cuisines; often into a kind of game, to decide *which* dish was more German or Jewish. Food as served among the Jewish merchant and banking kings like Lutz Katzenellenbogen, President of Schultheiss-Patzenhofer, Fritz Warburg of the international money family, and others.

Germany was the nest from which came the Deutsche Yehudim, as those Germans were called—also the Shayna Leit—the Beautiful People. They resented the later Russian and Polish Jews coming over. The names ring with famous gourmets; Belmonts, Guggenheims, Schiffs, Strausses, Gimbels, Rosenwalds, Lowensteins, Fleischmans, Sulzbergers, Lehmans. One finds among their European family records, letters, and gossip, many clues to German-Jewish cooking. Recipes for Graubrot (gray bread) and Kümmelbrot (caraway seed bread), both produced free of lard, and also, of course, the popular pumpernickel. Calories were no problem in those days when the German Jews lived normal lives, and potatoes took many forms, even as filled dumplings, the Kartoffel Klosse. Soups, like the lentil, were fortified with Wurstchen (frankfurters), Warmbier was a hot beer soup, and to balance it, there was Bierkaltesschale, a cold beer soup. ("Only the pure in heart can make a good soup . . ." Ludwig van Beethoven—1817.)

German is a heavy language and the hunter of recipes and the sampling, tasting of them, after being found, takes one past words such as Hollunderbeersuppe, Hagerbuttensuppe, which are fruit soups, some with elderberry, apples, plums, cherries, as basic items. Most of these are of interest only to collectors.

To the kasha, which had come from Russia, German-Jewish cooking added the Grutzwurst, a mixture of buckwheat, rye, and oats, *and,* in the Jewish version, beef fat. Smoked in steer casings, it was served with kale. Leberwurst (liver sausage) was another filling item, kept free of pork liver.

Actually, the major accepting of Jewish-German cooking as a valid cuisine, began with the witty salons of Jewish women, intellectuals, who between 1825 and 1845, were among the first emancipated grande dames of the Germanic Romantic period, friends and hostesses of Heine and Goethe. Memoirs record the food of these salons. The tables of Dorothea Viet (the daughter of Moses Mendelssohn), Rachel Levin-Varnhagen, Henriette Herz.

From these Berlin salons and attending dinners, the merits of German-Jewish food were established. In modern times, Max Liebermann, the Jewish painter, had a reputation as a great gourmet, but he feared the food of some of those who sat for their portraits. His rules for painting a picture were, "3,000 Marks without dinner, 5,000 Marks *with* dinner." Men like Walter Rathenau, foreign minister of the Weimar Republic, and Mendelsohn Batholdy, the famous banker between the two World Wars, both collected German-Jewish recipes.

The banker Katzenellenbogen was the second husband of the actress Tilla Durieux, and when forced into exile during the Hitler regime, they went to Yugoslavia, where they opened the Hotel Cristallo, famous for its Jewish dishes, among them various splendid forms of veal.

Veal was, in most of Europe, the popular meat dish—the reason being that the farmers disposed of the calves early, rather than bear the cost of feeding a steer to maturity. The result was the splendid Sauer-braten with red cabbage, the Schnitzel in its various forms—in Jewish kitchens free of bacon fat and sour cream. The Holsteiner Schnitzel was a favorite with Ernst Lubitsch and Max Reinhardt. It was a flashy production number, with an egg spread-eagled on top, and guarded by capers, sardelles, and pickle. The actor Conrad Veit favored the Garnieter Schnitzel, which was breaded and garnished with beets, pickle. Both usually were served with Liepzier Allerlei, very young vegetables in the Leipzig manner.

The goose, Heine had once said, should be the national German bird, rather than the war eagle. It was a favorite fowl roasted. The wings, feet, neck, and giblets became, when cooked together, Ganseklein (little hunks of goose). A goose neck skin stuffed in the style of kishka or derma in the Jewish manner, with bread or flour, or potato, even meat, became a holiday favorite.

Rather unappetizing, as to sound, is Ganseschwarzsauer (goose blood soup), which was actually bits of goose meat cooked with prunes, a bay leaf, clove, and a stick of cinnamon, goose blood being used to thicken the gravy.

Herring was eaten in many ways, rightly so, for tasty fillets of the fish were a Baltic and North Sea delight, and not merely the diet of poor Russian and Polish Jews. Salt herring with the brine soaked out of it a bit was mixed with chopped beef to become Koenigsberger Klops with a caper sauce added. Popular as a snack was a herring salad, or a more formal Herringskartoffein, made up of the fish and potatoes in a casserole.

Smoked were the buckling herring, and fish like the sprat, flounder, salmon, and the eel, which the ritual Jew did *not* eat.

There was once a plenty of the Rhine salmon, the carp is still around. The German-Jews obeyed the Northern European taboo; "Never cut fish with steel knives, and one doesn't cut the accompanying potato with a knife." "Everyone mopped up gravy," wrote a Warburg to an American cousin, "with a piece of bread."

The Kasesplatte (cheese platter) appeared in the more worldly Jewish homes at the end of the meal. There was also the Liebfraumilch, Burgundies, and other wines. While "Cold Duck" as a drink is a term new to us, Jewish-German children were given drinks of the kalte ente (Cold Duck, of course), a mixture, in its original form, of Moselle or Rhine wine with Selterwasser.

Victoria Wolff, popular German-American author, remembers the cheeses eaten at the end of a meal, such as Tilsiter, Munster, Allgauer, Harzerand, Emmentaler, and the strong, often the *so* strong, Limburger.

Milder was the Weiss Kümmelkaese; pot cheese with caraway seeds. This, if allowed to ripen in ceramic jars, became a very strong-smelling item indeed, and was called Harzerkaese.

Beer flowed freely in German-Jewish circles—few drank water, but ice water was an unknown item. Muenchen Hofbrauhaus beer was known all over the world. In a serious state of tipple, the German Jews would call out "Prosit!" and "Zum Wohlsein!" (Drink! and, To your health!) as they sipped a little Schnapps, a Steinhager, or Kümmel.

As so often in our survey of a Jewish gastronomic history, we are writing of the past. Of a time gone, when greatly talented Jews, *and* ordinary ones, geniuses or craftsmen, lovers and married folk, relatives and friends could come together as Germans and as Jews and toast each other in the Rhine or Saar Hock wines with words to a "Gesegnete" (a blessed mealtime).

Meat

SAUERBRATEN

German-Jewish wives prided themselves on their Sauerbraten—and rightly so. It differed slightly from the accepted form.

4 pounds boned shoulder beef
2 cups vinegar
1 cup Rhine wine
1 teaspoon whole cloves
1 teaspoon whole black peppers
1 bay leaf
1 clove garlic, bruised
2 onions, sliced thin

1 orange, with peel, sliced
1 tablespoon salt
$\frac{1}{2}$ teaspoon ground peppercorns
1 cup water
2 tablespoons vegetable
   shortening
1 cup tomato purée
6 Zwieback

Tie beef in a roll, place in bowl. Add to it vinegar, wine, cloves, peppers, bay leaf, garlic, onion slices, orange slices, salt, pepper, 1 cup of water. Cover tightly. Refrigerate 4 days, turning once a day. Take meat from marinade and dry. Put shortening in Dutch oven with meat and brown all sides. Add marinade, tomato purée; bring to a boil, cover, simmer 2 hours till meat is tender. Take out meat, strain, reserving 2 cups of liquid. Return meat and 2 cups liquid to pan and put in Zwieback, boil, stirring constantly, 3 minutes, add meat, and serve.
10 servings.

PEPPER STEAK

1 (1-pound) slice chuck steak,
   1 inch thick
2 onions, sliced thin
1 green pepper, sliced thin
$\frac{1}{4}$ pound button mushrooms

4 water chestnuts, sliced thin
1 teaspoon ground gingerroot
4 tablespoons soy sauce
$\frac{1}{2}$ cup cooking oil
2 tablespoons orange brandy

Preheat oven to 350°. Cut meat into 1-inch strips. Trim, discard fat. Combine all ingredients. Put on a cookie sheet with sides. Bake 45 minutes.

4 servings.

BAVARIAN MEAT LOAF

2 slices white bread	2 eggs
1 pound ground lean beef	1 cup chili sauce
1 pound ground veal	Salt, pepper to taste
1 onion, minced	3 hard-cooked eggs, cut in half
½ teaspoon ground coriander seeds	6 pimento-stuffed green olives, cut in half

Preheat oven to 350°. Soak bread in water, squeeze dry. Combine the bread, meats, onion, coriander, and the 2 eggs. Add ½ cup of chili sauce. Grease a loaf pan and put in half the meat mixture, set a row of the hard-cooked eggs down the center of the meat, cut side up, with olive halves. Add the remainder of the meat mixture. Pour rest of chili sauce on top. Bake in 350° oven, 1 hour.

6 servings.

SAUERKRAUT WITH BRATWURST AND PASTRAMI

¼ pound sliced fat pastrami	1 teaspoon caraway seeds
1 onion, finely chopped	1 bay leaf
2 pounds sauerkraut	1 tablespoon sugar
1 quart dry white wine	2 pairs bratwurst
1 potato, peeled	Parsley sprigs to garnish
5 juniper berries	

Cut the pastrami in cubes and fry in heavy kettle. Add chopped onion and sauté until the pastrami and onion are crisp. Add sauerkraut and fill kettle with wine until sauerkraut is covered. Stir, add potato, sliced, juniper berries, caraway seeds, bay leaf, and sugar. Bring to boil and simmer, covered, for 1½ hours. Add bratwurst; cover with sauer-

kraut. Simmer 30 minutes. Remove bratwurst and sauté it in frying pan until brown. Serve the sauerkraut on a platter with the cooked meats surrounding it. Top with fresh parsley sprigs.
4 servings.

POTTED BEEF ON NOODLES

4 tablespoons margarine
2 cups Chicken Soup
1 cup water
2 tablespoons dry sherry wine
1½ pounds round beef, cut in
   2-inch cubes

1 cup drained mushroom stems
3 carrots, quartered
½ pound medium noodles,
   cooked

In a skillet put margarine, 1 cup chicken soup, water, and sherry. Add meat. Cover. Simmer, stirring occasionally, for 30 minutes. Add remaining cup of chicken soup. Simmer until meat is tender, 1 hour. Add mushrooms and carrots 20 minutes before meat is done. Serve beef over hot noodles.
4 servings.

LAMB CHOPS WITH MUSHROOM-ONION SAUCE AND PARSLIED NOODLES

6 shoulder lamb chops, 1 inch
   thick
Salt, pepper to taste
3 tablespoons margarine
1 small onion, chopped

¼ pound mushrooms, chopped
2 tablespoons flour
1 cup Chicken Soup
2 cups noodles, cooked
1 tablespoon chopped parsley

Sprinkle lamb chops with salt and pepper and in pan broil 12 minutes, turning once. In a small skillet on low heat, in margarine, cook onion and mushrooms 10 minutes until onion is tender. Stir in flour, salt and pepper to taste, and soup. Mix, stir until thickened. Serve on chops and hot noodles. Garnish with parsley.
6 servings.

MATZO-STUFFED VEAL

4 matzos
¾ cup water
2 eggs, beaten
1 teaspoon salt
Pinch of ginger

Pinch of pepper
1 tablespoon chopped parsley
2 onions, chopped
4 slices veal

Preheat oven to 350°. Crumble matzos and sprinkle with ¼ cup water; add all other ingredients except meat and remaining water. Spread on thin slices of veal, roll up and skewer. Place in roasting pan, add ½ cup of water, and bake in moderate oven at 350° until done. 4 servings.

SHORT RIBS WITH SAUERKRAUT

3 pounds beef short ribs
1½ teaspoons salt
¼ teaspoon pepper

½ cup water
1 pound sauerkraut

Preheat oven to 300°. Brown short ribs slowly in a pan on all sides in their own fat. Pour away excess drippings. Season with salt and pepper.

Add water, cover, bake at 300° until meat is tender. Add sauerkraut and cook 10 minutes or until sauerkraut is heated through.
4 servings.

DOCK-SIDE COFFEE POT ROAST (HAMBURG)

3 tablespoons beef fat
1 (4-pound) pot roast
2 cups double-strength coffee
1/4 cup brandy

1 teaspoon each, salt, pepper, paprika, cinnamon
1/4 teaspoon thyme

Heat fat and in skillet brown pot roast over medium heat. Mix everything else and pour on roast. Cover and bring to boil. Reduce to a bare simmer, and cook for 4 hours. Check occasionally to add liquid if necessary. Remove the roast, skim fat off pot liquor, and serve the rest as gravy.
8 servings.

PEACH DUSSELDORF RIBS

3 pounds spareribs, cut into
   pieces
6 boiled peaches with juice
1 cup catsup
2 tablespoons Worcestershire
   sauce

1/2 cup minced onion
2 tablespoons flour
2 tablespoons Dusseldorf
   mustard
1/2 teaspoon ground cloves
Pinch of salt, pepper to taste

Preheat oven to 375°. Dry ribs and put in baking pan. Drain 1 cup of juice from peaches and mix with all ingredients. Bring sauce to boil, cook 4 minutes, stir until smooth. Pour the simmering sauce over the ribs and bake uncovered for 1 1/2 hours at 375°; baste and turn every 20 minutes.
6 servings.

FAMILY BRISKET IN LAGER BEER

5 pounds beef brisket
2 onions, sliced
4 whole celery stalks
½ cup tomato sauce

2 teaspoons salt
¼ teaspoon pepper
1 tablespoon brown sugar
1 can lager beer

Preheat oven to 325°. Put beef in roaster after covering with all ingredients *except* beer. Add 1 inch of water in bottom of roaster. Roast uncovered for 3 hours at 325°. Baste often. Add beer, cover, roast 2 more hours.
6 servings.

MÜNCHEN WINEBRATEN

2 cups cubed cooked beef roast
¼ cup wine vinegar
2 tablespoons mixed pickling
    spice, tied in cheesecloth
¼ teaspoon bottled meat sauce
½ teaspoon salt

⅛ teaspoon pepper
1 cup beef broth
1 medium onion, chopped
½ cup Rhine wine
1 tablespoon cornstarch

Mix it all in a saucepan. Simmer covered 1 hour until thickened, stir occasionally. Discard pickling spice. Serve with potato pancakes.
4 servings.

ROAST OF VEAL

1 (5-pound) veal rump roast,
    with bone
1 tablespoon dry Dijon mustard
1 teaspoon poultry seasoning
2 tablespoons flour
1 tablespoon brown sugar

1 tablespoon salt
Pepper to taste
3 tablespoons beef fat
½ cup Burgundy
1 onion, sliced
1 garlic clove, crushed

Dress meat with mixture of mustard, poultry seasoning, flour, brown sugar, salt, and pepper. In a pan with beef fat, brown on all sides. Add wine, onion, and garlic. Cover tightly; simmer 2½ hours until meat is tender. Serve with potato kugel.
4 servings.

VEAL IMPERIAL

This was a favorite dish of Stefan Zweig in his youth, and many famous German-Jewish authors such as Feuchtwanger, Werfel, Döblin, and others used to enjoy it in a keller on West Berlin's Kurfuerstendamm.

4 large potatoes, peeled, grated	1 (4-pound) breast of veal, with
3 onions	pocket
½ cup chicken fat	1 clove garlic, mashed
1 egg	1 tablespoon paprika
½ cup bread crumbs	1 cup dry white wine
Salt, pepper to taste	1 cup cider

Preheat oven to 350°. Set potatoes in a strainer and press out the water. In a bowl put grated potatoes, 1 grated onion, chicken fat, egg, bread crumbs, salt, and pepper. Combine thoroughly and press into veal pocket. Sew up pocket with heavy thread and set aside. In a bowl mix 1 grated onion, garlic, paprika, and salt and pepper. Mix to a paste and rub into all parts of the veal. Slice remaining onion and set in bottom of

a roaster. Put stuffed veal on top, pour wine and cider over veal. Roast in oven 1½ hours, basting frequently.
6 servings.

GIBLET FRICASSEE WITH MEATBALLS

3 onions, diced
½ cup chicken fat
Giblets and wings from 2
    chickens, cut up
3 cups hot water
2 teaspoons salt

1 teaspoon freshly ground pepper
1 pound ground beef
1 small clove garlic, minced
½ cup dry red wine
1 egg
¼ cup flour

In a 3½-quart pot with a lid, fry onions brown in chicken fat. Add giblets and wings and brown; stir constantly. Mix in 3 cups hot water, 1 teaspoon salt, and pepper. Boil, lower heat, cover, simmer until giblets are soft. For the meatballs: in a bowl combine chopped meat, garlic, 1 teaspoon salt, wine, and egg. Mix thoroughly and form walnut-sized meatballs. Put them in the broth. Cover, simmer 20 minutes. Mix flour with 2 tablespoons of broth. Add to pot, bring to boil. Serve.
4 servings.

DRESDEN STUFFED PEPPERS

4 green peppers, parboiled
1 egg
1 cup tomato sauce
1 teaspoon salt
¼ teaspoon oregano
Pinch of pepper

1 pound ground round beef
½ cup bread crumbs
2 onions
1 tablespoon dried parsley
½ cup boiling water

Preheat oven to 325°. Cut tops off peppers and reserve; clean of seeds. Beat egg, add half of tomato sauce, seasonings, and beat well. Add meat, bread crumbs, 1 onion, and parsley. Stuff peppers *lightly*. Slice 1 onion and set on bottom of a casserole. Salt. Put stuffed peppers on top. Replace their tops. Pour remaining tomato sauce over peppers and ½ cup of boiling water. Bake uncovered 1½ hours at 350°. Baste twice with liquid.
4 servings.

Fowl

YEHUDIM CHICKEN LIVER PÂTÉ

The German Yehudim, the rest of the European Jews suspected, looked down on all of them, as they were snubbed by the Spanish Sephardim. So the German chopped chicken liver became a pâté—and a very good one.

1 pound chicken livers	¼ pint Chicken Soup
3 tablespoons chicken fat	1 clove garlic, minced
Salt, pepper to taste	2 tablespoons brandy

Sauté livers in fat in a frying pan. Remove while still pink inside. Put through a food mill. Season with salt and pepper, add soup. Mix in crushed clove of garlic and brandy. Set in a dish in refrigerator overnight.
8 servings.

WHOLE CHICKEN LIVERS

A rich version of the popular chicken liver.

1 cup cooked carrots	1 cup margarine
1 cup cooked peas	1 cup Chicken Soup
1 pound chicken livers	2 tablespoons flour
Seasoned flour	¼ teaspoon poultry seasoning

Preheat oven to 350°. Drain vegetables, and put in 1-quart casserole. Pierce livers with a fork, roll in flour. Fry in half of margarine until brown, add vegetables. Put rest of margarine in skillet and add soup and flour, seasoning. Cook until thickened and pour over livers. Bake in moderate oven at 350° for 15 minutes.
4 servings.

GRIEBEN (RENDERED CHICKEN SKIN) IN HOT POTATO SALAD

4 pounds potatoes
3 onions, chopped
¾ cup sugar
Salt, black pepper to taste
½ pound diced grieben

1 cup hot water
½ cup cider vinegar
2 hard-boiled eggs, sliced, to
  garnish

In skins boil potatoes tender, peel and slice while warm. Add chopped onions to potatoes, and sugar, salt, and pepper. Fry grieben crisp. Add water and vinegar to grieben, bring to boil. Set over potatoes and onions and mix. Garnish with hard-boiled eggs.
8 servings.

CHAMPAGNE CHICKEN

Berlin grain merchants and brokers once had a Jewish club that featured this dish.

2 pounds chicken parts
½ cup flour
Salt, pepper to taste
½ cup olive oil
2 tablespoons curaçao

1 cup champagne
1 cup chicken consommé
1 cup sliced mushrooms
1 tablespoon cooking oil
½ cup Chicken Soup

Preheat oven to 350°. Dredge the chicken parts in flour, salt, and pepper, and brown in olive oil thoroughly. Move to a casserole and bake uncovered, 20 minutes at 350°. Add curaçao, champagne, and consommé, cover, and bake 20 minutes. Sauté the mushrooms in cooking oil 5 minutes over medium heat. Add chicken soup, heat, *but* without boiling; pour over chicken.
4 servings.

BREAST OF CHICKEN RHINE YEHUDIM

1 full breast of 4-pound chicken
2 tablespoons sliced pitted olives
Paprika, salt, pepper to taste
1 tablespoon bottled meat sauce
½ cup flour

1 egg, beaten
½ cup bread crumbs
½ cup salad oil
1 cup tomato sauce

Split breast of chicken in half, bone, and flatten. On each half of chicken breast place a tablespoon of sliced olives, sprinkle with paprika, salt, pepper, and meat sauce. Fold chicken pieces over, flour, dip into beaten egg, and roll in bread crumbs. Heat oil in a skillet over medium heat. Sauté chicken until browned on each side. Set on table with hot tomato sauce.
2 servings.

ROAST DUCKLING—BING CHERRY

Stuffing for ducklings
2 (4 pounds each) ducklings
1 pound (½-pint) can pitted
Bing cherries

½ cup red port wine
1 tablespoon cornstarch
2 tablespoons cold water

Preheat oven to 325°. Stuff ducklings with a favorite stuffing. Roast in 325° oven on rack for 3 hours until tender. Drain cherries, reserve

juice, add wine to liquid and bring to boil; thicken with cornstarch mixed with 2 tablespoons cold water. Return cherries to sauce, bring to a boil. Split ducklings lengthwise. Pour on hot cherry sauce.
8 servings.

STEWED GROUSE ROTHSCHILD

Unlike so many Rothschild-named dishes, this one *is* authentic.

MARINADE:

½ cup red wine	1 onion, sliced
½ cup olive oil	1 carrot, sliced
5 whole black peppercorns	2 sprays parsley
5 crushed juniper berries	1 bay leaf
2 (about 3 pounds each—dressed) mature grouse	4 small onions
1 cup beef or chicken fat	2 teaspoons salt
½ pound carrots	2 tablespoons allspice

Preheat oven to 375°. Mix all ingredients for marinade in pan, bring to boil. Set aside to cool. Pour on the grouse and marinate overnight in refrigerator. Next day put ½ cup of fat in a heavy casserole. Add the sliced onions and carrots. Stir for 2 minutes. Remove grouse from marinade, brown on all sides. Pour in the strained marinade. Add salt, allspice, all other ingredients, cover, and cook in oven 3 hours until birds are tender. To serve, cut grouse in half, "lay them on dish with the sauce."
6 servings.

Fish

POACHED CARP SELIGMAN

The early nineteenth century saw the emerging into the open of the great Jewish families in Germany. The Seligmans of Baiersdorf, August Belmont (nee Schonberg), other Jews in the Rhineland-Palatinate at Worms, Frankfurt. Their greater riches were to be made later in America, these Speyers, Bernheimers, Josephthals, Neustadts, Lewisohns, Heidelbachs; a group to be called the "Jewish Grand Dukes." One runs across accounts of their dinners, given by their grandes dames, all over Germany—and old recipes from their kitchens exist among more important family papers. It was already fine living. In the New World, the Morgenthaus, Altschuls, Ladenburgs, could state simply there were *two* kinds of Jews, "People *we* visit, people we *wouldn't* visit." Poor Haym Solomon of the American Revolution would not be acceptable. "He came from Poland."

1 pint vermouth, extra dry	12 whole black peppercorns
1 quart water	1/4 teaspoon thyme
1 large onion, sliced	1 teaspoon salt
3 stalks celery, sliced	1/2 cup heavy cream
1 carrot, chopped	3 egg yolks
3 sprigs parsley	1 (5-pound) carp
1 bay leaf	

Mix vermouth, water, onion, celery, carrot, parsley, bay leaf, peppercorns, thyme, salt, cream, and egg yolks. Cover, simmer slowly for 1/2 hour, and then strain. Wrap fish in cheesecloth and place in pan. Pour broth over fish, cover, simmer 25 minutes until tender. Peel off skin, get out most bones. Place on platter and serve with lemon wedges.
4 servings.

SWEET AND SOUR SALMON SCHONBERG

4 slices (about 2 pounds) fresh   1½ cups water
  salmon   ½ teaspoon sugar
1 pint cider vinegar   10 soda crackers
2 large onions, sliced   ½ teaspoon pickling spice

First marinate salmon in the vinegar in covered vessel overnight in refrigerator. In a pot put the sliced onions, 1½ cups water. Boil 10 minutes; lower heat and add fish, 4 tablespoons of the marinade, and sugar. Put crackers in a bowl, add 1 cup of hot fish liquid, and mix to paste with pickling spice. Spoon paste over fish in pot. Cover, simmer 20 minutes. Remove from heat and cool. Remove fish to new container, pour sauce over fish. Cover and set in refrigerator. Serve cold with lemon slices.

4 servings.

HERRING POTATO CASSEROLE

1 large onion, chopped   2 matjes herrings, cut in 2-inch
3 tablespoons margarine   pieces
6 medium-sized potatoes, peeled,   ¼ teaspoon pepper
  grated   ½ pint heavy cream

Preheat oven to 350°. Fry onion until soft in 2 tablespoons of margarine in a skillet. Arrange potatoes, herrings, and onion in greased baking dish, start and end with potatoes. Sprinkle with pepper. Pour cream over the potatoes. Dot with remaining margarine. Bake, covered, in oven at 350° for 1 hour.

6 servings.

SWEET AND SOUR FISH

1 (4-pound) carp or pike
1 onion, minced
1 tablespoon mixed spices
½ cup raisins
2 bay leaves

1 lemon, sliced
½ cup chopped almonds
5 gingersnaps, crumbled
1 cup sugar
1 cup white vinegar

Slice fish in small 2-inch-wide pieces. Combine onion and spices with raisins, bay leaves, and lemon. Cover with water, bring to a boil. Put in fish, almonds, gingersnaps, sugar, and vinegar. Cook at medium heat 1½ hours. Serve hot.
8 servings.

HERRINGS IN MATZO MEAL

8 salt herrings (2 herrings per person)
1 cup milk

2 cups matzo meal
½ cup butter
2 lemons, quartered

Preheat oven to 375°. Fillet the herrings; remove heads and tails, split open, take out backbones. Wash, leave in any roe, and dry on a cloth. Dip each fillet in milk, then in the matzo meal. Be sure they are *well* covered. Dot each one with butter and broil in oven 5 minutes, turn over; broil for 4 minutes. Serve with quarters of lemon on top.
4 servings.

Soup

SPLIT PEA SOUP

½ cup plus 1 tablespoon oil
1 large onion, chopped
2 pounds soup bones
1 clove garlic, crushed
3 inches stick cinnamon
2 whole cloves
2 cardamom seeds, crushed
¼ teaspoon whole black
  peppercorns
½ teaspoon minced gingerroot

1 teaspoon cumin
½ teaspoon paprika
½ teaspoon salt
2 tomatoes, peeled, chopped
1 cup split green peas, soaked 2
  hours
2 cups boiling water
1 onion, sliced
1 green onion, chopped, to
  garnish

Heat ½ cup oil and brown chopped onion. Add soup bones, garlic, cinnamon, cloves, cardamom, peppercorns, ginger, cumin, paprika, salt. Fry 5 minutes. Add tomatoes, cook 5 minutes. Add drained peas and stir for 4 minutes. Cover with boiling water, simmer, covered, for 3 hours. Before serving, brown sliced onion in 1 tablespoon oil and add to soup. Garnish with chopped green onion.
4 servings.

ZAYDE WEISS'S APPLE AND WINE SOUP

3 cups water
½ cup sugar
8 green apples, peeled, cored, sliced
2 inches stick cinnamon

1 square inch lemon rind
1½ cups dry white bread crumbs
2 cups dry red Rhine wine
Juice of ½ lemon

In a saucepan mix water and sugar and bring to boil. Add sliced green apples, cinnamon stick, rind of lemon, and dry white bread crumbs. Cook the mixture, stirring occasionally, for 10 minutes, until apples are tender. Remove cinnamon stick and lemon rind. Force the mixture through the fine disk of a food mill. Return the mixture to the pan, add red wine, lemon juice, simmer 3 minutes. Chill for 3 hours. Serve cold. 6 servings.

GERMAN-JEWISH SCHAV (COLD SORREL SOUP)

The Yehudim always claimed *their* schav (or shuff) was better than the Russian version cooked in the shtetlach, which soup some claimed was "flavored with bloote [mud]."

1 pound sorrel, stemmed, washed
2 quarts water
2 teaspoons salt
2 tablespoons sugar
1 tablespoon lemon juice

3 eggs
½ cup milk
1 cup sour cream
1 cup chopped cucumbers to garnish

Finely chop the sorrel leaves, put in a heavy saucepan. Add water and salt. Bring mixture to a boil, cook over low heat 30 minutes. Add sugar, lemon juice, cook mixture for 12 minutes. In a bowl beat eggs with ½ cup milk. Pour 1 cup of the hot soup over the eggs, and return mixture to saucepan. Take pan from heat and cool. In a bowl mix sour cream with ½ cup of soup and return to the saucepan. Chill soup, pour into bowls, garnish with chopped cucumber.
8 servings.

LUFTMENSH (DREAMERS) SPLIT PEA SOUP

3 cups Chicken Soup
1 cup split green peas
¼ teaspoon dried chervil
2 slices onion
Salt, pepper to taste

3 cups clear beef soup
½ cup dry sherry
1 teaspoon paprika to garnish
3 sprigs chervil to garnish

Mix chicken soup, peas, dried chervil, onion in a saucepan. Bring to a boil, cover, simmer 1 hour until peas are soft. Purée by forcing through a food mill. Season to taste with salt and pepper and thin with chicken soup if needed. Mix the pea soup with beef soup, heat until near boiling. Pour in sherry. Garnish with paprika and sprig of chervil.
6 servings.

SPINACH SOUP

3 tablespoons butter
1 tablespoon grated yellow onion
3 tablespoons flour
Salt, pepper to taste
2 cups sour cream
2 pounds fresh spinach

½ cup cooked puréed carrots
2 cups water
½ cup dry sherry
1½ cups toasted chopped
    almonds

Melt butter, add onion and flour, season. Cook slowly over low heat; stir gently, *not* browning the flour. Warm the cream and add all the vegetables and water. Bring to a boil, lower heat, and simmer, covered, 30 minutes; stir occasionally. Reduce heat, add sherry, and stir constantly for 1 minute. Add almonds. Serve.
6 servings.

BARON DE HIRSCH SOUP À LA CHAMPAGNE

6 yellow onions, sliced
2 tablespoons margarine
6 cups Chicken Soup
2 teaspoons cognac
1 bay leaf
¼ teaspoon nutmeg

Salt, pepper to taste
2 cups dry champagne
2 egg yolks
⅓ cup port
Toasted bread to garnish

Sauté onions over low heat with margarine, 20 minutes; stir frequently until deeply browned, not burned. Add soup, bay leaf, nutmeg, salt, and pepper. Bring to a boil, lower heat, simmer covered 25 minutes. Add the champagne, bring to a boil, reduce to a simmer 2 minutes. Combine beaten egg yolks with half of soup. Add port and cognac, and blend with rest of hot soup; stir on low heat until smooth and thick. Pour rest of soup in bowls and put bits of toasted bread on top.
4 servings.

LEBERKLOSE SOUP

3 slices white bread
5 cups chicken broth or soup
1 egg
1 onion, chopped
½ pound calf's liver, chopped

1 teaspoon chicken fat
Salt, pepper to taste
Pinch of marjoram
½ cup chopped chives to
   garnish

Soak the bread in half a cup of soup. Put egg and onion into a blender and make smooth. Add chopped liver to blender for 10 seconds. Put liver mixture into a bowl with the bread and fat. Season with salt, pepper, and a pinch of marjoram. Shape into balls the size of hazelnuts. In a pot bring chicken broth to boil, add liver balls. Reduce heat, simmer for 20 minutes. Serve with chopped chives.
4 servings.

DUCK SOUP

Once when Germany had a large population of upper class Jewish businessmen, intellectuals, and prominent political figures, their dinners often featured a traditional duck soup.

1 (5-pound) duck	2 sprigs parsley
2 onions, sliced	6 whole black peppercorns
2 carrots, sliced	½ bunch watercress
1 stalk celery	½ pint dry white wine
1 bay leaf	Salt, pepper to taste

Place cleaned duck in a pan with sliced onions and carrots, celery, bay leaf, parsley, peppercorns, and watercress. Pour in wine and enough water to cover. Bring to a boil. Simmer 1¼ hours until duck is cooked. Cut out the breast in 2 pieces. Strain stock and cool. Set aside 1 day and skim fat from stock and reheat. Season with salt and pepper well. Take breasts of duck, cut into sections. Heat duck meat and soup in pot 10 minutes. Pour into plates.
6 servings.

LENTIL SOUP

1 (1-pound) piece flanken, diced	1 tablespoon flour
2 quarts beef or chicken broth	2 cups lentils
2 stalks celery, chopped	2 bay leaves
1 leek, chopped	2 whole cloves in spice bag
1 carrot, chopped	¼ cup vinegar
1 onion, chopped	Salt, pepper to taste

Cook beef in 1 cup of broth until *lightly* browned in a saucepan. Add celery, leek, carrot, and onion, cook until vegetables are tender, not brown. Stir in flour, add broth, lentils, stir. Add bay leaves and cloves in cloth bag. Bring to a boil, reduce heat. Simmer, covered, 2 hours. Discard spice bag. Add vinegar, salt, and pepper. Heat to serving temperature.
8 servings.

LAMB-CORN MEAL SOUP

1 cup diced lamb
6 cups water
2 carrots, diced
2 potatoes, peeled, diced

1 large onion, diced
½ cup corn meal
Pinch of dried mint
Salt, pepper to taste

Cook diced meat in saucepan with water until tender. Add diced carrots, potatoes, onion, and corn meal. Simmer 15 minutes, add mint, salt, and pepper.
6 servings.

ZIONIST BEET-CABBAGE BORSCH

A club dish popular among Zionist members.

1½ pounds short ribs
1 onion, cut up
Margarine
Salt, pepper to taste
1 knuckle bone
1 head cabbage
4 cups boiling water

2 beets, sliced
1 tablespoon sugar
1 small potato
Juice of 1 lemon
2 cups stewed tomatoes
6 whole black peppercorns

Sauté meat and onion in pan in margarine, season to taste. Move to soup pot with bone. Shred cabbage, salt, and soak in boiling water 10 minutes, covered. Add more water and the cabbage to meat in soup pot with other ingredients. Simmer 1 hour, covered. Discard bone.
6 servings.

Vegetables

STUFFED CABBAGE

1 medium-sized cabbage,
washed, cored
2 onions, chopped
3 tablespoons oil
½ cup rice, cooked

2 eggs, beaten
1 teaspoon each, salt, pepper
2 tablespoons chicken fat
2 cups water
3 tomatoes, peeled, chopped

Cut off thick cabbage leaves and soften by putting in boiling water to cover for 4 minutes. Sauté onions in half the oil until light brown. Add the rice, beaten eggs, and stir. Add salt, pepper, and fat. Put 2 tablespoons each of mixture on a leaf, roll up, tuck in ends. Chop rest of cabbage and fry in remaining oil. Add stuffed leaves, water, salt, pepper, and chopped tomatoes. Cook 10 minutes.
4 servings.

CORN CABBAGE RELISH

1 quart corn cut from cobs
2 cups chopped cabbage
2 green peppers, chopped
2 sweet peppers, chopped
1 cup sugar

1 cup water
1 quart cider vinegar
1 tablespoon celery seeds
1 tablespoon pickling spice
2 tablespoons salt

Combine all the ingredients, cook 30 minutes, stir frequently. Place in hot, sterilized jars, *lightly* seal. Place in hot water 20 minutes, seal tightly.
Makes nearly 2 quarts.

EGGS IN TOMATOES

2 large tomatoes
2 eggs
Salt, pepper to taste

2 tablespoons oil
1 onion, chopped
½ cup water

Cut off the top of each tomato, scoop out pulp and reserve. Break an egg unbeaten into each tomato and add salt and pepper. Put oil in saucepan, add onion, fry until brown. Add tomato pulp, water, salt, and pepper, and boil. Add the egg-filled tomatoes, cover saucepan, and cook 10 minutes. Spoon sauce over tomatoes.
2 servings.

KOSHER GERMAN DILL PICKLES

½ cup pickling spice
8 cloves garlic, bruised
2-gallon stoneware jar
10 *firm* cucumbers

½ cup fresh chopped dill
½ cup white vinegar
1 cup salt

Place pickling spice and garlic in bottom of a stoneware jar. Pack cucumbers in tightly, put dill in the middle. Add vinegar, and the brine made of the salt and enough water to cover pickles up to top. Set in a cool place for 2 weeks.
Makes about 2 gallons.

BUTTERMILK HORSERADISH DRESSING

¾ cup buttermilk
2 tablespoons ground horseradish
1 tablespoon vinegar

1 tablespoon sugar
¼ teaspoon salt
½ teaspoon Düsseldorf mustard

Mix all ingredients thoroughly and chill.
Best for fish, salads, and as flavoring for potato, cabbage.
Makes 1 cup.

MUSHROOM CHEESE CASSEROLE

2 cups Chicken Soup
1 pound mushrooms
2 tablespoons flour
½ cup heavy cream
½ teaspoon salt

Dash pepper
½ cup bread crumbs
¾ cup grated Parmesan cheese
¼ cup butter

Preheat oven to 350°. In sauce pan heat the soup. Slice mushrooms into a casserole. To the soup add flour, cream, salt, and pepper. Cook until thickened and pour over mushrooms. Combine crumbs and cheese; sprinkle on top. Dot with butter, bake in moderate 350° oven 30 minutes, until browned.
6 servings.

PESACH (PASSOVER) GLAZED ONIONS

3 tablespoons margarine
3 tablespoons brown sugar

3 tablespoons ale or beer
1½ pounds onions, cooked

Melt the margarine in skillet. Add brown sugar and ale (or beer). Add drained onions, cook uncovered, stirring often, until onions are heated and glazed.
6 servings.

CUCUMBER-ONION RELISH WITH MUSTARD SEEDS

3 large cucumbers, peeled,
  chopped
1½ teaspoons salt
1 onion, minced

1 cup white vinegar
½ teaspoon mustard seeds
½ teaspoon freshly ground black
  pepper

Set cucumbers in a bowl with salt, drain after 1 hour, in a colander. Add all remaining ingredients and cover. Chill.
Makes 3 cups.

EGG SALAD

8 hard-cooked eggs
1 cup sliced celery
2 green onions, chopped
2 tablespoons chopped parsley

1 teaspoon salt
1 cup diced sweet red pepper
⅓ cup mayonnaise
Pepper, cayenne to taste

Slice eggs in large 1-inch pieces. Combine with celery, onions, parsley, salt, red pepper, and mayonnaise. Season to taste with the pepper and cayenne. Serve on lettuce.
4 servings.

STUFFED TOMATOES

4 large cucumbers
2 tablespoons salt
2 tablespoons sugar
1 teaspoon pepper
1 cup sour cream

½ cup mayonnaise
½ cup chopped dill
3 large tomatoes
2 hard-cooked eggs

Wash and peel cucumbers, cut in half lengthwise, scoop out seeds and discard. Slice cucumbers thin. Put in bowl, sprinkle with salt, and put in refrigerator for 2 hours. Pour off water, press out any additional moisture. Add sugar and pepper. Mix sour cream and mayonnaise and pour over cucumbers, toss lightly, add half of dill. Remove a circle from the stem ends of the tomatoes. Carefully scoop out all seeds and pulp of tomatoes; discard. Stuff them with cucumber mixture. Sprinkle rest of dill on top of tomatoes, garnish with slices of hard-cooked eggs.
6 servings.

BERLIN PICKLED EGGS

2 teaspoons dried ground ginger
2 tablespoons salt
6 pickled green chilies, sliced
1 pint vinegar
1 teaspoon sliced gingerroot

3 teaspoons mustard seeds
3 teaspoons crushed black
  peppercorns
Pinch of dill
10 hard-cooked eggs

Combine all ingredients *except* eggs, simmer 15 minutes. Prick eggs all over with fork and place in a glass jar. Pour in spiced vinegar mixture. Refrigerate until used.
10 servings.

HOT POTATO SALAD

¼ pound pastrami bits
1½ tablespoons flour
1 tablespoon sugar
1 teaspoon salt
Pinch of cayenne

⅓ cup vinegar
⅓ cup water
4 cups peeled, sliced, cooked
  potato
Chopped parsley

Fry pastrami for 1 minute. Remove. To fat in pan add flour, sugar, salt, cayenne, vinegar, and water. Cook, stir until thickened. Add potato and heat for 5 minutes. Sprinkle with pastrami bits and parsley.
4 servings.

APPLE-CARROT TZIMMES

It is hard to explain the vegetable and fruit stew called a tzimmes, but it is very tasty.

4 cups grated carrots
1 tablespoon bead barley
1 apple, peeled, grated
½ cup butter

½ cup water
½ teaspoon salt
2 teaspoons sugar
¼ teaspoon nutmeg

Mix all the ingredients together in a pan. Cook covered, simmering over low heat 2 hours until barley is soft. Add more water if needed.
6 servings.

PRUNE-HONEY TZIMMES

1 pound prunes
4 cups hot water
1 cup farina
1 teaspoon salt

Juice of 1 lemon
⅓ cup honey
½ cup butter

Pit prunes, soak in hot water for 2 hours. Set prunes and water in pot and bring to a boil. Add the farina, salt, lemon juice, honey, butter. Place mixture in baking dish, cover, bake in preheated oven at 370° for 45 minutes. Take off cover for last 15 minutes.
6 servings.

Doughs

GERMAN-JEWISH CHALLAH

The Friday-night challah once appeared on nearly every Jewish table in Europe and America. Each country had its *own* recipe—alike in most features—but with an item changed a bit here and there. This recipe is from the kitchen of a Frankfurt carpenter—made in this manner for generations.

1 package powdered yeast
1 cup warm water
1 egg
1 tablespoon sugar
½ tablespoon salt

2 tablespoons vegetable oil
4 cups flour
1 egg yolk
2 tablespoons sesame seeds

In a bowl put powdered yeast and add 1 cup of warm water, the egg, sugar, salt, oil, and flour. Mix well. Dust a board with flour, knead the dough well. Place the dough back in bowl, wipe with a little oil, cover with a cloth. Allow to rise 2 hours. Punch the dough down. Divide the dough into 4 pieces. Roll 3 into long pieces, thick at the center, thin at both ends. Simply braid these up and place on a greased tray. Take the fourth piece of dough and divide into 3 pieces. Roll these in the same way and braid. Place small braid on top of large braid, *press* to stick. Paint all this with egg yolk, and sprinkle sesame seeds on top. Let rise for ½ hour. Bake in preheated oven at 350° for 1 hour.

RAISIN PUMPERNICKEL

2½ cups cold water	2 envelopes dry yeast
1 cup corn meal	¼ cup warm water
2 teaspoons salt	1 teaspoon sugar
½ cup molasses	3 cups wheat flour
2 tablespoons vegetable shortening	3½ cups rye flour
	1 cup raisins

Put water into corn meal in saucepan, cook over medium heat; stir often until thickened and just coming to a boil. Remove and add salt, molasses, and shortening. Mix. Sprinkle yeast in warm water in a cup. Add sugar, stir to dissolve. Add yeast to corn meal mixture and stir in wheat and rye flours to make soft dough. Sprinkle flour on a board, and knead dough until it does not stick. Continue to knead for 10 minutes, add raisins and knead. Shape dough into a ball, place in a large greased bowl, grease top of dough. Cover, let rise 1 hour in warm place until doubled. Punch hard on dough, divide in halves. Shape each half into a ball and put on a greased baking sheet. Cover, let rise for 45 minutes until doubled. Bake in preheated oven at 375° for 45 minutes until light brown. Turn out on wire rack and cool.
Makes 2 loaves.

ONION KUCHEN

1 package yeast
1/4 cup warm water
3 cups sifted flour
1 teaspoon salt
1 1/2 teaspoons sugar
1/2 cup butter

1 cup milk
4 onions, sliced very thin
1 egg, beaten
1/4 cup sour cream
2 tablespoons poppy seeds

Preheat oven to 375°. Dissolve yeast in 1/4 cup warm water. Mix together flour, 1/2 teaspoon salt, sugar. Melt half the butter in saucepan, add milk. Bring to a boil, stir, and remove from heat; let stand 10 minutes. Add yeast and mix. Then add flour mixture, cover, let rise to double in size. Fry onions in 4 tablespoons butter, stir. Remove from heat. Mix beaten egg, sour cream, and 1/2 teaspoon salt. When dough has risen, knead dough. Roll into 3-inch balls, flatten on cookie sheet. Top with onion and sour cream mixture. Sprinkle on poppy seeds. Let rise 45 minutes. Bake until brown on top, for 25 minutes.
4 servings.

Dessert

RHINE NESSELRODE PIE

1 envelope unflavored gelatin
1 1/4 cups milk
4 eggs, separated
1 cup sugar
1/2 teaspoon salt
1/2 cup heavy cream

2 tablespoons rum
2 tablespoons each chopped
   maraschino cherries, dates,
   almonds
2 tablespoons grated citron rind
1 graham cracker crumb crust

Put gelatin in half of milk. Scald remaining milk in top part of double boiler. Beat egg yolks and beat in 1/2 of the sugar and salt. Stir in hot milk. Return to double boiler, cook over simmering water 5 minutes until mixture coats spoon. Stir constantly. Take from heat and add gelatin, stir until dissolved. Cook and add cream, rum. Chill 1 hour until mixture starts to set. Beat egg whites stiff, add remaining sugar. Fold in custard, fruit, and nuts. Pour into graham cracker crumb crust in a medium pan and chill until firm. Top with whipped cream and almonds.
4 servings.

HONEY DATE PUDDING

1 cup honey	½ teaspoon cloves
¼ cup margarine	½ teaspoon nutmeg
2 eggs	½ teaspoon salt
½ teaspoon vanilla	¾ cup chopped dates
2½ cups sifted cake flour	½ cup rough chopped walnuts
2½ teaspoons baking powder	1 cup evaporated milk
½ teaspoon ground cinnamon	

Add honey to margarine, eggs, and vanilla. Beat thoroughly. Mix flour, baking powder, cinnamon, cloves, nutmeg, and salt. Add 1 cup flour mixture to dates and nuts. Add rest of flour with milk to creamed mixture. Stir in the date mixture. Work batter stiff. Put into a greased 6-cup mold. Cover. Place mold on a rack in large kettle with 1 inch boiling water. Cover, steam 2¼ hours. Add hot water as needed. Let pudding stand in mold 7 minutes, and turn out. Serve warm with vanilla sauce.

10 servings.

MOCHA BUTTER CREAM

First the cream, then the cake.

½ cup butter	½ teaspoon vanilla
½ pound semisweet chocolate, melted	2 teaspoons cognac
1 egg yolk	1 teaspoon strong black coffee
	2 layers sponge cake

Cream butter and beat. Add melted chocolate, egg yolk, vanilla, cognac, coffee. Use between cake layers, and on sides and top.

YONTIFF (HOLIDAY) SPONGE CAKE

6 eggs   ¼ teaspoon cream of tartar
1½ cups sugar   1 teaspoon vanilla
2 cups flour, sifted

Preheat oven to 300°. First separate eggs, put whites in a bowl, yolks
in another bowl. Beat whites stiff, add 1 cup sugar. Beat yolks creamy,
add ½ cup sugar. Fold yolks into whites. Put flour, cream of tartar into
egg mixture, fold lightly. Add vanilla and bake 60 minutes in a medium
pan. Turn out of pan to cool. Add Mocha Butter Cream.
6 servings.

GESELTSCHAFT CHEESE PANCAKES

2 egg yolks   1 cup white flour
½ teaspoon salt   2 egg whites, stiffly beaten
2 tablespoons sugar   Butter for frying
2 cups drained cottage cheese

Combine and beat the egg yolks, salt, and sugar. Mix in cottage
cheese and flour, fold in egg whites. Heat 3 tablespoons butter in a skillet. Drop batter in it, 2 tablespoons at a time. Fry brown on both sides.
Serve hot with sour cream and/or jelly.
4 servings.

BRANDY APPLE FRITTERS

2 apples, peeled, sliced   1 teaspoon baking powder
½ cup sugar   1 egg
2 tablespoons brandy   1 cup milk
1½ cups flour   ½ cup butter, melted
½ teaspoon salt

Sprinkle apples with 4 tablespoons sugar and the brandy. Mix flour, salt, and baking powder in a bowl. Beat egg, milk, and half the butter, add to flour mixture, beat smooth. In a medium skillet in melted butter, pour 2 tablespoons of the batter. Put an apple slice on it. Cover with more batter. Brown both sides. Repeat for all batter and apple slices. Makes a dozen fritters.

FRUIT BREAD PUDDING

Next to a faith in chicken soup, the Jewish mother believed in puddings as the minyan of prayer-sayers believed in the Torah. Most puddings in the old days were milchedig (dairy), according to the kashruth (dietary laws).

2 eggs	4 cups milk, boiled
¼ cup sugar	3 cups bread cubes
½ teaspoon salt	1 cup thinly sliced apples
1 teaspoon vanilla	1 teaspoon butter
¼ teaspoon nutmeg	

Preheat oven to 350°. After you beat the eggs, add sugar, salt, vanilla, and nutmeg, then the milk. Add bread cubes, fruit. Pour into buttered baking dish. Set dish in oven in a pan of hot water and bake 45 minutes. Serve with heavy cream.

4–6 servings.

RAISIN-RICE PUDDING

1 cup rice, uncooked	½ teaspoon mace
1½ quarts milk	¼ teaspoon ground cinnamon
¾ cup sugar	¾ cup raisins
¼ teaspoon nutmeg	

Preheat oven to 325°. Butter baking dish and wash, drain rice. Add milk, sugar, nutmeg, and mace. Pour in baking dish, sprinkle on cinnamon, bake 2 hours at 325°. Add raisins and bake ½ hour.
6 servings.

AUSTRIA

Es war einmal ein Walzer
Es war einmal Wien . . .
Once there was a waltz
Once there was a Vienna . . .
Song, 1920

One of the compilers of this book had a Great-Aunt Longstrasse, who was the hostess in a huge household in Alt Wien where the first strains of the oversweet waltzes were heard with much Schlamperei, and there was the drinking of Rhine wine and seltzer. The corseted officers of the Kaiserschritzen were happy to be invited to eat at Tante Longstrasse's. She—in a couturier's robe décolleté—lived a very long and rich life, and kept for many years a series of kitchen daybooks in which she listed the dishes her two cooks and three kitchen helpers prepared under her hussarlike eye.

The books, passing through several family hands, for a short period were on loan to us. One can almost hear in them the court Jews at Bad Nauheim praising the memory of her dishes to the sound of the "Balenweiler March" and talk of how Mittel-europa was once a different kind of a place. The guest lists included names of Austrian, German, Hungarian Jews, famous or notorious in their day, mostly unknown to us now. Here and there one comes across an Arthur Schnitzler, a visiting Rothschild ("It must be terrible to be a Jew and *not* be a Rothschild." Lionel de Rothschild), Max Reinhardt (born Goldmann), the older and younger Schildkraut. So many actors, actresses, poets, bankers, some shady characters too. And in a hurried pencil line, *Hr. Dr. S. Freud und Frau*, who came, it is noted, only for a Jause, the afternoon coffee hour. The Herr Doktor was a notorious lover of Schlagobers (whipped cream).

The great Jewish families, "the Ring Millionaires," entertained the waltz kings, the Johann Strausses, father and son (both of Jewish descent). The musicians were proud to appear and eat at the Baron Moritz Todesco's (the younger Strauss repaid all this by carrying off and marrying the Jewish baron's mistress, Jetty Treffz). The waltz was found with the best cuisine at the Jewish mansions of the Arnsteins, the Werteimsteins, the Konigswarters, a haute monde, as Schnitzler wrote, "of fashion, intellect and fine food that had a great deal to do with the Austrian glamour that delighted the cosmopolitan gourmet." And exposed him to Kipferln pastries and Pressburger Beugel.

Austria was the great absorber of *other* cuisines. German, Hungarian, Russian, and there was once an Austrian queen whose daughter became a French queen and was reported to have said, "If they do not have bread, let them eat cake . . ." *"Si le peuple n'a pas du pain, qu'ils mangent la brioche . . ."* (only it was J. J. Rousseau around 1738 who said it, *not* the queen).

The goulash became Gulasch in Vienna—fried chicken became Wiener Backhahdel, sauerkraut was mixed with caraway seeds.

The Jews of Austria, high and low, were sophisticated. Many kept some of their dietary ritual laws, but made their own versions of Beuschel, a sort of hash of calf's lungs with a pickle in it. The Jewish version of the famed Wiener Schnitzel (veal steak with an egg on top) was often a main course. The Austrian rivers provided Friday Sabbath-night fish: carp, pike, trout. The Jewish geniuses of violin, piano, medicine, and theater ate with relish of the Saltzburger Nockerl (Salzburg spoon pudding) that Tante Longstrasse, the salonnarde and gourmet, produced.

Afterward, over the good Viennese coffee, Upmann, Hoyo de Monterrey cigars, there was worldly talk of scandal, politics, art, the eternal Jewish question, accompanied by a native red wine (Voeslauer), white wine (Gumpoldskirchner), to settle the pancakes (Kaiserschmarren) and the plum dumplings (Pflaumenknodel).

There are records of picnic trips to the Weinhauser—with hampers of cold duck, goose, or Schnitzel, a potato salad. The winery owners around Nussdorf and Grinzing encouraged one to visit the houses where Schubert and Beethoven wrote some of their music. The new green wine season was the best of times for all classes—janitors to bankers—when a green wreath, the Ausgesteckt, hung out of the wine shops.

The singers called the Schrammein sang sentimental music to a world soon to come apart at the seams.

Few of the Jews of the glory of their society in Austria survived. There are other changes. Johann Strauss's *Blue Danube* is too often a recording today at Innsbruck. But diners, in lederhosen and the American Jews still play at the casinos at Baden, Bad Gastein, and Kitbühel, and order the roast goose cooked as it used to be on the High Holidays when there was a large Austrian-Jewish population and a rabbi dipped his Semmel (roll) in the good coffee in the Konditorei in the First Bezirk. They were all mighty feeders—before terror came—taking the second or fork breakfast (Gabelfruhstick), lunch at noon, as usual, of course. Then at five in the afternoon, the Jause. And after a grand dinner, if one still wanted to nibble, there were the street sausage stands (Wurstel-stands). Some were set up across from the Opera and the Sacher Hotel. For the nosher before bedtime there was the café Sachertorte with an apricot jam layer. And who can resist Apfelstrudel? *Where* did they put it all?

The Austrian Jews would gather at Grinzing in the Weiner Wald— Vienna Woods—to drink draft beer in a mug called the Krugel (a half liter) or a Seidel (nearly a liter); a liter is just a little over a quart. Or offer a glass of Kremser or Durnsteiner wine.

The great Austrian-Jewish families of pre-Anschluss days have few survivors. The cooking of those who have returned is just as good as it once was. But something is missing as one walks down the Karntner-strasse, the Ringstrasse, or drives out to the Schönbrunn Palace. For all the solid well-cooked food, somehow the past of the Austrian Jews seems to have been a façade, a marvelous surface done in Austrian Baroque. One notes in Tante Longstrasse's daybooks a line suggesting the world is a masquerade: "Erich von Stroheim, cinema person. I knew his father, a Jewish hat-maker here, named Nordenwald . . ."

Meat

WIENER SCHNITZEL

This upper class Jewish version is from the families who lived near the Mariahiferstrasse and observed the dietary laws in meat being cooked *without* butter.

4 thin veal cutlets	1 egg
Juice of 1 lemon	½ cup very dry bread crumbs
Salt, freshly ground pepper to	2 tablespoons vegetable oil
taste	6 lettuce leaves
¼ cup flour	1 lemon, cut in quarters

Pound cutlets with mallet or knife handle. Sprinkle with lemon juice, marinate 10 minutes. Season with salt and pepper and dredge in flour, shake off excess. Dip in beaten egg, then in bread crumbs. Heat the oil in a frying pan, brown cutlets well for 3 minutes on each side. Serve on a bed of lettuce, wedges of lemon on top.
4 servings.

PRUNE-TONGUE

1 pound dried prunes	Juice of 1 lemon
1 (3-pound) fresh beef tongue	Peel of 1 lemon, thin sliced
2 cups tomato purée	½ cup brown sugar
1 onion, sliced thin	

Preheat oven to 350°. Soak prunes overnight. Boil the tongue in water for 3½ hours until tender. Cool, peel, set in a casserole. Drain and pit the prunes. Add with rest of ingredients to tongue. Cover, bake 45 minutes. Slice at once.
6 servings.

VEAL CHOPS INNSBRUCK (GOLDENER ADLER INN)

4 loin veal chops
½ cup margarine
2 tomatoes, sliced
4 shallots, minced
1 cup button mushrooms
5 cloves garlic, peeled

1 green pepper, chopped
10 ripe olives
½ teaspoon salt
Pepper to taste
¼ cup Marsala

Preheat oven to 400°. Coat the chops with melted margarine (reserving 2 tablespoons) and broil 4 minutes on each side; also broil tomatoes at the same time. Put remaining margarine in a skillet, and add everything but wine. Fry 10 minutes over medium heat. Stir. Add the Marsala wine, cook 5 minutes. Put mixture in a baking dish, add tomatoes and chops. Bake in oven 20 minutes, uncovered, at 400°.
4 servings.

BURGUNDY OVEN BEEF

2 tablespoons flour
2 pounds stew meat
4 carrots, sliced
2 large onions, sliced
1 cup thinly sliced celery

1 clove garlic, minced
½ teaspoon each, pepper,
  marjoram, thyme
1 cup dry burgundy wine
1 cup sliced mushrooms

Preheat oven to 325°. Put flour in 3-quart baking dish. Cut meat into 2-inch cubes, add to flour, and toss to coat meat. Add carrots, sliced onions, celery, garlic, pepper, marjoram, thyme, and red wine. Stir to mix. Cover, cook in 325° oven 1 hour. Add mushrooms, stir, cover tightly, and cook 2 hours until the meat and vegetables are tender.
6 servings.

INNSBRUCK SAUERBRATEN

2 tablespoons salt	1 cup red wine vinegar
4 pounds sirloin butt	2 tablespoons pickling spice
2 tablespoons oil	½ cup currants
2 celery stalks, sliced	1 pint tomato purée
1 carrot, sliced	2 tablespoons paprika
1 onion, sliced	1 tablespoon flour

Salt the meat, brown in skillet in oil. Combine remaining ingredients except tomatoe purée and paprika in a bowl, and add meat to mixture. Marinate 5 days in refrigerator. Move everything into a cooking pot, add purée and paprika. Simmer slowly about an hour or until meat is tender. Strain off juices and thicken for gravy with flour. Serve sliced thick with potato pancakes.
6 servings.

DER PRATER BEEF

Der Prater district of the second Bezirk of Vienna is the fun city, with once good Jewish eating places.

1 pound boneless beef chuck
2 large onions, sliced
4 medium potatoes, peeled, cut
    in slices
1 bay leaf
Salt, pepper to taste
1 quart boiling water
Chopped parsley

Cut fat from beef and reserve. Cut meat into 1-inch slices and flatten with flat side of knife. Put fat in Dutch oven and heat to render. Remove pieces of fat, cook onions in drippings until crisp. Add meat, brown on both sides. Add potatoes, bay leaf, salt, and pepper to taste. Add boiling water to cover, simmer, covered, 1½ hours until meat is tender. Sprinkle with parsley.
4 servings.

JEWISH BEINFLEISCH ODER TAFELSPITZ (BOILED BEEF AUSTRIAN STYLE)

The old guidebooks will tell you this is the traditional Viennese dish. It was always Gemütlichkeit at the White Swan—Weisser Schwan— served with grated horseradish, also good in the best Jewish homes.

2½ pounds beef brisket
Salt to taste
2½ quarts water
8 whole black peppercorns
2 bay leaves
½ celery root
3 carrots, sliced lengthwise
2 parsnips, sliced
1 stalk celery
1 teaspoon sugar
1 large red onion, unskinned

Do *not* slice beef. Put the whole cut of meat to boil in salted water. Skim, let simmer 1 hour. Add peppercorns, bay leaves, vegetables, sugar, and the onion (red outer skin gives color to the soup). Continue to cook at a simmer for 1½ hours till meat is tender. Remove meat and slice. Place on a heated platter with cooked vegetables. Serve with grated horseradish on the side.
6 servings.

MEAT TZIMMES

3 pounds cooked flanken pieces   Grated rind and juice of 1
2 bunches carrots, sliced   orange
¼ cup flour   Salt to taste
½ cup brown sugar

Preheat oven to 350°. Cut meat in pieces after removing all fat.
Grease casserole, put in a layer of carrots and meat, mixed. Sprinkle
with flour and brown sugar, some of orange rind. Repeat layers until all
carrots are used. Pour in orange juice, cover, and cook 50 minutes in
350° oven. Stir twice during cooking.
6 servings.

Fowl

TANTE LONGSTRASSE'S ROAST DUCK AUX PÊCHES
(PEACHES)

She liked the sound of Court French.

1 (5–6 pound) duck, unstuffed   1 cup peach brandy
1 cup ice water   1 cup beef consommé
½ cup beef soup   2 teaspoons arrowroot dissolved
¼ cup chicken fat   in a tablespoonful of soup
¼ cup sugar   8 ripe peaches
½ cup white vinegar

Preheat oven to 400°. Set duck in a roasting pan. Dribble water over
duck. Roast uncovered for 40 minutes, discard pan fat. Heat beef soup
over low flame. Add chicken fat, pour over bird, return to oven 30 minutes, basting every 10 minutes. Mix sugar and vinegar in saucepan, set
over heat, stir until sugar melts. Add the brandy, stir until blended
with sugar. Add consommé to arrowroot and stir until thickened. Peel

and halve peaches. Add with consommé and arrowroot to the sauce; heat for 10 minutes. Arrange the fruit with some of the sauce around the duck on platter, put rest of the sauce in a boat to add after duck is carved.

4 servings. (For a large dinner party, of course, add 1 duck for each extra 4 guests.)

ZWEIG CHICKEN GIBLETS

A prominent Jewish family's dish.

2 pounds cleaned chicken
  gizzards, cut in 2
1 pound chicken hearts
½ pound chicken livers,
  quartered
⅓ cup vegetable oil
2 tablespoons mustard seeds
1 large onion, chopped
5 cloves garlic, chopped

2 tablespoons curry powder
1 teaspoon cardamom powder
½ teaspoon ground cinnamon
½ teaspoon cayenne
1 teaspoon black pepper
1 cup Chicken Soup
2 tablespoons chopped parsley to
  garnish

Wash and dry chicken parts. Set aside. Heat oil in saucepan, add mustard seeds. Cover pan over medium heat until seeds pop. Add onion, garlic, sauté until tender. Mix in curry powder and other seasonings, spices. Stir for 2 minutes. Add chicken gizzards, hearts. Stir together. Add enough soup to just cover giblets. Simmer over low heat 2 hours until meats are tender. Add chicken livers, continue to simmer 15 minutes. Garnish with parsley.

8 servings.

CHICKEN FRAULEIN

4 chicken breasts
½ cup flour
Salt, and pepper to taste
2 ounces chicken fat
1 green pepper
1 clove garlic, chopped fine

1 medium onion, chopped
1 large potato, peeled, sliced
1 cup sliced cooked mushrooms
4 ounces Durnsteiner wine or
   any good red wine

Dredge chicken in flour, salt, and pepper, brown pieces in fat. Place chicken in Duch oven with green pepper, garlic, and onion. Put potato slices on top. Add mushrooms. Cover, cook over low heat 45 minutes. Add wine, let stand 10 minutes before serving.

4 servings.

ROAST PHEASANT

2 pheasants, dressed
Salt, fresh pepper to taste
4 sprigs parsley
2 celery leaves
1 onion
1 apple, cut in quarters
5 tablespoons chicken fat
2 tablespoons finely chopped
   shallots

1 carrot, chopped
1 stalk celery, sliced
½ cup Chicken Soup
1 cup dry red wine
1 tablespoon Bad-Voslau (or
   California) red wine
1 bay leaf
2 slices white bread
1 tablespoon flour

Rub the pheasants well with salt and pepper—inside and out. Stuff each with a parsley sprig, celery leaf, ½ onion, ½ apple. Sew up opening with white thread. In a large casserole heat fat until hot, add the pheasants. Sauté till brown on all sides. Remove and put aside. Add shallots, carrots, and celery to pot—sauté 3 minutes. Add chicken soup,

wines, and bay leaf. Bring to boil, put pheasants into sauce. Lower heat, cover casserole, simmer for 40 minutes. Toast 2 slices of white bread without crusts, and place in the middle of preheated serving platter. Put pheasants on the toast. Garnish with parsley sprigs. Mix flour with sauce to thicken. Bring to boil, strain into gravy boat.
4 servings.

COURT JEWS' SQUAB

There were a special group of important figures in the Austro-Hungarian Empire: the Court Jews. As bankers, brokers, contractors, or just old families, they had a solid feeling of their importance. They mixed with Jewish journalists, violin performers, historians, playwrights, and they set a gourmet table. The following dishes come from Tante Longstrasse's kitchen daybooks.

4 fat squabs	1/2 teaspoon salt
2 tablespoons chicken fat	1/4 pound sliced mushrooms
2 teaspoons olive oil	1/3 cup Tokay wine
1 cup minced onion	4 slices buttered toast
1 carrot, diced	

Tie the squabs up neatly. In fat with oil brown the birds with onion, carrot, and salt. On low heat cook 12 minutes. Add mushrooms and wine. Cover pan, simmer 40 minutes, check occasionally to add liquid if necessary. Serve squab on buttered toast. Use pan juice as gravy.
4 servings.

FOIE GRAS SQUAB STUFFING

2 tablespoons chicken fat	1 teaspoon chives
3 chicken livers	1 tablespoon minced parsley
1/2 cup mushrooms, minced	Salt, pepper to taste
1 (2-ounce) can foie gras	1 cup cooked rice

In fat sauté livers and mushrooms 10 minutes over low heat until livers are well cooked. Purée livers and mushrooms, mix with foie gras and seasonings. Add rice, mix again. Stuff and cook squab, following directions for Court Jews' Squab.
Makes stuffing for 4 squabs.

Fish

FISH STEAKS IN WINE

2 pounds fish steaks, any kind
3 tablespoons olive oil
Pinch of salt
2 tablespoons bread crumbs

2 tablespoons chopped blanched
  almonds
1/8 teaspoon ground coriander
1 cup dry sherry

Preheat oven to 350°. Put fish in oiled baking pan. Brush with olive oil, sprinkle on salt. Mix crumbs, almonds, coriander; sprinkle over, and pour on half of sherry. Bake 25 minutes at 350°, using the rest of the sherry to baste often.
4 servings.

BREADED LAKE PIKE

1 clove garlic, chopped
1/2 cup olive oil
1 cup bread crumbs
1/2 cup grated Romano cheese

2 tablespoons chopped parsley
Salt, pepper to taste
2 pounds pike fillets
2 eggs, beaten

Sauté garlic in oil and discard. Combine bread crumbs, cheese, parsley, salt, and pepper. Dip fish in eggs, then into crumbs. Set in hot oil, fry crisp. Serve hot.
4 servings.

HIGH HOLIDAYS TROUT AND HAZELNUTS

2 pounds trout
¼ cup melted butter
3 shallots, minced
½ cup ground hazelnuts

Juice of ½ lemon
¼ cup brandy
1 lemon cut in wedges

Preheat oven to 450°. Put fish in baking pan, add melted butter, sprinkle with shallots and hazelnuts. Bake 25 minutes at 450°, basting often. Move to platter. Pour lemon juice over the fish. Bring to table. Heat brandy, light and pour over the fish. Return to oven 3 minutes. Serve with lemon wedges.
4 servings.

KARPF IM ROTWEIN (CARP IN RED WINE)

This dish on Friday nights, at Jewish bankers' tables, proved that not all carp ended up as chopped fish.

2 pounds carp
2 cups dry red wine
1 teaspoon freshly ground black
    pepper
Salt to taste
1 bay leaf

1 teaspoon chopped parsley
1 sprig thyme
4 mushroom caps
2 tablespoons butter
1 teaspoon flour

Slice the fish crosswise into 2-inch strips, but *not* through all the way. Put in a saucepan, pour red wine over it, add pepper, salt, bay leaf, parsley, thyme, and mushrooms. Bring to boil, reduce heat, simmer for 10 minutes. Move fish to a serving platter. Reserve liquid. Make the following sauce: Heat butter in a pan and brown flour. Pour in the liquid in which the fish was cooked, stir to thicken. Pour sauce over fish and top with the mushrooms.
4 servings.

DANUBE RICE-FISH FILLETS

½ cup rice, cooked	¼ cup chopped parsley
2¼ cups milk	1½ pounds fish fillets
½ teaspoon salt	¼ cup butter
1 teaspoon curry powder	

Preheat oven to 350°. Mix rice with 1½ cups milk, salt, and heat until milk is absorbed. Add curry powder, parsley and blend. Spread mixture on fish fillets, roll up jelly-roll fashion. Secure with toothpicks. Put in buttered baking dish, dot with butter, pour remaining milk over it. Bake at 350° for 35 minutes until fish flakes with a fork.
4 servings.

FRANZ JOSEF BIRTHDAY CAVIAR PIE

A Jewish holiday, of course.

2 white onions, chopped fine	1 (6-ounce) jar caviar
6 hard-boiled eggs, coarsely chopped	½ cup cream cheese
2 tablespoons mayonnaise	1 cup sour cream
	Minced watercress

Add onions to eggs with mayonnaise. Spread on a shallow plate. Spread with 1 inch of caviar. Mix cheese and sour cream, spread it over the caviar. The minced watercress makes a border. Cover and chill for 4 hours. Serve with pumpernickel.
8–10 servings.

Vegetables

RADISH AND CHICKEN FAT RELISH

2 black radishes
2 tablespoons salt
½ cup rendered chicken fat

2 small onions, chopped
½ teaspoon black pepper

Wash radishes well, remove outer skin with knife. Shred on coarse side of grater. Sprinkle with salt and set in refrigerator, covered, for 2 hours. Remove, put shredded radishes in a strainer. Rinse with water and press out as much water as you can. Place in bowl. Add chicken fat, onions, and pepper. Mix. Pack in jar, cover tightly, store in refrigerator.
6 servings.

HIGH HOLIDAYS ONION RELISH

4 onions, fine diced
Juice of 3 lemons
1 teaspoon coarse ground red pepper

Put onions in a bowl, add lemon juice partly to cover onions. Add coarse red pepper. Mix. Keep covered in the refrigerator. Best on meats. Makes nearly 1 quart.

SACHER MARINATED CAULIFLOWER

1 head cauliflower
1 clove garlic, minced
2 tablespoons oil
2 tablespoons white wine vinegar
1 teaspoon salt

½ teaspoon freshly ground black
   pepper
½ cup chopped onion
½ cup chopped parsley

Tear a head of cauliflower into its sections. Cook in a pot of water until barely tender. Make a marinade of all ingredients, pour over cauliflower in a covered bowl, let stand for 2 days refrigerated.
4 servings.

BAKED ONIONS

6 medium onions, unpeeled
2 tablespoons salt

½ cup olive oil
1 teaspoon paprika

Preheat oven to 350°. Set onions, unpeeled, on baking sheet. Bake in moderate oven for 1½ hours until tender. Peel onions, serve them hot with salt, olive oil, and paprika.
6 servings.

TANTE'S APPLES AND RED CABBAGE

1 head red cabbage, cored,
   coarsely shredded
6 large grieben (rendered
   chicken skin)
1 onion, chopped

1 teaspoon salt
Pepper to taste
¼ cup vinegar
2 medium apples, peeled, sliced

Add shredded cabbage to grieben, onion, salt, pepper, and vinegar. Mix, cover in saucepan, simmer 10 minutes. Stir in the sliced apples. Cover, cook 15 minutes until cabbage is crisp-tender. Spoon cabbage on a platter, discard grieben.
8 servings.

Doughs

THE TRUE BAGEL

Ten cities claimed to be the birthplace of the poet Homer. As many claim to be the place where the modern bagel first was baked. Sophisticates, cosmopolitans, as well as ordinary Jewish citizens, give it fame. Balbatim (Hebrew for masters of their houses) demanded a supply always be at hand. And *who* was the Columbus of the bagel? Tante Longstrasse gives us the following information.

Bagel-making started in 1683 in Vienna when an eager coffee shop owner, name not given, sold stirrup-shaped rolls in honor of the King of Poland's favorite pastime—riding. The Austrian word for stirrup is "buegel." Viennese bakers, enterprising fellows, took on the "buegel," and began turning them out in the shape of rings. Here is the original recipe:

1½ cups warm water	½ teaspoon salt
1 cake yeast	4¼ cups flour
3 tablespoons sugar	1 gallon water

Pour warm water into a large bowl. Sprinkle and stir yeast until dissolved. Add sugar, salt, and flour to produce a soft dough. Turn onto floured surface, knead until smooth, elastic, 10 minutes. Cover, let rise 15 minutes. Flatten on a floured surface, roll dough 1 inch thick. Cut into strips a foot long and 1 inch wide. Roll each strip ½ inch thick, cut in half. Pinch together ends of strips to form the bagel. Cover, let rise 20 minutes. Bring 1 gallon water to a boil. Lower heat, add 4 bagels (at a time), simmer 7 minutes. Remove with spoon and cool. Repeat until all bagels are cooked. Place bagels on an ungreased baking sheet, bake in preheated oven at 375° for 30 minutes.
Makes 12 bagels.

FOR SALTED BAGELS:

Sprinkle cooked bagels with coarse salt. Bake.

FOR SEEDED BAGELS:

Sprinkle cooked bagels with sesame seeds, poppy seeds, or caraway seeds. Bake.

SPAETZLE

The Spaetzle—*how* to describe it? It's bits of doughy dough to Jew and Gentile; tasty, served with roast chicken, duck, goose, game birds, venison, and beef. Its home is Mittel-europa. And to do it by rule, you need a Spaetzle machine, which you can buy, among many other places in this country, at Bremen House, 200 East 86th Street, New York, N.Y. 10028. Or you can chop the dough by hand into short pieces.

4 cups all-purpose flour	5 eggs
1 teaspoon salt	½ cup water

Place the flour in a bowl, make a small pit in the center. Sprinkle salt on the flour and break the eggs right into it. Beat into a batter until smooth, adding the water as needed. You want a heavy, thick mixture.

Knead the dough well with vigor. Bring 2 kettles of salted water to a boil. Put dough in the Spaetzle machine and push it through into boiling water. As the spaetzle swim to the top in a few minutes, lift out with a slotted spoon and put them into the second pot. Continue making and cooking spaetzle until all dough is used up. Drain and serve.
10 servings.

Dessert

VIENNA APPLE STRUDEL

Vienna, strudel, Strauss music, May wine, and a sight of the Danube seem to form a montage when one thinks of that city. The best makers of the strudel were the Jewish cooks, so claimed Franz Liszt when he went to hear the cantors (chazzonim) sing their virtuoso Hebrew falsettos in the Vienna synagogues. It would appear he *tasted* as well as listened.

2 sheets packaged strudel	¾ cup golden raisins
1 cup melted margarine or vegetable shortening	½ cup chopped walnuts
	5 bitter almonds, chopped
4 tablespoons bread crumbs, fried in oil	½ cup sugar
	1 teaspoon ground cinnamon
3 apples, peeled, finely sliced	Confectioners' sugar

We use packaged sheets here, as we have already given the recipe for making them (see Index for Jewish-Russian Strudel).

Preheat oven to 400°. Put a sheet strudel on a cloth. Brush with melted margarine, sprinkle with bread crumbs, top with another sheet. Brush again and sprinkle with crumbs. Combine remaining ingredients, except confectioners' sugar, to make filling. Spread filling lengthwise, leaving an inch bare along sides. Lift, use cloth as base, and roll like a jelly roll. Place on baking sheet, brush with margarine. Bake at 400°, 30 minutes, then 350° for 30 minutes until golden. Let cool on a rack 30 minutes, sprinkle with confectioners' sugar.
6 servings.

LONGSTRASSE CAFÉ SCHLAG

2 teaspoons chocolate syrup   2 jiggers crème de menthe
2 mugs double-strength hot coffee   2 scoops whipped cream

Pour chocolate syrup into 2 tall continental cups—1 teaspoon each—and fill cups three fourths full with hot coffee. Pour a jigger of crème de menthe into each cup. Add whipped cream.
Makes 2 drinks.

BAD GASTEIN SAUTERNE FRUIT COMPOTE

Jewish gamblers at the casino treated their nervous digestion with this dish.

3 ripe peaches   ¼ cup orange juice
6 apricots   2 cups Haut Sauterne wine
1 cantaloupe   Maraschino cherries to garnish

Wash and peel peaches, cut into thick slices. Peel, cut apricots in half, remove pits. Remove rind from melon, remove seeds, cut into balls. Place fruits in dish; pour on orange juice, wine. Set aside for 1 hour. (Do *not* refrigerate.) Garnish with cherries to serve.
6 servings.

HUNGARY

Since Eve ate apples, much depends on dinner . . .
Byron, 1823

It was the Turks, who overran Hungary from time to time searching for white maidens for the harems, and loot, who brought in exchange the small oriental peppers called paprika. Becoming acclimated, the paprika, like the Hungarian Jews, had a lively flavor, a high color, and a sense of being pleasantly unique. The women were beautiful and gay. The men, legend claims, were wits, writers, hard-working businessmen, cattle dealers, seducers, confidence men, dandies—*and* usually sitters in cafés of the cities of Buda and Pest that face each other across the Danube (brown, not blue), reading the newspapers, sipping coffee, remembering the freshly caught Fogas (fish sent from Lake Balaton), or visiting the pastry café, the Gerban, to eat a slice of Dobos Torta.

The ancient Magyars and the Jews may have come into Hungary together. And so, busy with the battling Turks, or the Holy Office Inquisitor, the country was always in turmoil. Yet it was a bountiful land, even as part of the dying Austro-Hungarian Empire; fertile plains, fine cattle, hard-working peasants, and usually absent landlords.

The paprika gulyas (goulash) has only been around a hundred years, but it is a sort of national symbol of the Hungarian gourmet *and* ordinary citizen. There is sweet paprika gulyas and rose paprika gulyas, which are usually the two kinds made by the Hungarian Jews with their own minor or major changes, and a gulyas soup. "Of soup and love, the first is the best." T. Fuller, 1737. . . . Advanced Jews who did not follow the Orthodox rituals cooked the szekelu gulyas, made with pork, sour cream, and sauerkraut. Tokany gulyas had smaller bits of meat, less onions and paprika and was favored by the older Jews. One had to use meticulous judgment deciding among the gulyas.

The European Jews were always fisheaters and the Danubian carp and the salmonlike whitefish, the Lake Balaton fogas, were in every Jewish cooking list. (Just *what* a fogas fish is scientifically, no one has been able to tell us. A loyal Hungarian, it does not seem to migrate to other waters.)

Hungarians were noodle lovers and were expert noodle (lokshen) makers. In Hungary, noodles go with all meats, geese, ducks, chickens. But they also are eaten alone, mixed with cheese, cinnamon, and nuts. Jewish cooks flavored them with chicken fat mixed with some slightly overbrowned bits of onions. Hungarian flour is a splendid product of the country, and in some ways superior to our own overrefined machine product.

A good Jewish Hungarian breakfast would end with korozott liptoi, a homemade mixture of pot cheese and paprika. Hungarians are not raw vegetable eaters. Cooked vegetables at the Friday-night Sabbath meal (while the candles were blessed) were usually part of the meat dish. Later a platter of fruit was served, usually apricots and marilles (a yellow plum), white Tokay grapes. And Tokay wine, of course, which in some Jewish households was drunk with charged water.

In Budapest cafés we heard much food gossip. Did some Jewish Hungarians of genius invent the true original strudel, the retes? Did it go from here to Austria and then to Germany? Hungarians claim it did. The favorite cake with the Jewish sweets lovers, and other Hungarians, was Dobos Torta, fifteen layers at least of fine sponge cake with latherings of chocolate and mocha creams. In the Jewish version that we've eaten in the village of Tichany, the caramel icing was thick and had just a hint of vanilla.

Meat

THE SZEKELY GOULASH

Experts on Hungarian cooking, gourmets of Budapest we have talked to, and in the better eating places from Debrecen to Szeged, where we have tasted the cuisine, have all given us different figures as to the number of goulashes available in Hungary. The high count was 72, the low 21. We shall set down here only those goulashes that have felt a Hungarian-Jewish touch, and are among the most popular in those households. From all the various spellings, we shall settle on goulash for this text. The Jewish-Hungarian version does use sour cream (so they are Jewish but not kosher). However, they do not use lard or pork, which the traditional formal szekely goulash usually does.

3 pounds sauerkraut
3 large onions, chopped
4 cloves garlic, minced
⅓ cup beef or chicken fat
4 tablespoons paprika
2 tablespoons caraway seeds
2 cups drained, chopped, stewed tomatoes

3 pounds beef, cut in 1-inch sections
Salt, pepper to taste
3 cups beef soup or beef stock
3 tablespoons flour
1 cup sour cream
½ cup chopped dill to garnish

Wash the sauerkraut in cold water, press out all the moisture you can. In a deep pot, fry onions and garlic in fat until soft. Mix in paprika, caraway seeds, add tomatoes, beef, salt, pepper, sauerkraut. Toss to mix. Pour in 2 cups of soup, cover, and simmer slowly 1½ hours until beef is tender. Stir remaining soup into flour. Add sour cream. Stir into meat-sauerkraut mix until entire pot is thickened. Garnish with chopped dill.
6 servings.

BEEF GOULASH

3 pounds beef chuck	Salt to taste
3 tablespoons margarine	2 cups water
3 cups sliced onion	½ pound wide noodles
1 tablespoon sweet paprika	2 tablespoons poppy seeds

Cut meat into 1½-inch bits. Heat margarine in kettle. Add onion, and cook 3 minutes. Season meat with paprika, salt; add to onions. Add 1 cup water. Cook, uncovered, stirring occasionally, 20 minutes, until onion and liquid cook down. Add other cup of water. Cover, simmer 2 hours until meat is tender, add more water if necessary. Cook noodles tender in boiling salted water. Drain and sprinkle with poppy seeds. Serve with goulash.
6 servings.

RICH SHVER (FATHER-IN-LAW) VEAL PAPRIKA

Served in hopes he'll settle something impressive on the newlyweds. There are five varieties of paprika—and this dish uses the "Exquite"— the kind made for export.

3 tablespoons oil
2 pounds cubed veal
¼ cup flour
1 cup hot water
1 cup dry sauterne wine
1 cup mushrooms, cooked

2 tablespoons chopped parsley
1 onion, sliced
1 teaspoon "Exquite" paprika
Salt, pepper to taste
1 cup sour cream

Heat the oil in a skillet and add veal; brown on all sides. Add flour, hot water, and wine. Mix and cook; stir constantly until mixture is thick and smooth. Add mushrooms and their liquid, parsley, onion, paprika, salt, and pepper. Simmer 1 hour, covered. Before serving, pour in sour cream. Heat through again.
4 servings.

KIDNEYS WITH JUNIPER BERRIES

"Gentiles use juniper berries to flavor gin, Jews to cook kidneys" (Hungarian cook). Actually the dish is not too well known, but very tasty.

6 veal kidneys, soaked, sliced
½ teaspoon each, salt, pepper
¼ teaspoon each thyme, dry
   Dijon mustard
¼ cup oil

½ onion, grated
1 tablespoon flour
¼ cup dry white wine
12 juniper berries, crushed

Take up kidney slices, sprinkle with mixed seasonings. To oil add onion and kidneys, sauté 5 minutes over medium heat, cook both sides. Sprinkle with flour, and stir until brown. Add wine and juniper berries, blending with pan juice. Stir until it comes to a boil. Reduce heat to minimum, cover, simmer 3 minutes.
4 servings.

LENTIL-RICE STEW

3 pounds beef chuck
3 onions, diced
2 tablespoons chicken fat
1 cup lentils, soaked 2 hours

2 teaspoons salt
½ teaspoon pepper
4 cups hot water
½ cup rice, uncooked

Slice beef in 2-inch bits and sauté with onions in fat. Mix the lentils with salt, pepper, and water. Cover and simmer over low heat 1½ hours. Add rice, cover and cook 25 minutes.
6–8 servings.

VEAL HONGROISE

2 pounds fresh veal tenderloin   ¼ teaspoon pepper
1 clove garlic, pressed   ½ teaspoon rosemary
1 teaspoon caraway seeds   1 quart dry white wine
1½ teaspoons paprika

Get the tenderloin ¾ inch thick. Set slices in a baking dish. Add the seasonings, including garlic, and pour on sufficient wine just to cover the meat. Marinate in refrigerator for 6 hours. Bake in preheated oven 1 hour at 300°, until wine is used up and meat is fork-tender.
4 servings.

LAMB CRÈME DE MENTHE ROTHSCHILD

4 pounds lamb shoulder, boned   1 (4-ounce) jar kumquats and
1 pint bottle white crème de   juice
    menthe

Paint one side of the lamb with liqueur, set a row of drained kumquats in the middle. Roll up lamb. Paint again with crème de menthe until you've done the outside of the meat. Roast in preheated oven at 325° for ½ hours. Baste with liquid in the pan, mixed with kumquat juice.
6 servings.

WEDDING FEAST TOLTOOT KAPOSZTA (STUFFED SAUERKRAUT)

No real Jewish-Hungarian country wedding would leave it out. As is often usual with the Magyars' best meat dishes, it contains sour cream, making it non-kosher, but *very* Jewish in Hungary.

8 big green cabbage leaves
2 pounds fresh sauerkraut
1½ pounds ground beef
¾ cup rice, uncooked
Salt, pepper to taste
2 cloves garlic, crushed

½ cup warm water
4 tablespoons beef or chicken fat
2 teaspoons sweet red paprika
1 large onion, chopped
2 cups water
1 cup sour cream

Carefully soften the cabbage leaves in boiling water. Drain, add sauerkraut, and keep for 24 hours in a bowl. Remove sauerkraut. Mix the ground beef, rice, season with salt, pepper, and garlic. Make into a paste with warm water. Put 2 tablespoons of the filling in the middle of each softened leaf, roll up, tie with a string. Drain the sauerkraut. In a saucepan heat fat, sprinkle with paprika. Fry chopped onion lightly. Place the sauerkraut and onion on top of the filled leaves. Pour in a cup of water. Bring to a boil, cover, simmer at reduced heat ½ hour. Add 1 more cup of water, cook slowly for 1½ hours. Add more water if needed. Before serving, pour the sour cream over it.
6 servings.

Fowl

MAGYAR-HEBREW CHICKEN LIVERS

1 pound chicken livers
½ teaspoon salt
⅛ teaspoon pepper
½ cup sifted flour
¼ cup chicken fat

½ cup dry white dinner wine
6 grieben, crisply fried (rendered chicken skin)
2 tablespoons finely chopped fresh parsley

Dredge chicken livers in mixed salt, pepper, flour; brown lightly in fat. Turn heat to simmer, add wine; cover and steam 5 minutes, until cooked. Sprinkle with grieben and parsley. Serve on crackers, matzos, or crisp toast.
8 servings.

HERBED BAKED CHICKEN

1 (3½-pound) fryer	1 teaspoon thyme
5 tablespoons margarine	1½ teaspoons sage
3 tablespoons flour	2½ cups Chicken Soup
1½ teaspoons salt	1 tablespoon chopped parsley
¼ teaspoon pepper	1 tablespoon chopped chives

Preheat oven to 325°. Wash chicken and dry. Brown in hot skillet on all sides in 2 tablespoons margarine. Remove to a casserole. Melt rest of margarine in skillet, blend in flour. Add all remaining ingredients. Cook until slightly thickened, stir constantly. Pour over chicken. Bake uncovered in oven at 325° for 50 minutes, until the chicken is tender.
4 servings.

CHIEF RABBI'S CHICKEN STEW (FROM MISKOLC)

2 tablespoons salad oil	1 bay leaf
2 tablespoons chicken fat	½ teaspoon thyme
2 (2½ pounds each) broiler-fryers, cut in serving pieces	¼ teaspoon oregano
	1 tablespoon capers
2 tomatoes, seeded, chopped	1 clove garlic, minced
2 onions, sliced	1½ cups dry white wine
2 cloves garlic, chopped	Salt, ground pepper to taste
¼ cup chopped beef	

In an oven casserole with a lid, heat oil and fat, sauté chickens until golden. Add tomatoes, onions, chopped garlic, beef, bay leaf, thyme, oregano, minced garlic, and capers. Add wine barely to cover and season to taste with salt, pepper. Cook, covered, over low heat until chickens are tender to a fork jab, about 1 hour.
6 servings.

ROAST WILD DUCK

2 ducks, cleaned and trussed	1 bay leaf
2 teaspoons salt	½ lemon, thinly sliced
3 cups cracker stuffing	1 clove garlic
2 cups Tokay wine	1 medium onion, chopped
2 carrots, sliced	½ cup chicken fat or margarine

Preheat oven to 450°. Rub the ducks with salt. Stuff lightly with cracker stuffing, moistened with 1 cup of wine. Place carrots in a greased baking pan. Add bay leaf, lemon slices, garlic, onion, and fat. Arrange ducks in pan breast side *up*. Roast until lightly browned at 450°, about 40 minutes. Pour rest of wine over ducks, cover with lid, reduce temperature to 325°. Cook 1½ hours until tender, baste occasionally.
6 servings.

BONELESS STUFFED CHICKEN

"Kashrut—to keep the kosherness of Jewish dietary laws," is fully observed in this popular dish.

½ cup chopped or sliced
  mushrooms
2 tablespoons chicken fat or
  margarine
¼ cup white rice, cooked
¼ cup brown rice, cooked

2 tablespoons poultry seasoning
Salt, pepper to taste
2 broilers, boned and halved
½ cup oil
1 teaspoon paprika
½ cup dry white wine

Preheat oven to 375°. In skillet sauté mushrooms with fat until tender. Mix rice, mushrooms, poultry seasoning, salt, and pepper as a dressing. Place portions of dressing between breasts and thighs of chicken halves. Fold flesh over and press together to keep dressing in place. Place breast side up on greased pan. Brush chicken pieces with oil. Sprinkle with paprika. Roast at 375° for 60 minutes until done, basting with wine from time to time.
4 servings.

CHICKEN GIBLET PAPRIKASH

½ cup chicken fat
2 onions, chopped
3 cloves garlic, minced
3 pounds mixed chicken gizzards,
  hearts
1 tablespoon flour

5 tablespoons sweet paprika
1 cup Chicken Soup
½ cup tomato purée
Salt, pepper to taste
1 pound chicken livers, diced
½ cup chopped dill

Put chicken fat in a pot and add onions, garlic, and fry until soft. Mix in gizzards and hearts. Heat, but do not brown. Add flour with paprika, chicken soup, and tomato purée. Season with salt, pepper. Cover pot and allow to simmer 1½ hours until meats are nearly tender. Add chicken livers, continue to cook till meats are tender. Dust with chopped dill.
6 servings.

KOSHER HUNGARIAN GREEN APPLE STUFFING

For chicken, turkeys, and ducks.

1 pound seasoned bread crumbs
3 green apples, but ripe, peeled,
cored, diced
1 cup margarine
1 cup chopped celery

1 cup pineapple juice
1 teaspoon curry powder
½ cup chopped pecans
½ cup chopped parsley

Mix bread crumbs, apples, margarine, celery, pineapple juice, curry powder, pecans, and parsley. This is enough for two 6-pound chickens or a 12-pound turkey.

STUFFED CHICKEN HELZEL (NECK)

½ cup flour
Salt, pepper to taste
1 small onion, diced

¼ cup chicken fat
1 chicken neck skin from 6-pound
chicken

Preheat oven to 375°. Mix ingredients, fill neck but not *too* bulging. Sew up both ends. Put in roasting pan in ½ inch of water. Roast for 35 minutes until neck is light brown. Slice in ¼-inch slices.
4 servings.

CHICKEN PAPRIKASH

1 (4-pound) chicken
½ pound margarine
¼ cup sliced carrots
¼ cup chopped celery
¼ cup chopped onions
½ clove garlic, crushed

1 cup flour
2 teaspoons paprika
Salt, pepper to taste
1 quart Chicken Soup
¼ pint sour cream
Cooked noodles

Cut chicken into 4 sections, brown on all sides in skillet in margarine. Drain, place in baking pan. Back to the skillet, where you sauté the carrots, celery, onions, and garlic until tender. Remove. Add remaining margarine, cook flour, paprika, salt, and pepper until light brown; add the chicken soup and vegetables. Cook until smooth, mix in sour cream. Pour sauce over the chicken, bake in 325° oven 45 minutes. Serve on cooked noodles.
8 servings.

Fish

YONTIF (HOLIDAY) SALMON

4 pounds salmon, sliced thick	2 bays leaves
1/2 cup vinegar	1/2 teaspoon thyme
2 medium onions, sliced	1 tablespoon salt
1 carrot, sliced	8 whole black peppercorns
2 sprigs parsley	1 lemon, sliced
2 stalks celery	4 sprigs parsley

Take slices of fish and place in a large saucepan with water to cover and all ingredients except lemon slices. Simmer until boiling. Take from fire and cool. Remove salmon from pan, take out the bones, remove skin. Put slices on a platter; set lemon slices and parsley around in a pattern. Serve cold with tartar sauce or Russian dressing, and new potatoes in cream.
6 servings.

DANUBE FISH CAKES

2 cups flaked cooked codfish	1/2 teaspoon paprika
2 cups matzo meal	2 eggs, beaten
3/4 cup butter	1/2 cup milk
2 teaspoons salt	1/2 teaspoon black pepper

Reserve ¼ cup butter for frying. Combine well all the rest of the ingredients. Shape in 6 or 8 cakes and chill 3 hours. Fry in butter, brown both sides. Serve with a sharp relish.
4 servings.

SWEET-AND-SOUR PIKE

2 onions, sliced
2 lemons, sliced
⅓ cup brown sugar
¼ cup seedless white raisins
1 bay leaf
1½ pounds pike, sliced

2 teaspoons salt
2 cups water
6 soda crackers, crushed
⅓ cup cider vinegar
¼ cup sliced almonds

In a saucepan combine and mix the onions, lemon slices, brown sugar, raisins, bay leaf, fish, salt, and water. Cover and simmer on low heat 25 minutes. Set fish on a platter. To the fish sauce add the soda crackers, cider vinegar, and almonds. Cook over low heat until smooth. Pour over fish. Can be eaten hot or cold.
6 servings.

Soup

MUSHROOM-BARLEY SOUP

At Jewish weddings in Hungary, at one time, they threw barley
at the bride and groom for fertility, rather than our habit of hurling rice.

3 quarts water
2 cups dried mushrooms
1½–2 pounds flanken
Salt, pepper to taste

1 cup pearl barley
4 green onions, sliced
3 tablespoons oil
1 quart chicken or beef soup

Mix water, mushrooms; flanken, salt, and pepper in a kettle. Bring
to a boil, reduce heat, simmer 45 minutes. Rinse and drain barley.
Sautè it with the green onions in oil until barley is lightly toasted. Add
soup. Simmer 45 minutes until barley is tender. Taste, correct salt and
pepper if necessary. Serve with meat and mushrooms on the side.
8 servings.

YESHIVA BUCHER (TALMUD STUDENT)
POTATO MUSHROOM SOUP

12 dried mushrooms
1 quart water
1 cup dry white wine
2 onions, chopped
2 carrots, sliced

4 potatoes, peeled, diced
Salt, freshly ground black pepper
  to taste
2 tablespoons chopped parsley

With water cover mushrooms, soak 1 hour. Drain, place mushrooms
in saucepan with 1 quart water, wine, onions, and carrots. Bring to a
boil, cover, cook over low heat 1 hour. Press the mixture through a
sieve. Add potatoes, salt, and pepper. Cook over low heat 15 minutes,
add water if too thick. Correct seasoning. Add parsley and serve.
4 servings.

JEWISH-HUNGARIAN GOULASH SOUP

3 pounds stew meat
6 tablespoons margarine
2 large onions, diced
2 tablespoons sweet paprika
2½ tablespoons salt

½ teaspoon pepper
2½ quarts water
1 pound stewed tomatoes
1 cup sour cream

Slice meat into 1-inch cubes. Melt half the margarine in a large saucepan, add onions, cook until tender, not browned, stir often. Skim out onions with slotted spoon, set aside. Melt rest of margarine in pan drippings, add meat and brown on all sides. Return onions to pan, sprinkle with paprika, salt, pepper. Add water, tomatoes, cover, simmer 2 full hours. Readjust seasoning, simmer soup ½ hour longer. Stir in sour cream. Heat, do *not* boil.
10 servings.

POT CHEESE SOUP

1 onion, chopped
1 stalk celery, chopped
2 green peppers, sliced thin
½ cup butter
Pinch salt
¼ teaspoon pepper

½ teaspoon paprika
4 cups water
2 cups milk
¼ cup heavy cream
1 cup pot cheese

Sauté onion, celery, and green peppers in butter 15 minutes. Combine with salt, pepper, paprika, water, milk. Cover and simmer on low heat 1 hour. Add cream and cheese. Heat. Do *not* boil.
6 servings.

Vegetables

BAKED FENNEL

1 large fennel bulb
⅓ cup melted butter
⅓ cup fresh grated Parmesan cheese

Preheat oven to 450°. Slice thin the fennel, set in steamer basket over steaming water, cover, and steam for 8 minutes. Move to a buttered casserole. Pour over butter, sprinkle with cheese. Cover, bake 10 minutes at 450°.
4 servings.

ASPARAGUS

2 packages frozen asparagus tips   ½ cup grated Parmesan cheese
¼ cup olive oil   1 teaspoon nutmeg

Preheat oven to 350°. Cook asparagus according to package directions. Drain. Put in a greased baking dish. Pour olive oil over asparagus, coat well. Sprinkle with cheese and nutmeg. Set in the 350° oven for 15 minutes.
6 servings.

CARROT KNAYDL

1 bunch carrots, scraped, cut fine,   ½ cup potato flour
  cooked   2 tablespoons chicken fat or
1 large sweet potato, cooked,   margarine
  peeled, diced   Salt to taste

Combine carrots and potato. Brown potato flour in hot pan, stir in fat, salt. Add carrot-potato mix. Stir to let mixture form. Cover pan. Add some water, let steam 3 minutes. Cut into sections for soup.
4 servings.

POMEGRANATE ELIJAH

Elijah is supposed to have at one time lived on pomegranates—not this dish of course.

5 pomegranates
1 small (3-ounce) bottle
  grenadine syrup
1 package (2-ounce) unflavored
  gelatin

1 cup water
½ cup sugar
1 egg white
1 cup heavy cream
½ teaspoon almond extract

With palm of hand roll pomegranates on a surface for pulp softening inside, but do not break the skin. Hold pomegranate pointing over a bowl and pierce the end with a knife. Beware of squirts. Squeeze out all the juice. Strain out the seeds from juice. Add grenadine syrup to make 2 cups. Soak gelatin in 1 cup water, add sugar to pomegranate juice. Boil juice over medium heat, stir to dissolve sugar. Lower heat, add gelatin, dissolve. Cover and chill until just beginning to set. Beat egg white stiff and fold in. Separate to serving dishes and chill until firm. At serving time, beat cream stiff with almond extract. Set a big spoonful on each dish.
6 servings.

NEW POTATOES IN CREAM

2 pounds new potatoes
2 teaspoons salt

½ teaspoon Szeged paprika
1½ cups heavy cream

In a kettle boil potatoes in skins in salted water to cover, 20 minutes, until tender. Drain, peel, cut into 1-inch cubes. Set cubes in top of double boiler, sprinkle with salt and paprika. Pour cream over them, cook, uncovered, over low simmering water, stirring occasionally, 1 hour.
4 servings.

Wedding Wines

Besides champagnes, guests drank the wines of Lake Balaton vine-yards—wines like Badacsonyi Kéknyelü, Szürkebarát, and Hárslevelü. All are now imported to our country.

ROMANIA AND THE BALKANS

All the labor of man is for his mouth,
and yet the appetite is not filled.

Ecclesiastes 6:7

The mythical Romanian cookbook that began a recipe with the words,
"First steal a chicken," was not in its telling a Jewish cookbook. What
can be said in this text of the cooking of that nation and its influence
on Jewish cooking can be said of nearly all the Balkan nations; of
Slovenes, Croats, Montenegrins, Dalmatians, Bosnians, and a few others
in a conglomerate population. To generalize, the coffee is usually Turk-
ish style, small cups of wet grounds. There is a great deal of lamb and
mutton cooked on open charcoal fires. Fennel and cumin, garlic and
peppers flavor the food. Sour milk, buttermilk, curds and wheys make up
a good part of the diet. Good food, not sumptuous.

The Jews came early to the Balkans in their great exile, and once
in Romania—and finding maize imported—they took over the ground
corn meal that made the native mamaliga a popular food, which as
corn meal mush with butter or meat or fish, or eaten in various other
ways, is part of the staple diet. But Romanian Jews also put their
touch on the appetizers; ikre (carp roe), patlagele vinete (an eggplant
dish), salamure (yellow pike broiled with dried red peppers). The Jews
refined the ciorbas (sour soup), proving food habits are based on the
influence of social, economic, physical forces.

The Romanian Jews' food problem in that country was the avoiding
of the national love of pork: smoked, spiced, stuffed in cabbage, in
garlic aspic, in sausages. The overuse was unhealthy. The purging of
the more gross food improved the cuisine.

In our travels we have tried a dish favored by some hardy Jewish
families. Drob de miel. As raunchy as it sounds. It is fried calf's stomach,
stuffed with boiled lamb lung, heart, liver. All chopped, mixed with beef
fat, green onions, peppers, eggs, and parsley.

Actually Romanian and Balkan Jewish food was greatly influenced by
Russian and German-Jewish cookery. The upper class families served
the best of both cuisines. The great test for a Jewish wife was her ability

to make the mamaliga just right. Beginning by pouring the ground corn meal properly into the boiling pot of salted water, simmering it *just* long enough, pouring it out to use it cold, cut up as slices with fish or meat, or baked crisp and golden brown to use instead of bread.

Mushrooms marinated in fennel could complement the Sabbath challah, and olives soaked in Tzuica brandy accompany the family pot of cholent. The usual European beef stew would be cooked with slices of quinces, the chicken soup's noodles would be served with a dusting of chopped hazelnuts. And the breakfast pancakes might (and did for us in Mamaia on the Black Sea) come with breaded and fried calf's brains.

The Romanian-Balkan Jews (according to gossip, either cattle drovers *or* composers) did not all the time take too much to the national habits of grilling nearly every kind of meat over charcoal. But they liked the native plum brandy called Tzuica in Romania, and it was drunk at native Jewish affairs and to whet the appetite after services on the holidays of Tsom Gedaliah, Succoth, Tisha Bov, or to greet a greedy official.

Advanced Jews, usually called "the intelligentsia," ate with the rich the caviarlike white carp eggs called ikre, with hard-boiled eggs and onion slices, or feasted on the Greek tarama, the red pike caviar.

The Jewish eating places, the better ones in the old days, on the Danube, the Black Sea resorts, at the summer resort Poiana Brasov, featured Russian borsches, hot and cold: sarmales, the vine or cabbage leaves filled with chopped meat, rice.

Romanian wines and all Balkan vintages, no great treat, were *not* for bouquet sniffing. The Jewish homes indulged in spritz, a mixture of dry white wine and mineral charged water. Bucharest was once a gay wild city with many Jewish businessmen, merchants, exporters, who could be seen celebrating some family event or hosting special guests at the Bucaresti, La Doi Cocosi, and the Pescu Pescarul. But today, the best Balkan-Jewish dishes are found in the homes of those who have survived or stayed on in the changing decades. Some remember a time when a return on a Sabbath from the synagogue meant "the candles lit, the bed made, *and* the table set . . . Truth is, it wasn't the Jews who kept the Sabbath, the Sabbath kept the Jews . . ."

Meat

LAMB WITH ANCHOVIES

Fine as Romanian dishes were, the Romanian Jews, very Orthodox, had to turn them into recipes free of pork, lard, creams, and butter. In most cases, old gourmets say, they improved them.

1 (3-pound) half leg of lamb	½ cup dry red wine
4 tablespoons olive oil	2 cups water
1 onion, minced	6 anchovy fillets, chopped
Salt, pepper to taste	1 tablespoon chopped parsley
1 tablespoon flour	1 clove garlic, crushed

Mix the meat, oil, onion, salt, and pepper in a large pot. Brown meat on all sides. Spread the flour over the meat and add wine. Cook 10 minutes. Add water, cover, and simmer 1½ hours until meat is done. Mix anchovies, parsley, garlic into the pot, simmer 4 minutes. Serve with hot gravy.
3 servings.

SHNUR (DAUGHTER-IN-LAW) STUFFED BEEF HEART

1 beef heart	Salt, pepper to taste
2 tablespoons olive oil	½ cup white raisins
3 tablespoons chopped fresh parsley	1 hard-boiled egg, chopped
	½ cup cooking oil
1 clove garlic, minced	1½ cups tomato sauce

Buy beef heart ready for stuffing. Cut 1-inch slits down from center but *not* through. Rub inside and out with olive oil. Mix all ingredients except oil and tomato sauce; stuff heart with mixture. Bind string around meat so stuffing stays in. Brown on all sides in hot oil. Add tomato sauce, simmer 1 hour. Slice across and serve.
4 servings.

BALKAN VILLAGE LAMBS' TONGUES

5 pounds lambs' tongues,
   trimmed
4 tablespoons chicken fat
2 large onions, chopped
5 cloves garlic, minced

3 tablespoons paprika
⅔ cup stewed tomatoes
Salt, pepper to taste
½ teaspoon sugar

Put lambs' tongues in a pot and cover with water. Bring to a boil, lower heat, simmer 1 hour. Drain, reserving pot liquid. Skin tongues. Heat chicken fat in a pot. Add onions, garlic, and fry until soft, just beginning to brown. Add paprika and tongues, and mix. Add tomatoes, 1 cup of tongue liquid, salt, pepper, and sugar. Cover, simmer over low heat 1 more hour until tongues are fully tender. Add more pot liquid if needed.
6 servings.

SPICY LAMB (ALBANIA)

2 small onions
½ teaspoon grated gingerroot
¼ teaspoon cumin
½ teaspoon cayenne
2 pounds lamb shoulder, cut in
   2-inch cubes

3 cloves garlic, crushed
3 tablespoons vegetable oil
Pinch of ground cloves
Salt to taste
2 tablespoons water
Juice of ½ lime

Grate 1 onion and mix with the ginger, cumin, and cayenne. Add to meat and stir to mix. Slice 1 onion. Sauté *light* brown with garlic in oil. Add ground cloves and fry 2 minutes. Add spiced meat and salt. Cover, slow fry 30 minutes. Sprinkle on water, frying uncovered until meat is tender, water evaporated. Five minutes before serving, add lime juice.
6 servings.

MISHPOCHEH (RELATIVES) LIVER PIE

A treat when in-laws get together to talk over the young married, or when a will (yerisha) or inheritance is to be read.

½ onion, diced
½ cup margarine
2 cups diced calf's liver
1 cup rice, cooked
1 cup water

1 egg
4 tablespoons corn syrup
1 tablespoon salt
¼ teaspoon pepper
1 cup white raisins

Preheat oven to 350°. Fry onion soft, not brown, in 1 tablespoon margarine. Combine all ingredients in a greased casserole. Bake 1 hour. Serve from platter in wedges on toasted rye bread.
8 servings.

ESSIG FLEISH (SOUR BEEF)

1 tablespoon oil
3 onions, diced
2½ pounds chuck, cut up
1 cup tomato sauce
1 pint water

1 tablespoon brown sugar
½ teaspoon salt
1 bay leaf
Juice of 1 lemon
2 tablespoons sugar

Heat oil in a skillet. Lightly brown onions on low heat. Push to one side and sear meat. Add all ingredients but lemon juice, sugar. Cover, simmer on low heat 3 hours until meat is tender. Combine sugar and lemon juice. Mix with pot gravy and put in preheated moderate oven, 350°, uncovered, ½ hour.

6 servings.

Fowl

YUGOSLAV SMOTHERED PIGEONS

In ancient times, the Hebrews offered doves to the Temple in sacrifice, and the birds were eaten by the high priests, or so it was assumed. In Yugoslavia, the Jews ate the squabs themselves.

1 clove garlic, halved	Salt, pepper to taste
4 adult pigeons, cleaned	½ cup hot water
4 tablespoons olive oil	1 tablespoon chopped parsley
4 tablespoons margarine	1 onion, sliced
½ teaspoon sage	1 cup sliced mushrooms
⅛ teaspoon marjoram	1 lemon quarter

Rub the garlic over pigeons inside and out. Wash birds with olive oil. Coat with margarine, and sage, marjoram; salt and pepper the interiors of pigeons. Brown pigeons in a pot on all sides quickly in oil. Add water, parsley, onion, mushrooms, and lemon. Cover, simmer 30 minutes until tender.

4 servings.

If you desire stuffing for the birds—oven-cooked—here is a Black Sea recipe.

SQUAB STUFFING AND SAUCE

½ cup oil
2 shallots
4 mushrooms, sliced
2 tablespoons bread crumbs
4 raw squab livers chopped
2 raw chicken livers, chopped
2 tablespoons butter

1 tablespoon chopped parsley
Salt, pepper to taste
⅓ cup port wine
1 cup cooked white rice
1 cup chicken fat
1 cup dry sherry

Preheat oven to 400°. To oil, add shallots, mushrooms, bread crumbs, cook over medium heat 2 minutes. Add chopped livers, and cook 2 minutes, stir, brown the livers. Add all other ingredients except chicken fat and sherry. Stuff and truss 4 squabs and grease birds with chicken fat. Place in a greased pan. Roast 45 minutes at 400°. *Watch* to prevent overbaking. Baste every 10 minutes. Use roasting pan juices mixed with 1 cup of sherry for sauce.
Makes stuffing for 4 squabs.

BULGARIAN ROAST MINT DUCK

1 (5-pound) duck, cleaned, drawn
1 orange, peeled, in segments
1½ teaspoons salt
¼ teaspoon pepper

½ teaspoon ground ginger
½ teaspoon allspice
1½ teaspoons dried mint leaves
1 cup orange juice
½ cup dry red wine

Preheat oven to 325°. Dry and stuff the bird with the orange segments and put duck, breast side up, on a rack in an uncovered roasting pan in oven. Roast 1½ hours. Skim off the fat. Combine all other ingredients and 30 minutes before duck is done (takes about 1½ hours), pour mixture over and baste frequently. Orange segments in cavity can be used as garnish.
4 servings.

HONEYED CHICKEN BREAST

2 tablespoons lemon juice
8 whole chicken breasts, boned
½ teaspoon salt
Matzo Meal-Prune Stuffing

½ cup orange juice
¼ cup dark honey
Orange slices to garnish

Preheat oven to 350°. Splash lemon juice all over chicken, salt lightly. Put breasts skin side down on table and place 3 tablespoons stuffing mixture on each and fold together. Put skin side up on buttered baking pan. Bake at 350° 40 minutes, baste with orange juice and honey. Serve whole on heated platter. Garnish with sliced orange.
8 servings.

MATZO MEAL-PRUNE STUFFING

2 cups pitted prunes
1 cup orange juice
2 onions, diced
½ cup butter
1 pound matzo meal

2 eggs
1 large carrot, grated
1 tablespoon chopped parsley
½ cup water
Salt, pepper to taste

Soak prunes in orange juice for 3 days. Fry onions in butter. Mix with matzo meal. Drain prunes, leave some liquid. Add to meat mixture with eggs and remaining ingredients. Makes stuffing for 10 chicken breasts.

Fish

CHOPPED SCHMALTZ HERRING

2 schmaltz herrings, split and
cleaned
1 thick slice rye bread, soaked in
vinegar
1 big apple, peeled, cored, sliced

3 hard-boiled eggs
Dash of white pepper
Pinch of sugar to taste
1 onion, sliced

Place herrings in water to cover. Refrigerate 12 hours in covered container. Change water 3 times. Drain herrings and discard water. Remove skin from fish, and fillet. Rinse under cold water. Press vinegar out of bread. Chop fish in wooden bowl. Put through grinder twice. Mix fillets, apple, 2 hard-boiled eggs, chopped, dash of pepper, and rye bread. Season with sugar to taste. Top with a crumbled hard-boiled egg, add slices of raw onion.
4 servings.

FRIED FLOUNDER

3 pounds sliced flounder
1 1/2 cups matzo meal
1 teaspoon salt
1/2 teaspoon pepper

1 teaspoon minced chervil
1 teaspoon minced parsley
1/2 teaspoon paprika
1 pint oil

Wash and drain the fish. Dredge with matzo meal, salt, pepper, chervil, parsley, and paprika. Put fish in a fry basket and set in 375° oil 2 minutes. Drain and serve hot or cold.
6 servings.

STEWED WHITEFISH WITH VEGETABLES

3 pounds whitefish, cleaned, cut
   into 4 pieces
¼ cup dry white wine
1 onion, sliced
3 stalks celery, chopped

3 carrots, sliced
1 tablespoon salt
¼ teaspoon pepper
1 pint cold water

In a deep dish marinate the fish in the wine for 1 hour. Put onion, celery, carrots, salt, pepper in a Dutch oven with water and bring to a boil. Add fish to the mixture, cover, simmer ¾ of an hour. Remove fish to platter. Strain liquid, save carrots, and pour over fish. Serve with the carrots as garnish. The liquid will jell when chilled to serve with the cold fish.

4 servings.

ALBANIA OVEN-POACHED TROUT

Juice of 1 lemon
1 teaspoon chopped parsley
Pinch of dill
1 bay leaf
½ teaspoon sugar
½ minced onion

Salt, pepper to taste
1 cup oil and vinegar salad
   dressing
2 tomatoes, sliced
2 pounds trout fillets

Combine everything but the tomatoes and fish. Marinate fish in the mixture 4 hours in refrigerator. Preheat oven to 350°. Put the fish in baking dish, pour marinade over it. Cover with sliced tomato, extra salt and pepper. Put in preheated oven for 40 minutes.
4 servings.

POACHED FISH ROE

2 pounds fresh shad roe or *any*
   roe available
½ pound sweet butter

Salt, pepper to taste
1 cup chopped parsley
Lemon slices to garnish

Put the roe in ½ of butter in a skillet. Fry slowly until roe is nearly firm on both sides. Remove from skillet before it is brown. Turn up heat in skillet. Add rest of butter and salt and pepper. Add parsley. Pour mix over roe. Serve garnished with sliced lemon.
4 servings.

Soup

ROMANIAN TCHORKA (SOUR SOUP)

1 tablespoon oil
1 onion, minced
1 carrot, diced
2 sprigs parsley
2 stalks celery
1 cup water
2 pints sauerkraut juice
1 pound ground veal

1 egg, beaten
1 slice bread soaked in water,
   drained
¾ teaspoon salt
½ teaspoon pepper
1 teaspoon chopped dill
2 tablespoons rice, cooked

To oil in a saucepan, add onion and carrot, sauté 5 minutes, stir occasionally. Add parsley, celery, water, bring to boil. Add sauerkraut juice, cook 10 minutes. Mix the veal, egg, bread, salt, pepper, and dill. Make into nut-size balls and add to boiling soup. Add rice. Cook on medium heat 30 minutes.
8 servings.

YENTA'S (GOSSIP'S) EGG-LEMON SOUP

5 cups beef soup
¼ cup rice, uncooked
2 egg yolks
1 teaspoon cornstarch

Juice of ¼ lemon
1 teaspoon chopped parsley
Salt, pepper to taste

Put soup in a kettle, bring to boil. Put in the rice, cover, cook 30 minutes until rice is tender. Combine egg yolks with cornstarch and add to soup. When mixture thickens, add lemon and chopped parsley, salt and pepper to taste.
6 servings.

EGGPLANT SOUP

½ onion, chopped
½ cup sliced mushrooms
1 large tomato, sliced
½ cup olive oil
1 eggplant, peeled, diced
2 cups beef or Chicken Soup

1 cup water
1 teaspoon chopped parsley
Salt, pepper to taste
¼ teaspoon thyme
½ teaspoon grated nutmeg

Sauté the onion, mushrooms, tomato in olive oil 5 minutes. Combine all remaining ingredients except nutmeg, bring to a boil. Reduce heat, cover, simmer ½ hour until vegetables are tender. Sprinkle with grated nutmeg.

4 servings.

MUSHROOM SOUP

1½ pounds mushrooms, sliced
1 cup sweet butter
1 onion, chopped
Salt to taste
2 teaspoons chopped parsley

3 cups half and half
3 tablespoons flour
2 cups water
1 cup dry white wine
¼ cup chopped fresh dill

Slice mushrooms into small pieces. To 3 tablespoons butter in a skillet, add the onion, mushrooms, salt, parsley, and fry until mushrooms are tender. In a saucepan put remaining butter and add half and half, flour, blend smooth. Add 2 cups water and the wine, stir. Heat just to boiling, but do *not* permit to boil. Add mushroom mix, heat 10 minutes, stir often. Top with chopped dill at serving.

6 servings.

PLOESTI TURKEY-MATZO BALLS SOUP

1 onion, minced
3 cups sliced, peeled potato
4 cups turkey soup
1 carrot, cooked, sliced
2 tablespoons margarine
⅛ teaspoon crumbled sage

Salt, pepper to taste
2 cups diced cooked turkey
1 dozen Matzo Balls
Paprika
Chopped parsley

Cook onion and potato in soup 20 minutes: add carrot, cook 10 minutes. Add margarine, sage, parsley, and salt and pepper to taste. Add turkey and matzo balls, and heat. Serve with a sprinkling of paprika and parsley.

4 servings.

Doughs

MAMALIGA (CORN MEAL BAKED MUSH)

Call it corn meal, maize, corn, be it ground or cut from the fresh cob, roasted on the ear, Romanian and Balkan Jews could depend on it, the way the Irish depended for so many years on the potato. It was eaten by the poor and by the well-off people. For it was tasty, filling, and a kind of addiction, so that a generation later, in America and elsewhere, some middle-aged tycoon could sigh and remark, "No one turns out a mamaliga like *my* mother used to make. All she needed was a fistful of corn meal, a pot of hot water, and as quick as that a michel [delicacy] was ready." It *wasn't* that simple.

4 cups water	1 teaspoon salt
1½ cups corn meal	¼ teaspoon white pepper
2 tablespoons butter	2 tablespoons melted butter

Preheat oven to 400°. Set water to a rapid boil in a pot, stir in corn meal. Reduce heat to medium and cook, stirring, until mixture thickens. Add 2 tablespoons butter, salt, pepper, and take the mush right from the boiling pot. Put it onto a baking sheet, brush with melted butter. Bake at 400° until lightly browned. Serve in slices.
Makes 8 slices.

MAMALIGA SPOON BREAD

1½ cups boiling water	1 teaspoon baking soda
1 cup corn meal	1 egg, separated
1 tablespoon chicken fat	1½ cups buttermilk
½ teaspoon salt	

In a pot mix water, corn meal, and fat; add salt, soda, egg yolk, and buttermilk. Mix again. Fold in stiffly beaten egg white. Pour into greased casserole. Bake in preheated moderate 350° oven for 1 hour, until firm. Serve hot with butter.
6 servings.

YOGURT FRIED BREAD

3 cups whole wheat flour
1 teaspoon salt
½ cup butter

1–1½ cups yogurt
½ cup cooking oil

In a bowl mix the flour and salt well. Melt the butter and pour into the flour mixture. Mix, and add the yogurt—to make a stiffish dough. On a floured surface knead dough for 5 minutes. Form into a ball, and let it stand for half an hour, covered. Divide into 10 sections, and roll each into a ball. Set the balls into a skillet with the hot oil and fry light brown.
10 servings.

Dessert

BALKAN STRUDEL STUFFINGS

The traditional Jewish-Russian Strudel dough (see Index) might be made in the Balkans as we have set down, *but* the filling includes a few changes.

POPPY SEED STRUDEL FILLING

1 pound poppy seeds, ground
¾ cup honey
½ cup light cream

½ cup raisins
1 tablespoon grated lemon rind
½ cup melted butter

Cook together poppy seeds, honey, cream, and raisins until a thick mass. Add lemon rind and cool. Set on the oiled strudel dough and roll up; paint with butter.
6–8 servings.

CHERRY STRUDEL FILLING

1½ cups finely ground hazelnuts
4 cups sour red cherries, pitted
1 cup sugar

Plaster the nuts over the buttered strudel dough and top with cherries. Sprinkle with the sugar. Roll up for baking.
6 servings.

In baking, follow the traditional strudel recipe in this book (see Jewish-Russian Strudel in Index).

ITALY AND THE
MEDITERRANEAN

Eat in Poland, drink in Hungary, sleep in Germany,
and make love in Italy . . .

Jewish Travel Advice—1912

Anyone who has read, or seen Vittorio De Sica's film version of the
novel, *The Garden of the Finzi-Continis,* must be aware that the Italian
Jews, long settled there and mostly assimilated, were different, in their
attitudes and in their philosophy of events, from the Jews of the rest
of the world. They had merged more fully into the Italian life over
their Campari and soda, and lost much of their dependence on the
old orthodoxies; lost, too, a great deal of their vigor, unable to take action
in a political crisis that might, and did, turn against them.

The tragedy of the Finzi-Continis, and the middle and upper class
Jew of Italy, was in part created by their remoteness from modern life, its
strife and drama. They existed in their mansions and gardens, positions
and honors, as well-mannered, overeducated folk, unaware of the foul
winds blowing from the burning edges of Europe. They retained a
touching connection with their religion, and the Passover scene in the
film is not festive, but rather like some secret ritual guarded from
the intruding eye of the town. Their food remained, at least during
the holidays, traditionally what is called Jewish.

We, in gathering recipes for this book from many such families and
in sitting at their tables as guests (Italian dinner hours are usually
from 9 or 10 P.M. and last two hours, often), were able to see the
blending of the Jewish and the best of the Italian dishes. The Jewish-
run rosticceria (delicatessen) also shows this blend.

The ancient Jewish historian Flavius Josephus mentioned a colony
of Jews in Rome observing ritual food procedures. They were part of
the Roman population where Nero hastened the Decline and Fall. One
of Christ's Jewish traveling disciples had the honor of being martyred
there.

When their Catholic Spanish Majesties, Ferdinand and Isabella, and
the Holy Office Inquisitor expelled the Spanish Jews (known as the
Sephardim Jews, and who looked down, and still do, on their Ashkenazic
brothers of Eastern Europe), many of the Spanish-Portuguese exiles

settled in Italy. Here, for generations, they did not mingle socially or genetically with Ashkenazic Jews.

One of the expelled families was that of the famous artist Amedeo (Beloved of God) Modigliani, whose forefathers, driven from Spain, first settled in a little town south of Rome called Modigliana—a name they took as their own when they set themselves up as dealers in commodities. In Paris, the artist is still remembered by some French Jews as talking of the food in his mother's house, as she blended traditional Jewish dishes with the cuisine of Italy.

Italian-Jewish food is more than the usual pastas, the polenta or minestrone. The wines at a Jewish-Italian table after the antipasto are not all raffia-covered bottles of Chianti. The antipasto is made up of black and green olives, anchovies and capers, artichoke hearts, radishes, fennel, green and red peppers, sardines, cold veal, salami. But the ham is often missing, as is the hog headcheese, the pork sausages. Olive oil, salt, vinegar, and lemon juice are used on the antipasto in the high class Jewish-Italian ristorante and trattoria (eating places.)

Jewish-Italian dried mushroom soup and gnocchi (corn meal balls) were a treat. The salads of romaine, chicory, escarole, with Lucca olive oil were usually missing from the tables of Russian or German Jews. As were the dried chestnut purées.

Italy has a varied and different cuisine for various sections of the country. Risotto alla Milanese was not eaten in the south; the Venetian Jews stuck to a rice with green peas called risi-bisi. Ritual Jews once did not eat scampi (shrimplike crustaceans), but times have changed. In Rome today, the Jewish dish can be a carciofi, artichokes fried in oil, in Sicily, the tiny sciabacheddu; in Naples, the scaloppine (veal cutlets) is the treat (the secret is beating the veal with a wooden hammer for a full five minutes).

The Italian-Jewish mother, of course, has the traditional chicken soup ready, but she is also an expert with Chicken alla Cacciatore seasoned often in an un-Italian way. And after the Sabbath tzimmes, you will be served the formaggio—those gorgonzola, Bel Paese, or Pecorino cheeses.

Espresso coffee is not a traditional Jewish drink, but true Italian coffee is deadly. Jews in Rome brew up Vienna-style coffee. There is no Russian-Jewish tea drinking, but there is "teatime" for the ladies and their guests, often on the Hassler Hotel terrace in the late afternoon.

In Roman-Jewish life, the surprise can be a Roman idea of a Vienna strudel, or an Italian version of chopped liver with chicken fat at a bar mitzvah. You will be served native wine; white Falerno, white Torra Giulia, Verdicchio, Orvieto, or Soave, at a Succoth holiday dinner, and an after-dinner liqueur, Crema di Timo, tasting of thyme. The frutta fresca (fresh fruit) will come to table with a deep dish of water, and you are expected to dip each piece into the dish and wash it. The gelato (sherbet) in Jewish homes is usually milk-free, no whipped cream.

Unlike among many other European Jews, a large portion of Italian-Jewish culture has merged and disappeared into Italian society, inter-married, even joined the church. It is neither snobbery nor social status seeking, nor fears greater than most of us bear for the future. But rather a comfortable belonging. As one old Jewish grandmother told us, "My granddaughters are more Catholic than the Pope, but if you want a well-fried latke, stuffed kishka, have dinner with Bianca. And I, myself, taught her how to use matzo meal to make the family's sogliole alla marinara—fried pickled sole."

Meat

Latin Jews on the land, like most of the farmers, could not afford to raise full-grown beef—so calves, as veal, came on the market at an early age.

VEAL TARRAGON

2 tablespoons chicken fat
2 pounds veal, cut in 2-inch cubes
Salt, pepper to taste
2 tablespoons finely chopped
   shallots
2 cups Chicken Soup

1 cup dry white wine
1 tablespoon dried tarragon
   leaves
1 bay leaf
Freshly chopped parsley to
   garnish

Put fat into a heavy pot. Add veal seasoned with salt and pepper. Fry until veal is brown on all sides. Add shallots and cook for 3 minutes. Add chicken soup and wine, which have been mixed with tarragon and bay leaf. Bring to a boil, reduce heat, simmer, covered, for 2 hours, or until veal is tender. Garnish with chopped parsley.
4 servings.

TRUFFLE PÂTÉ

To the Latin Jews, *this* was one special form of chopped chicken livers, at least among the upper classes, and always a delight to the gourmets. The chicken breasts added a nuance of flavor, the pistachio nuts a crispness.

1 pound cooked lean boneless
    veal
½ pound cooked tongue
2 pounds cooked chicken livers
4 eggs
⅓ cup cognac
½ cup chopped black truffles
½ cup pistachio nuts

4 teaspoons salt
1 teaspoon white pepper
1 teaspoon allspice
½ teaspoon ground cinnamon
2 whole cloves
½ cup flour
4 cooked chicken breasts, sliced,
    boned, skinned

Put veal, tongue through grinder. In blender put half the chicken livers with eggs, cognac. Turn on, add the ground meats. Mix well with ground meats. Add truffles, nuts, seasonings, and flour. Mix. Fill a 3-quart mold less than half full of paté mixture. Put chicken breasts on top, cover with rest of pâté. Chill well.
10 servings.

BRAINS WITH TOMATO

Europeans learned to make fine food out of the parts of animals that Americans ignored—because of the overabundance of meat on the American frontiers. But now with rising inflated prices, it's time we all tasted these gourmet dishes.

1½ pounds calf's brains
3 tablespoons oil
1 onion, chopped
½ teaspoon Spanish paprika

3 tomatoes, peeled, chopped
8 sprigs fresh coriander
Salt, pepper to taste

Soak the brains in water to cover for 2 hours. Remove membrane, veins. Set in boiling, salted water. Reduce heat, simmer slowly 30 minutes. Cool, drain, slice. Heat oil in a skillet and fry the onion. Add paprika, tomatoes, coriander, salt, and pepper. Cook on moderate heat, stir often until ingredients are a blended sauce. Add brains, bring only *just* to a boil.
4 servings.

BROILED KIDNEYS

1 cup oil	Pepper to taste
¼ cup minced chives	1 teaspoon dried basil
3 tablespoons minced parsley	6 veal kidneys, soaked
1 tablespoon salt	½ cup dry vermouth

Mix the hot oil with herbs and seasoning. Split, flatten out kidneys. Roll in herb mixture, broil in a pan set 5 inches below heat 7 minutes. Turn kidneys from side to side. When lightly browned remove to lower heat on top of stove; add vermouth. Stir just to heat.
6 servings.

POLENTA STEW

To Jews, it's called mamaliga—corn meal—but along the Mediterranean, it's polenta to the Italians. So top the mamaliga given earlier in the book with this:

1 teaspoon cooking oil	½ teaspoon caraway seeds
1 onion, minced	1 teaspoon salt
2 pounds veal cutlet, cubed	⅛ teaspoon pepper
1 clove garlic, peeled	1 cup water
2 teaspoons paprika	3 tablespoons tomato sauce

Set oil in skillet and heat. Fry the onion for 4 minutes, push aside. Sauté the meat and all ingredients but the water and tomato sauce. Cover, simmer over low heat 1 hour. Remove. Mix tomato sauce and water, pour over the meat. Heat, do not simmer. Serve on hot mamaliga.
6 servings.

VEAL-PRUNE CUTLETS

1½ cups chopped pitted prunes
1 pint dry red wine
1 cup margarine
6 veal cutlets
2 chopped onions

1 minced clove garlic
3 tomatoes, peeled, chopped
Salt, pepper to taste
⅛ teaspoon ground nutmeg

First soak prunes in the wine overnight. Heat margarine in a skillet. Fry cutlets on both sides, brown. Set in a flameproof casserole with a lid. Add the onions to the margarine in the skillet, and fry. Add the garlic, tomatoes, salt and pepper, nutmeg. Pour over cutlets; cover. Cook over a low heat until tender, 1½ hours. Add prunes and wine they were soaked in. Cook uncovered 10 minutes.
6 servings.

YOUNG KID—EGGPLANT

If you can't buy young roasting goat—use lamb meat.

2 tablespoons oil
1½ pounds kid meat
2 eggplants
1 cup melted margarine
1 cup tomato sauce

¼ cup water
½ tablespoon mixed spices
½ teaspoon red pepper
Salt, pepper to taste

In casserole heat oil. Add kid meat, cook until brown. Peel, slice eggplant 1½ inches thick, brush slices with margarine. Put in a baking pan, bake in preheated oven at 375° for 15 minutes until eggplant is golden. Place over meat in casserole. Mix tomato sauce, water, mixed spices, red pepper, and salt and pepper to taste. Pour over eggplant. Bake 45 minutes in 375° oven until meat and eggplant are tender.
6 servings.

SWEETBREADS

1 pound calf's sweetbreads
1 quart water
1 tablespoon vinegar
½ pound mushrooms, sliced
¾ cup chopped parsley
1 clove garlic, minced

½ cup butter
1 teaspoon dried oregano
½ cup Madeira wine
1 tablespoon grated horseradish
Salt, pepper to taste

Soak sweetbreads for 1 hour in water to cover. Change water twice. Drain, place in saucepan with 1 quart water and 1 tablespoon vinegar. Bring slowly to boil. Reduce heat, simmer for 5 minutes, and cut into sections. Remove excess tissues. Fry mushrooms, parsley, and garlic in butter 5 minutes. Add sweetbreads and sauté 4 minutes. Add oregano, Madeira, and horseradish. Simmer 15 minutes. Salt and pepper to taste.
4 servings.

Fowl

HOT SHERRIED CHICKEN LIVERS

Here is a Spanish-Jewish hot liver-sherry dish (or brandy if you like it tangy).

2 pounds chicken livers
1 cup chicken fat
½ cup Oporto or Jerez sherry

2 teaspoons chopped parsley
½ teaspoon salt
½ teaspoon pepper

Fry livers in fat over low heat until brown. Add all other ingredients, simmer 10 minutes. Serve hot on pilot crackers.
10 servings.

POLLO À LA ESPAÑOLA
(CHICKEN IN WINE AND FRUIT)

¼ cup chicken fat
2 chicken breasts, halved
2 teaspoons olive oil
1 tablespoon curaçao

2 cups manzanilla wine
1 cup seedless white grapes
2 peeled, sliced oranges

Preheat oven to 350°. In fat brown unfloured chicken. Transfer to baking dish, add all the rest of the ingredients. Cover, bake 50 minutes until tender, basting.
4 servings.

BREAST OF CHICKEN SHEBA

2 (½ pound each) whole
   boneless chicken breasts
1 cup flour
1 egg, beaten

1 cup bread crumbs
1 cup vegetable oil
2 slices toast
1 sprig parsley to garnish

Preheat oven to 400°. Place breasts of chicken on board. Flatten with cleaver. Flour pieces, dip into egg, roll in bread crumbs. Preheat frying pan with oil. Place chicken breasts in pan, sauté on both sides. Remove and place in medium pan in 400° oven. Bake each side 10 minutes. Place toast on serving dish, add chicken. Serve with sprig of parsley.
2 servings.

CHICKEN PARMESAN

From a non-Orthodox family kitchen book.

6 chicken breasts, halved, boned
2 eggs, beaten
½ cup seasoned bread crumbs
1 teaspoon each, salt, pepper
½ cup margarine

1 quart tomato sauce
½ pound mozzarella cheese,
   grated
½ cup grated Parmesan cheese

Preheat oven to 350°. Dip breasts in egg, roll in bread crumbs and seasoning. Brown in margarine. Put in shallow baking pan. Pour half of tomato sauce over pieces. Top with mozzarella cheese and put remaining sauce on. Sprinkle with Parmesan cheese. Bake 1 hour until tender.
6 servings.

PURIM CHICKEN ON THE VINE

10 chicken breasts, halved, skinned
1 cup flour seasoned with salt, pepper
1 cup margarine
1 cup undrained sliced mushrooms

4 tablespoons flour
Salt, pepper to taste
2 tablespoons grape juice
1 cup Chicken Soup
1 cup seedless grapes
1 cup dry sherry

Preheat oven to 350°. Dredge chicken with flour. Sauté in margarine, turning occasionally until tender and light brown. Put in a casserole. Stir undrained mushrooms into drippings left in pan. Mix flour, salt, and pepper. Add grape juice to form paste. Stir into mushrooms and drippings, add chicken soup, grapes. Simmer 10 minutes, stir occasionally. Pour in wine, simmer 1 minute. Pour over chicken; bake in 350° oven for 30 minutes.
8 servings.

Fish

TISHA BOV ROCKFISH

During the nine days leading to Tisha Bov—a time of mourning for the disasters and catastrophes of the Jews in history, no marriages are performed and *no* meat is eaten. Fish is permitted.

2 pounds fish fillets
1 teaspoon salt
⅛ teaspoon pepper
1 tablespoon prepared mustard

3 tablespoons chili sauce
1 onion, chopped
Parsley to garnish

Preheat oven to 350°. Cover fish fillets with salt and pepper. Roll up and fasten with skewers, and place on a greased baking dish. Mix mustard, chili sauce, onion and blend. Spread on fish rolls. Bake uncovered 30 minutes until fish flakes to a fork. Move to serving dish. Garnish with parsley.
6 servings.

RED SNAPPER IN SAUTERNE

2 tablespoons olive oil	½ onion, chopped
5 potatoes	5 pounds red snapper fillets
Salt, pepper to taste	1 cup dry sauterne
2 tablespoons chopped parsley	½ cup tomato sauce
2 cloves garlic, chopped	

Preheat oven to 375°. Put oil into baking dish. Peel, slice potatoes lengthwise ½ inch thick. Lay on bottom of dish. Season with salt and pepper. Mix parsley, garlic, and onion. Sprinkle half of mixture over potatoes. Salt the fish, put over potatoes. Sprinkle with remaining half of mixture. Add wine and tomato sauce. Bake, uncovered, in moderate 375° oven 1½ hours, basting.
8 servings.

FISH IN DILL

6 peppercorns	½ cup olive oil
1 bay leaf	4 cloves garlic, peeled
1 teaspoon salt	1 small onion
½ cup water	1½ cups fresh dill
1 pound fish fillet (carp)	½ cup chopped fresh parsley
1 pound fish fillet (pike)	½ cup dry white wine

In a large saucepan mix peppercorns, bay leaf, salt, and water. Bring to boil, simmer 5 minutes. Add fish. Simmer 20 minutes. Remove fillets from liquid and set aside. Turn up heat, reduce liquid to ½ cup. Put olive oil in blender. Add garlic, onion, dill, and parsley. Turn on blender, add pot liquid and wine. Pour over fish. Chill.

HOLIDAY ANCHOVY-PEPPERS

3 pounds Italian frying peppers
12 anchovy fillets
2 pints olive oil

Dry peppers in sun or air 1 week, until they are wrinkled, soft. Make 1 slit in each pepper, get out seeds, and stuff 2 anchovies into each pepper. Put anchovy-stuffed peppers into a strainer. Place a plate on top and weight it down with a stone. Stand overnight to drain into a bowl. Pack peppers into jars already sterilized in boiling water. Heat olive oil and pour to cover peppers completely. Screw tight.
Makes about 2 quarts.

Soup

JEWISH-ITALIAN CHICKEN SOUP

The un-Orthodox add ¾ cup of grated Parmesan cheese to this version of Jewish Chicken Soup International, also endive.

3 quarts Chicken Soup	Salt, pepper to taste
½ cup chopped celery	3 cups cut-up fresh endive
½ cup chopped onion	2 eggs
¼ cup chopped carrot	¾ cup grated Parmesan cheese
½ teaspoon oregano	1 cup chopped, cooked chicken

Get chicken soup to a boil, add celery, onion, carrot, oregano, salt, pepper. Cook 15 minutes, add endive, simmer 10 minutes. Whip eggs with grated cheese, add with chicken to soup. Simmer 15 minutes until done.

6 servings.

AFTER PRAYER SOUP (ITALY)

4 cups Chicken Soup	1 carrot, sliced
1 yellow onion, sliced	4 ounces wide pasta
2 tablespoons sliced green pepper	1 cup red kidney beans
2 tablespoons minced mushrooms	½ cup freshly grated
¼ cup sliced fresh green beans	Parmesan cheese
1 cup shelled fresh peas	

Mix all but cheese in a pot, set on low heat, simmer covered 35 minutes. Add Parmesan cheese halfway.

Said to act like a blood transfusion on the tired and aged.

4 servings.

SPANISH-JEWISH DANDELION SOUP

You can use spinach instead of dandelions if you have no lawn.

¼ pound dried chick-peas
¼ pound dried white beans
Water for soaking
½ pound corned beef
2 tablespoons cooking oil
¼ pound garlic beef sausage
8 cups water
2 cloves garlic, finely chopped

2 tomatoes, chopped
1½ teaspoons ground cumin
2 potatoes, peeled, diced
Salt, pepper to taste
½ pound chopped dandelion
  greens or spinach
½ cup margarine
1 cup croutons

Soak chick-peas and beans overnight in water. Drain. In a large pot sauté beef in oil and add sausage. Sauté until cooked. Remove from pot. Slice sausage. Add rest of ingredients to pot except the dandelion greens, margarine, and croutons. Simmer 3 hours or until chick-peas, beans are tender. Melt margarine in a skillet, add meats and greens on high heat. Stir, toss greens well until wilted. Add with meats to soup. Serve with crisp croutons.
10 servings.

Vegetables

WHITE CABBAGE WITH BUTTER

1 head white cabbage
¾ cup butter

¼ cup water
Salt, ground pepper to taste

Preheat oven to 350°. Pull off outer leaves, cut cabbage into quarters. Remove center core and shred cabbage into medium slices as for cole slaw. Put ½ of butter in a casserole and add water. Set in a layer of cabbage. Sprinkle with salt and pepper, dot with more butter. Repeat layers until all cabbage has been used. Add 1 tablespoon butter on top. Cover, bake for 30 minutes.
6 servings.

MELAMED (TEACHER) TOMATO PANCAKES

2 cups tomato juice   ¼ teaspoon ground cinnamon
1½ teaspoons baking soda   ¼ teaspoon nutmeg
1 cup buttermilk   2 eggs, slightly beaten
2 cups pancake flour   ¼ cup melted butter

Mix tomato juice with soda in a bowl. Add buttermilk and flour, cinnamon, nutmeg, eggs, and butter. Beat until blended. Pour batter, using 3 tablespoons at a time to form 1 pancake, on hot griddle. Turn when bubbles appear on cake, brown other side. Serve with honey.
6 servings.

PRESERVED AEGEAN OLIVES

½ pound each, green olives, black   ⅓ cup mustard seeds
   olives, brown olives   4 cups olive oil
3 garlic cloves, crushed

In a bowl mix Greek olives of various colors with garlic cloves and mustard seeds. Cover mixture with olive oil. Pack into jars, seal tightly. Keeps indefinitely. Ready to eat in 2 weeks.
Makes about 2 quarts.

ONIONS IN GOD'S HONEY

8 white onions   8 teaspoons honey
1 pint tomato juice   4 tablespoons butter

Preheat oven to 350°. After you peel the onions, slice off ¼ inch of bottoms to sit well in a casserole dish. Pour in ¼ inch tomato juice. Drop teaspoon of honey on each onion, dot with butter. Cover, and bake in oven for 1 hour.
6 servings.

Dessert

ROMAN SHUL PRUNE CAKE

1 cup butter
1½ cups sugar
3 eggs, beaten
1¼ teaspoons baking soda
1 cup sour milk
1 cup stewed prunes, pitted,
  chopped

2 cups flour
½ teaspoon ground cloves
½ teaspoon ground cinnamon
½ teaspoon ground nutmeg

Preheat oven to 350°. Mix butter and sugar; add eggs. Mix baking soda and sour milk. Add to above the prunes. Mix dry ingredients together and add. Bake 35 minutes at 350°.
6 servings.

PEARS IN WINE

6 firm pears, peeled, halved
½ cup Crema di Timo liqueur
1 cup water
1 teaspoon grated lemon rind

2 teaspoons lemon juice
1 teaspoon ground ginger
1 3-inch stick cinnamon
1 cup sugar

Put pears in saucepan with liqueur and 1 cup water. Bring to boil, simmer 10 minutes. Add lemon rind, lemon juice, ginger, cinnamon, and sugar. Cover and continue cooking until pears are tender. Chill, serve in its own sauce.
4 servings.

FRANCE

"Qui vivra, verra . . . [who lives will see]," Max Jacob, the Jewish-born poet and friend of Picasso, is said to have remarked on sitting down to a Paris Rothschild dinner.

It would be foolish to assume that the French were ever intrigued by any great additions to their national cooking by Jewish influences brought to them by exiles from Spain and elsewhere, settling in, or moving on to Holland—there to cut diamonds, or grind lenses, as Spinoza did. The greatness of the French cuisine, its splendor of sauces and spicing, fully seduced many important French-Jewish families, from the Prousts to the Bergsons.

Yet the Passover seders we attended as guests in Fontainebleau just last year recalled the ritual respect such artists as Soutine, Chagall, and Pascin paid to some of the dishes of their youth, showing that there existed, exists, a pull toward a memory of Jewish food.

Jacques Offenbach, whose music made the Second Empire dance the cancan, was devoted to a special fried herring; the grandmother of Marcel Proust, according to an old bit of gossip, served fried matzo at one déjeuner; Léon Blum claimed one of his aunts made the best potato kugel in France, *si Dieu veut.*

But in the main, the French dishes in the houses of the important or well-off Jewish families were tied to the culinary grace of France. However, it took time. Even the French Rothschilds, as they drifted more and more away from their Hebrew roots, took two generations for the full departure. Their various chefs often produced recipes echoing German-Jewish and Russian- and Polish-Jewish dishes. Several dishes were to be immortalized by the family name. An old cookbook lists Rothschild Caneton Bigarde, one version of duck with orange, and Edmund de Rothschild Soupe Verte, a green soup related to the Jewish schav (cold sorrel soup) with basil, watercress, spinach, and chicken added. But certainly Rothschild Cuisses des Grenouilles (fricassee of frogs' leg) or Rothschild Coquilles St. Jacques (scallops in shells) can *hardly* have any connection with Jewish cooking.

> The discovery of a new dish does more for the human happiness than the finding of a new star . . .
>
> *Anthelme Brillat-Savarin, 1825*

The middle class, or workingman, French Jew, ritual or free-thinking, made attempts to retain some Jewish dishes, even if adapted to a blending of older tastes with the French recipes. But as with the famous, the notorious, the talented Jews of the artists, or the upper classes, no large solid French-Jewish cuisine emerged.

The *haricots verts et blancs,* green and white beans, might be made with chicken fat instead of bacon grease by the Jewish hostess of Sarah Bernhardt or Anatole France, and their hors d'oeuvres might leave out the lobster and the crab meat, the oysters and mussels, and present pickled mushrooms, spiced artichoke hearts, fillets of anchovy, but no cockscombs in aspic, *escargot* (snails in shell). Still, all this did not make it a Jewish dish, even if there was a tin of Imperial Golden Russian Caviar, 16 ounces for $150.

At a special meal, a *dîner et fête,* the pâté would recall the chopped liver of the Pale, the herring fillets an older taste. From the time of the Second Empire and into the twentieth century, a great many of the more famous Paris salons, and dinners, were dominated by Jewish hostesses. Their names appear again and again in the famous journals of Edmond de Goncourt. Madame Émile Strauss, nee Halévy, "collector of Princesses and Duchesses." Madame Maurice Lippman. . . . "Masters of France," De Goncourt called their husbands—which was untrue; "dictators of taste," he called their wives. Yes. "Only Jewesses read—and *dare* to admit it." He attended the dinners of the Countess Albert Cahen, Madame Cahen d'Anvers, Madame Maria Kann, Baroness Alphonse Rothschild, to eat splendid food off their turquoise Sèvres porcelain.

The best dinners were at the mansion of Geneviève Halévy-Bizet-Strauss (she had been married to, among others, the composer of *Carmen*). Marcel Proust uses her conversation as that of the Duchess de Guermantes in his great novel.

Guy de Maupassant was friendly with all the society women of Jewish origin, including the Countess Potocka, Madame Lecomte du Nouy, Gisele d'Estoc, and they inspired some of the characters in his novel *Notre Coeur.*

The kitchens of these trend-setters contained the best chefs in France, and one journal records that now and then "a delicious dish would appear that was decidedly of the Jewish mode."

Crêpes suzette could have some kasha in the dough, and, notes a Lehman guest from America, "butter in the crêpe *after* the meat courses, along with the flaming Grand Marnier." The Chablis and the dry sauterne had replaced a taste for Rhine wines, just as the fiery silvowitz, the Polish plum brandy of the old Orthodox tippling, was replaced by Calvados, or a liqueur such as Benedictine or Cointreau.

In our visits to French-Jewish families, after Passover, in time would come Bastille Day, *Le Quatorze Juillet,* and a toast to the Republic by our host—then the strong black coffee with a bit of *chicorée* (chicory) added, and hot milk, *café au lait,* hardly ever cream.

The French Jews felt that for all their problems, and the usual burdens of a minority, they were citizens of a great nation. Our Jewish host —one of the heroes of the French Resistance Underground—led us in a toast—full glasses of Dom Pérignon Cuvée champagne that day—after a magnificent carp dish with Périgourdine truffles, *"À bon vin point d'enseigne,* L'Chayim!" Any comment we could have made on French-Jewish toasting would have had a very wrong Gallic accent. And the cheeses were coming on the table; Gruyère, Roquefort, Camembert, Brie. But the youngest grandchild we noticed, was eating a slice of smoked salmon on a spread of Port-Salut cheese.

Meat

PÂTÉ ROTHSCHILD

This dish, Max Jacob, poet, swore to us in our art student days, was the *true* chopped liver of the French branch of the international banking house, and he had eaten it as a guest. "Many times, *faire venir l'eau à la bouche*" (to make the mouth water).

2 pounds calf's liver	1 clove garlic, crushed
½ pound chicken livers	1 bay leaf, crushed
¼ pound veal liver	Salt, freshly ground pepper to
2 eggs, beaten	taste
¼ cup heavy cream	1 cup chicken fat
Juice of 1 lemon	½ cup fine brandy

Preheat oven to 325°. Clean livers, put them through a grinder twice on the finest blade. Add all ingredients to livers *except* brandy, and mix into a paste. Warm brandy in a pan, light, pour flaming over liver mixture. Mix. Grease with extra fat a pâté mold, put in mixture. Cover mold, and set it into a roasting pan that has 2 inches of water on its bottom. Let stand in the 325° oven 2 hours. Remove and chill overnight.
10–12 servings.

SUCCOTH OXTAIL STEW

4 pounds oxtail, cut at the joints	3 cups beef soup
2 onions, chopped	1 pinch of basil
4 teaspoons margarine	2 dashes of angostura bitters
1 clove garlic, minced	6 carrots, quartered
Salt, pepper to taste	

In a pot brown the oxtails and onions in margarine. Add garlic, salt, and pepper. Add all remaining ingredients, simmer 3 hours.
4 servings.

Oxtail is not Orthodox, but very French-Jewish.

BURGUNDY BEEF RIBS

2½ pounds short ribs
1 tablespoon salt
½ cup burgundy wine
⅓ cup dry red wine vinegar
1 cup catsup

2 tablespoons oil
2 tablespoons honey
1 tablespoon Worcestershire sauce
1 tablespoon prepared mustard
1 clove garlic, minced

Put ribs in kettle with water to cover and 1 tablespoon salt. Bring to boil, cover, and simmer ½ hour. Combine wine, vinegar, catsup, oil, honey, Worcestershire sauce, mustard, garlic, and simmer 15 minutes. Drain ribs and place in a pan. Brush with sauce and roast in preheated oven at 350° for 20 minutes. Baste. Turn ribs, brush with sauce, and roast 20 minutes.
4 servings.

Fish

FRENCH-JEWISH CHOPPED HERRING

6 salt herring fillets
1 onion, chopped
1 apple, chopped
2 hard-cooked eggs

3 tablespoons cider vinegar
2 slices white bread, no crusts
1 teaspoon sugar
2 tablespoons salad oil

Soak the herring in cold water 12 hours. Change water 2 times. Chop onion, apple, eggs, and herring and mix well. Pour vinegar over bread, add to herring, also sugar and oil. Chop very smooth. Chill for 6 hours.
8 servings.

HERRING SALAD GERTRUDE STEIN

Members of the La Stein cult may not be aware of this item in the
Great One's long life in Paris.

4 salt herring fillets	1 cup shredded lettuce
4 scallions, sliced	1 cup cider vinegar
4 radishes, cubed	3 tablespoons salad oil
2 tomatoes, sliced	1 teaspoon sugar
2 green peppers, diced	Pinch each, paprika, black pepper

Slice the herring into 1-inch pieces. Toss scallions, radishes, tomatoes,
and peppers together; add the lettuce, vinegar, oil, sugar, paprika, and
pepper. Top with herring bits. Chill well.
6 servings.

FISH KUGEL (PUDDING)

½ cup butter	1½ teaspoons salt
2 onions, sliced	½ teaspoon pepper
3 potatoes, peeled, sliced	2 eggs
3 cups cooked flaked fish	1½ cups heavy cream

Preheat oven to 350°. Melt butter in a skillet and brown onions. Set
alternate layers of potatoes, fish, and onions in a buttered baking dish,
ending with potatoes. Sprinkle the potatoes with salt and pepper. Beat
eggs, cream together, pour over contents of baking dish. Bake in oven
45 minutes until firm.
6 servings.

FILLET OF SOLE MARGUERITE

This Jewish version differed from Maxim's and Voisin's by leaving
out the 2 tablespoons of chopped shrimp. At least it used to.

4 sole fillets

½ cup butter or margarine

2 cups dry white wine

Salt, pepper to taste

½ cup sliced mushrooms

2 tablespoons flour

1 cup heavy cream

3 egg yolks

1 cup heavy cream, whipped

6 cored baked apples

Slice fillets into serving bits. Roll and fasten with toothpicks. Grease skillet with 2 teaspoons butter. Set fillets in pan and cover with wine. Sprinkle with salt and pepper. Simmer 8 minutes until fillets are tender. Remove fish and save 1 cup liquid. Melt rest of butter in same pan. Add mushrooms, cook until tender. Stir in flour till smooth. Gradually add saved fish liquid and cream. Cook and stir smooth. Remove from heat, stir in egg yolks. Fold in whipped cream. Stuff fish rolls into baked apples. Arrange in casserole. Spoon sauce on apples. Place under broiler for sauce to glaze, for 10 minutes.

6 servings.

Soup

VICHYSSOISE MEYERBEER

4 leeks

4 tablespoons margarine

4 potatoes, peeled, thinly sliced

4 cups Chicken Soup

1 teaspoon salt

1 teaspoon white pepper

1 cup heavy cream

½ cup chopped fresh chives

In a pot fry the white part of the leeks in margarine. Add potatoes, chicken soup, salt, and pepper. Bring to a boil. Reduce heat, simmer 40 minutes. Pour the soup into a blender (Meyerbeer's cook didn't have one—only a strainer), and mix smooth. Return soup to pot to chill, add the cream. Serve chilled, with a sprinkle of fresh chives.

6 servings.

CHILLED LEMON SOUP

Another favorite of the upper class Jews during the Second Empire. This one also contains cream with the chicken soup. A sinful era.

4 cups Chicken Soup
2 cups light cream
2 tablespoons cornstarch
5 egg yolks

Juice of 3 lemons sweetened with
1 teaspoon sugar
Pinch of cayenne

Mix soup and cream, heat, add cornstarch and stir. Cook until thick over low heat, stirring. Beat egg yolks and add to the soup with lemon juice and sugar, cayenne. Stir as the soup thickens a bit. Pour into a bowl, cover, chill overnight.
6 servings.

Vegetables

MONTPARNASSE FRIED TOMATOES

Great favorites of Soutine and Pascin (Pincus), Jewish painters with very tender digestions.

4 medium tomatoes, stems
   removed, sliced
2 tablespoons sugar

1 teaspoon crushed sweet basil
Salt
2 tablespoons butter

Cut tomatoes into 3 thick slices and coat with sugar, sprinkle with basil and salt. Melt butter in a large skillet on medium heat; slowly fry tomatoes until *light* brown and glazed.
2 servings.

STUFFED MUSHROOMS

1 pound mushrooms, stems
   removed
2 tablespoons butter
1 tablespoon chopped parsley

1 teaspoon chopped shallots
1 slice truffle, chopped
1 clove garlic, chopped
Salt, pepper to taste

Pick 12 mushroom caps for stuffing. Chop the remaining mushrooms and stems and sauté until brown in butter with parsley, shallots, truffle, garlic clove, salt, and pepper, for 5 minutes. Put mixture to one side. Sauté mushroom caps on both sides for 2 minutes. Stuff mushrooms with mixture, put under broiler for 5 minutes until brown.
4 servings.

Doughs

POTATO KNISHES

The French Jews say the Russian and German refugees brought this recipe with them.

1 onion, minced
1 cup chicken fat
4 cups mashed potatoes
½ cup potato flour

3 eggs
1 teaspoon salt
¼ teaspoon pepper

Sauté onion in 4 tablespoons chicken fat and cool. Knead together remaining fat, potatoes, potato flour, eggs, salt, and pepper. Roll out and cut into 2-inch squares. Place a teaspoon of browned onions on each, fold, pinching edges together. Place on a greased baking sheet. Bake 25 minutes.
Makes about 2 dozen.

PRUNE-POTATO TZIMMES

1 pound pitted prunes
3 cups water
6 potatoes, peeled
⅓ cup brown sugar
Juice of 1 lemon

1½ teaspoons salt
3 tablespoons potato flour
2 tablespoons melted fat (beef or
    chicken)
⅛ teaspoon pepper

Preheat oven to 350°. Soak prunes in the 3 cups water 1 hour. Bring to a boil. Slice 5 potatoes into a casserole, pour the undrained prunes over them. Add brown sugar, lemon juice, 1 teaspoon salt. Cover, bake 1 hour. Grate remaining potato, add the potato flour, fat, pepper, remaining salt. Spread mixture on top of casserole. Cover and bake 1¼ hours more, remove the cover for last ½ hour.
8 servings.

Dessert

CRÊPES SUZETTE CITROËN

Gourmet historians come to blows—nearly—over just *who* invented crêpes suzette. Americans accept the legend that a French chef in New York created them for the gourmand fresser (crude feeder) Diamond Jim Brady. The French give the credit to André Citroën, the Jewish Henry Ford, who made auto history in France. So:

FOR THE CRÊPES:

2 cups milk	Pinch of salt
4 eggs	2 teaspoons melted butter
2 cups sifted all-purpose flour	½ tablespoon cognac
1 tablespoon sugar	½ cup butter for frying

FOR THE SAUCE:

4 lumps sugar   ½ cup Cointreau
1 orange   3 tablespoons brandy, heated
1 cup sweet butter

FOR THE CRÊPES: Mix well, with vigor, milk and eggs, add all remaining ingredients, except butter for frying, stir smooth. Pour into a bowl and let stand unchilled, 2 hours. Heat a small-size frying pan very hot. Brush pan with butter. Pour in 2 tablespoons of batter. Tilt the pan in all directions so as to spread batter evenly over the pan. Cook for about 30 seconds, turn the crêpe over, cook for 15 seconds. Place crêpe on warm plate. Repeat this, buttering the pan lightly for each crêpe.

FOR THE SAUCE: Rub lumps of sugar hard on the rind of the orange. Press the orange, reserve the juice. Melt butter in chafing dish. Add the sugar, orange juice, and Cointreau, and bring to a boil. Fold crêpes into quarters, put into sauce. Pour warm brandy over dish and light liquid. Spoon flaming sauce over crêpes and serve when the flames die out.
6 servings.

FRENCH LAKACH (HONEY CAKE)

3½ cups flour   ½ teaspoon ground ginger
¼ teaspoon salt   4 eggs
1½ teaspoons baking powder   ¾ cup sugar
1 teaspoon baking soda   4 tablespoons salad oil
½ teaspoon ground cinnamon   2 cups dark honey
¼ teaspoon ground nutmeg   ½ cup strong coffee
⅛ teaspoon powdered cloves   1½ cups walnuts

Preheat oven to 325°. Combine flour, salt, baking powder, baking soda, cinnamon, nutmeg, cloves, and ginger together. Beat eggs, sugar. Beat thick and light. Beat in the oil, honey, and coffee. Add the flour mixture and nuts. Turn the batter into greased pan. Bake in oven 1¼ hours until browned. Cool on a rack before taking from pan.
8 servings.

CREAM CHEESE TARTS

¼ pound melted margarine
1 cup graham cracker crumbs
1 pound cream cheese
2 teaspoons vanilla

2 eggs
½ cup sugar
1 cup heavy cream, whipped

Preheat oven to 375°. Mix margarine with graham cracker crumbs, set aside. Mix cream cheese, vanilla, eggs, and sugar together. In cupcake tins place 1 tablespoon of graham cracker crumb mixture into each cup. Then put 2 tablespoons of cream cheese mixture on top of crumbs. Bake in oven for 10 minutes. Cool, flip out with knife blade. Top with whipped cream.
4 servings.

ENGLAND

"The English take their pleasures sadly," once wrote a French historian, and it could be added they took their meals with serenity. The Jews had been to England before William the Conqueror, had been exiled, and come back—Queen Elizabeth I had a Hebrew doctor. In time, they became as solid as any native there with brolly and bowler, and often had a taste for fish and chips. Each wave of the people as they came—Spanish Jews; exiles from Germany's early nineteenth-century uprising; in the great flight from the Czar's oppressions; the final migration in the 1930s—in the end produced not a minority in harmony together, but various groupings separated by land of origin, class, and tastes.

They modified English cooking for their own use—a cooking which William Kite had described as "food boiled to death in live steam and sauce with white wallpaper paste." But in Soho, in Whitechapel, in the dining rooms of Mayfair—with the Bentley out front—English-Jewish cooking (with stopovers in Germany and France) had a taste of its own, the flavors of many countries. Early Disraelis came into it; Heine as a visitor, and people like Karl Marx, Trotsky; such descendants of Jews as Sir Beerbohm Tree and Max Beerbohm; George du Maurier, an artist and writer; Epstein; the poet Sassoon (of the China tycoons Sassoons); Zangwell; Weizmann; the husband of Virginia Woolf; Sidney Webb, who was a kingpin in turning the Empire toward socialism; Alexander Korda; South African diamond kings; pushcart hucksters; Lord Samuel; *all* had families that gave English cuisine a spicy Jewish lift.

England never showed a love—or perhaps a knowledge of lettuce until that Jewish gourmet, Lord Duveen, talked of it as food in *other* places. The Jews accepted the Yorkshire pudding, the grilling of giant mutton chops, and stole the famous roast beef of England, wedges of Stilton, Cheshire, and Cheddar. If they avoided, in the main, the Northumberland hot pie of tripe, the Welsh cawl of leeks and mutton, the Melton Mowbray pies, and winkles and whelks (eaten with a pin), they *did* see the merits of kippered herring, crimping cod, and snacking at "Eleven," and tea at "Five." Scones, crumpets were accepted, but their apple nut strudel outfaced the raspberry fool, the trifle, *and* the Canterbury savory (fried bread, apple rings, sausage cakes, Bar-le-Duc currant jelly).

English-Jewish cooking was often a mixture of the Russian, German—some Spanish—dishes of their forefathers, and so we will skip those—it would be a repetition of recipes we have already given. Where the cooking merged with the English, we have hunted out and tasted the dishes, and the result is good eating, and most think superior to the average English food.

The great restaurants of London and elsewhere, often with Jewish-Continental gourmet food, are as good as any place, if one avoids such places as the Hilton-type hotels and the chain eating places.

The potato pancake, as the universal latke, is also, in the company of Jewish corn beef (in England called *salt beef*); available too are lokshen (noodles) and Galitzianer sorrel soup. In the best families—even among Jewish lords—the fried matzo, the gefilte fish is often on the table at the proper time. The true Orthodox kosher households are the minority, as elsewhere in the world. Yet in the older sections of the cities of Britain the synagogues still exist in isolation, and the chanting is the full recited Hebrew, the fringed prayer shawls, worn large and long, *not* the mere scarf symbols of Reform Judaism. And in those households, the chicken fat and grieben, the boiled beef with red horseradish are still served.

When the poet Kipling wrote, "What should they know of England, who only England know?" that could be extended to a view of its cooking; what should anyone know of its dishes, who doesn't know those that are Scottish, Welsh, Irish, *or* Jewish?

Meat

LOIN LAMB CHOPS

George du Maurier was said to be of Jewish descent, and Du Maurier, author of *Trilby,* introduced his dear friend Henry James to the proper loin lamb chop.

1 tablespoon fresh lemon juice
4 loin lamb chops
Salt, freshly ground black pepper to taste

Press the lemon juice over the lamb chops and rub in all over. Let stand for ½ hour. Season with salt and pepper and place under a hot broiler for 4 minutes on each side. The thickness of the chops decides how long they will take to brown properly. *Don't* overbroil.
2 servings.

LONDON BOILED FLANKEN

4 pounds beef flanken
½ cup chicken fat
1½ quarts boiling water
2 onions, sliced
2 carrots, cubed

3 stalks celery
3 sprigs parsley
1 tablespoon salt
6 whole black peppercorns

Sauté beef in fat. Drain. Add water, onions, carrots, celery, parsley, salt, peppercorns. On low heat cover and cook 2 hours until meat is tender. Strain the soup. The main dish is the meat with horseradish.
6–8 servings.

CHATEAUBRIAND DISRAELI
(EARL BEACONSFIELD, 1804–1881)

Often called (in error) Chateaubriand Edward VI. Disraeli as a young man is said to have invented it.

3 pounds filet mignon
1 cup dry burgundy
2 slices guinea hen breasts (or chicken breasts)

2 tablespoons pâté
1 large mushroom cap, sautéed

Preheat oven to 400°. Sauté the steak for ½ minute in the wine. Place steak, guinea hen breasts, pâté, and mushroom cap on a baking sheet, but first seal it in aluminum foil (Disraeli's chef had to use a covered pan; you can too). Bake in oven for 25 minutes—5 minutes longer for medium well done.
2 servings.

ENGLISH-JEWISH KIDNEY SAUTÉ

12 lamb kidneys—sliced in half, cleaned
1 cup cold water
1 cup wine vinegar
1 medium onion, sliced
1 cup sliced celery
1 cup chicken fat

3 tablespoons flour
1 cup small sliced mushrooms
1½ teaspoons salt
Pepper
1 teaspoon Worcestershire sauce
¼ cup dry sherry

Cover kidneys with cold water and wine vinegar, soak 1 hour. Sauté onion and celery in fat. Add kidneys, simmer 5 minutes. Stir in flour, add mushrooms, salt, pepper, Worcestershire sauce. Simmer, covered, 30 minutes. Add sherry.
8 servings.

LIVER BALLS

1 onion, minced	⅛ teaspoon pepper
2 teaspoons chicken fat	2 tablespoons potato flour
½ pound beef or chicken livers	1 egg yolk
1 teaspoon salt	1 egg white, stiffly beaten

Sauté the onion in the fat. Grind the livers with the onion. Stir in the salt, pepper, potato flour, and egg yolk. Fold in the egg white. Drop by the half tablespoon into boiling soup (or salted water). Cook 15 minutes until they rise to the surface. Best in hot soup.
8 servings.

SAUERKRAUT STRUDEL FILLING

These 2 fillings for the strudel are certainly *not* what most expect. But they are very good and belong with meat dishes.

2 pounds sauerkraut, drained	2 teaspoons sugar
½ onion, minced	¼ teaspoon pepper
½ cup butter	

Sauté sauerkraut and onion in butter 15 minutes. Mix in sugar and pepper. Cool and spread on strudel dough (see Index), roll up.

LIVER STRUDEL FILLING

1½ pounds chicken livers   1½ teaspoons salt
2 onions, diced   ½ teaspoon pepper
½ cup chicken fat

Rough slice the livers, and sauté with onions in chicken fat until liver loses color. Chop the liver, not too fine, and add the salt, pepper. Spread out on oiled strudel dough, roll up.

The making of the strudel dough, and the baking, is the traditional method set down in the Index.

Fowl

PETTICOAT LANE CHICKEN GARLIC STEW

Don't let the garlic scare you—it's discarded after baking. *Very* tasty.

3 tablespoons olive oil   1 teaspoon ground white pepper
10 cloves garlic, peeled   ½ teaspoon allspice
½ cup chopped parsley   ¼ teaspoon ground cinnamon
½ cup chopped celery leaves   1½ cups dry white wine
1 teaspoon dried tarragon   6 chicken leg and thigh pieces, cut
1 tablespoon salt   in 2

Preheat oven to 375°. Pour olive oil in a pot with cover. Add garlic and all ingredients including chicken. Cover tightly, place in oven for about 1¼ hours. The chicken does *not* brown. Discard garlic. Serve with bread.
6 servings.

SHEVUOTH FRICASSEE OF GIBLETS

1 cup chicken fat
2 onions, diced
2 pounds mixed giblets, cleaned, cut up
2 tablespoons flour
½ teaspoon garlic powder
4 cups boiling water

3 teaspoons salt
½ teaspoon pepper
½ clove garlic, crushed
1 pound beef, ground
¼ cup cold water
½ cup raw rice

Heat chicken fat in saucepan and sauté the onions. Add giblets and brown for 5 minutes. Sprinkle on flour, garlic powder; add boiling water, 2 teaspoons salt, ¼ teaspoon pepper, and garlic. Cover, cook on low heat 1 hour. Combine beef, ¼ cup cold water, and rest of salt, pepper. Shape into balls, add to giblets and rice. Cook 20 minutes.
6 servings.

Fish

GRAPES AND FLOUNDER

3 pounds flounder fillets
½ teaspoon paprika
Salt, pepper to taste
3 tablespoons butter

1 cup seedless grapes, sliced in halves
2 cups water
½ cup dry white wine

Coat flounder with paprika, salt, and pepper. Fry in butter until flaky, 4 minutes each side. Cook grapes at a boil in water, 2 minutes. Add to skillet with wine, simmer 2 minutes. Serve at once to keep grapes hot and firm and juicy.
4 servings.

BAKED HERRING

4 salt herring fillets   1 cup sweet butter
½ cup milk   3 onions, sliced
⅓ cup flour

Preheat oven to 375°. Soak herrings 12 hours in cold water to cover.
Change water twice. Dry and dip herrings in milk, then in flour. Melt 2
tablespoons butter in baking dish and set herrings in it. Cover with onions. Dot with remaining butter and milk. Bake in oven 30 minutes.
4 servings.

WHITECHAPEL BAKED GEFILTE FISH

3 pounds pike fillets   1 egg
1 onion   2 tablespoons salad oil
2 slices white bread, water-soaked   2 onions, sliced
½ cup water   1 green pepper, sliced
1 teaspoon salt   1 cup tomato sauce
½ teaspoon pepper

Preheat oven to 325°. Grind together fish and onion. Move to a
chopping bowl. Add soaked bread squeezed dry, salt, pepper, and egg.
Chop smooth. Make into 12 balls. Mix oil, sliced onions, green pepper,
tomato sauce in a baking dish. Set balls on top. Bake in oven 45 minutes. Baste.
6 servings.

VEGETARIAN CHOPPED LIVER

It's a not too shameful secret, but a lot of non-liver chopped liver is
eaten. If it's the *only* game in town, play it.

1 onion, sliced   ½ cup hazelnuts
3 tablespoons butter   1 teaspoon salt
3 hard-cooked eggs   ¼ teaspoon pepper
2 California sardines in tomato
    sauce

Sauté the onion in the butter 15 minutes. Put in a chopping bowl, add the eggs, sardines, nuts, salt, pepper. Chop very fine. Chill. Serve on lettuce.

4 servings.

Soup

Some Jews have an idea basil has some ritual meaning in their texts —but no one, we found, could explain it.

BASIL SOUP

1 pound cut green beans
2 cups cooked white beans with
　bean liquid
3 carrots scraped, sliced
1 cup sliced zucchini
2 quarts Chicken Soup

2 cloves garlic, finely chopped
Salt, pepper to taste
1 cup elbow pasta
4 tablespoons chopped fresh basil
4 tablespoons grated Parmesan
　cheese

Mix the green beans, white beans (and liquid), carrots, zucchini, soup, and garlic in a pot. Bring to a boil. Lower heat; simmer, covered, until carrots go tender. Season with salt, pepper. Add pasta, simmer till tender. Add basil to soup. Simmer till basil is wilted. Sprinkle in plates with grated Parmesan cheese.

10 servings.

COLD CUCUMBER SCHAV (SORREL)

1 pound sorrel
1 tablespoon salt
4 cups water
1 cucumber, peeled, diced

1 hard-cooked egg, sliced
¼ cup chopped chives
½ cup sour cream

Be sure to wash sorrel well in water and drain. Cut off part of stems and chop up the leaves. Add salt to water, bring to a boil, and add sorrel to pot. Simmer 5 minutes. Cool and refrigerate. On serving, cucumber, egg, and chives are divided among the soup plates. Garnish with sour cream.

6 servings.

Vegetables

TRUFFLES ROTHSCHILD

The truth is this is the best way to prepare truffles—and no Rothschild monopoly—but their name is usually connected to this recipe by English Jews.

At their best, truffles must be fresh, not woody in texture. Ideally, round. The king truffles are French, (the Périgord, the Vaucluse), but also good is a different variety from Italy (the Umbria, the Piedmont). Fresh truffles now fly the Atlantic to our markets.

1 pound fresh truffles	1 tablespoon sweet butter
3 tablespoons minced vegetables:	½ quart Madeira
carrot, celery, onion	

Clean (it's a bit of a job) the truffles. Soak in salted warm water—1 teaspoon salt to 1 quart water. Soak 45 minutes. Drain, scrub them with a stiff brush under cold water. In a pan simmer mixed vegetables in butter until soft. Add truffles and 2 inches of wine. Cook, covered, over low heat 20 minutes; do *not* overcook. Cool, slice, to grace the main dish.

Not for fressers (crude eaters) but for true gourmets. Enough to flavor a big dinner.

ISRAEL

> You shall be a peculiar treasure unto me . . .
>
> *Exodus 19:5*

One must begin by saying that there is splendid food in Israel, *but* it is European and Oriental. The native cuisine of Israel itself is little better than the food served in the Wild West of the American frontier a hundred years ago. In private homes in Jerusalem, Tel Aviv, where the background is German, Austrian, Hungarian, Romanian, Russian, or Polish, the food is as tasty as the Jewish dishes of those countries. But they cannot be called Israeli dishes, and their preparation is costly, so for only special events are they most bountiful, such as for Yom Ha'atzmant —Independence Day.

Israeli food is closest to the Arab nations. The Israeli bread, the pita, the flat wheat round, which can be filled with cooked vegetables, spiced meats, is a simple food and eatable. The Israeli version of couscous is good, but a copy of Yemenite recipes. In the settlements of the Negev and along the Sea of Galilee, they eat good vegetables, fine fruit, usually in community dining rooms. It is filling, but hardly eating for the pleasures of subtle tastes. There is fish, and it is cooked in native style or in a European-Jewish manner.

Because of a rigid rabbinal control in this country of much of the ritual rules and ancient dogma, the hotel food is all kosher. The food cannot be called good at the King David, the Eden, or at the Dan Hotel in Tel Aviv, at the Ramat Aviv. Nor at the Acadia Grand at Herzliya-on-the-Sea. The Hilton is like all Hiltons, an ordeal of overpriced poor eating. There are good Arab eating places in Haifa, and in the Jezreel Valley. But Israel itself is still too much a pioneer nation fighting for survival to produce a fine cuisine of its own. That takes leisure, prosperous classes who delight in taste and variety. Today, from the Plains of Sharon to Caesarea, to the Galilee hills, one can find items from the best of Jewish-European dishes sometimes infiltrating the bland, monotonous diets of the second- and third-generation Israeli tables.

As a Hasidic rabbi wearing a shtreimel (round velvet hat trimmed with fox) told us in the Negev, "There was a miracle working tzaddik [wise saint] here who fasted for six months. He used to eat in private— but what the people eat here was such—he began to also fast in private."

Actually, desert shish kebab is splendid eating.

Meat

ISRAEL-ARAB MINCED MEAT

This is a dish of the well-off city Arab, or the Muslim leader of a village or desert tribe. In the city it is often beef, but other places lamb or mutton.

4 tablespoons olive oil
2 pounds chopped lamb
2 onions, chopped
1 clove garlic, chopped
Salt, pepper to taste
2 apples, peeled, cored, chopped
1 pound tomatoes, chopped
½ cup raisins
¼ cup pimento-stuffed olives, halved
⅛ teaspoon ground cinnamon
⅛ teaspoon ground cloves
2 tablespoons slivered almonds
4 tablespoons olive oil

In 4 tablespoons olive oil, in a large skillet, brown the meat and add onions and garlic. When brown, season with salt and pepper, add all other ingredients except the almonds. Simmer, uncovered, 20 minutes. Fry almonds in 4 tablespoons olive oil. Sprinkle on almonds. Cook for 2 minutes.
6 servings.

DESERT SHISH KEBAB

1½ cups olive oil
⅓ cup wine vinegar
Juice of 2 lemons
1 garlic clove, crushed
1 cup chopped onion
2 teaspoons salt
1½ teaspoons dried oregano
1 teaspoon pepper
½ teaspoon ground thyme
1 (5-pound) leg of lamb, boned, cut in 1-inch cubes
1 green pepper, cut in slices
16 mushroom caps
16 cherry tomatoes

Mix oil, vinegar, lemon juice, garlic, onion, seasonings in bowl. Add meat cubes and coat. Cover and place in refrigerator overnight. Drain meat, skewer with pepper, mushrooms, and tomatoes alternately. Broil 4 minutes on one side, and broil other side 5 minutes.
8 servings.

JAFFAI PETCHA

2 pounds veal leg, with foot bones
  cut up
3 cloves garlic, minced
1/4 teaspoon mint
3 sprigs parsley

3 onions, minced
1 bay leaf
2 teaspoons salt
1/4 teaspoon pepper
2 hard-cooked eggs, sliced

Place meat in kettle with water to cover. Add garlic, mint, parsley, onions, bay leaf, seasonings. Simmer, uncovered, on low flame 3 hours, until meat separates from bones. Remove from liquid. Cut meat into small bits and set on a plate. Strain liquid and pour over meat. Place sliced eggs over meat and chill firm. Lift off congealed fat and slice.
6 servings.

Fowl

SESAME SEED CHICKEN

1 egg
1/2 cup water
1 (2 1/2-pound) fryer, cut up
1/2 cup matzo meal
1 tablespoon baking powder

1 teaspoon salt
2 teaspoons paprika
1/2 cup sesame seeds
1/2 cup melted margaine

Preheat oven to 375°. Mix egg with water. Dip chicken pieces in egg and then in matzo meal mixed with baking powder, salt, paprika, and

sesame seeds. Place chicken in baking dish and add margarine. Bake in 375° oven for 1 hour until crisp.
4 servings.

PINEAPPLE CHICKEN

1 (3-pound) broiler, cut up
2 tablespoons soy sauce
1½ teaspoons salt
1½ teaspoons sugar

Flour
1½ cups margarine
2 cups undrained crushed pineapple

Preheat oven to 350°. To coat chicken make mixture of soy sauce, salt, sugar. Dip chicken in flour. Melt margarine in baking pan. Roll chicken pieces in margarine, arrange skin side up in pan. Bake 30 minutes. Pour undrained pineapple over chicken. Bake 45 minutes until chicken is tender.
4 servings.

CHOPPED LIVER (ISRAELI STYLE)

2 pounds broiled beef liver
1 onion, sliced
2 tablespoons chicken fat

4 hard-boiled eggs
1 avocado, ripe
Salt, pepper to taste

Remove all veins from liver. Sauté onion lightly in chicken fat. Grind liver, eggs, onion in food chopper. Add mashed avocado. Salt and pepper to taste and mix well. Serve on Israeli pita bread or matzos.
8 servings.

Fish ·

POACHED FISH

4 pounds halibut fillets, sliced | 2 onions, sliced
4 cups boiling water | 1 sprig fresh dill
1 teaspoon allspice | Salt to taste
1 bay leaf | 1 pound peeled, boiled potatoes

Put fish fillets in half of water, simmer for 12 minutes. Combine all other ingredients except potatoes in another pan of the rest of the boiling water. Pour on fish. Serve with boiled potatoes and natural juices.
4 servings.

FISH AND TOMATO-YOGURT SAUCE

2 pounds flounder fillets
6 tablespoons vegetable oil
1 onion, chopped
1 clove garlic, crushed
2 tablespoons crushed coriander
   leaves

1 green chili, chopped
2 teaspoons ground coriander
1/8 teaspoon turmeric
1/2 cup tomato sauce
2 cups yogurt
Salt to taste

Brown fillets in hot oil; remove and set aside. Add onion and fry brown. Add garlic, coriander leaves, green chili, coriander, turmeric. Fry for 3 minutes, stir constantly. Combine tomato sauce, yogurt, salt, add to other mixture. Simmer 5 minutes. Add fish, cover, simmer 5 minutes.
4 servings.

Soup

HAIFA SEAFOOD POT

2 pounds fillet any fleshy fish
3 cups cooked rice
1 onion, chopped
1 teaspoon salt
1 teaspoon crushed basil
1 clove garlic, minced

1/4 teaspoon nutmeg
1/8 teaspoon pepper
1/4 cup chili sauce
2 tomatoes, sliced
1/2 cup shredded hard cheese

Preheat oven to 350°. Mix rice, onion, salt, basil, garlic, nutmeg, and pepper. Add chili sauce to mixture. Spoon into greased casserole. Roll up fillets, place on rice. Top with tomato slices. Bake at 350° for 30 minutes. Sprinkle with cheese. Bake 10 minutes more.
6 servings.

Vegetables

PEPPERS STUFFED WITH BEANS

6 bell peppers
3 cups fried, mashed baked beans
2 eggs, separated
Flour

½ cup oil
1 cup heavy cream
¼ pound mild Cheddar cheese,
  shredded

Boil the peppers in water 10 minutes, cut off tops, clean out seeds. Stuff with the beans. Beat the egg yolks thick, then beat the whites until stiff. Fold into the yolks. Dust peppers with flour; dip into eggs. Heat the oil in a skillet and fry peppers light brown. Arrange in an ovenproof pan, pour on cream, sprinkle with cheese; cook in a preheated 350° oven until cheese is melted, 20 minutes.
6 servings.

STEWED EGGPLANTS HEBRON

3 peeled eggplants
4 tablespoons cooking oil
2 pounds beef in 1½ inch cubes

1 onion, minced
4 cups water
Salt, pepper to taste

Slice eggplants thin. In oil in a pot sauté meat and onion. Add water, salt, and pepper, bring to a boil. Add eggplant, cook 40 minutes over low heat until eggplant is soft and mixture is stew thick.
6 servings.

ISRAELI COUSCOUS

Simpler than the traditional Arab version. Enjoyed by the Sabras—native-born Israelis.

1 pound lamb, cubed	½ cabbage, shredded
1 onion, minced	3 turnips, diced
½ cup tomato sauce	3 green onions, sliced
3 tomatoes, peeled, chopped	1 sweet potato, diced
3 cups water	1 slice pumpkin
Salt, pepper to taste	1½ pounds millet couscous
1 *bouquet garni*	

Sauté meat with onion. When brown, add tomato sauce and the tomatoes. Add water, salt, pepper, *bouquet garni*. Bring to a boil. Add vegetables. Simmer 1 hour. Remove meat and vegetables and *bouquet garni*. Add the couscous to sauce, simmer until thoroughly cooked. Serve hot with meat and vegetables.
6 servings.

MOCK STUFFED DERMA

Popular (like hot dogs in the U.S.A.) on Yom Hashoa Y'Hagvurah (Day of Remembrance).

2 carrots	½ pound flour
1 onion	1 egg, beaten
2 stalks celery	3 tablespoons chicken fat
½ pound matzo meal	Salt, pepper to taste

Put the vegetables through a food grinder. Mix together matzo meal and flour, vegetables, egg, fat, and seasonings. Shape into 2-inch rolls. Bake on rack in preheated oven at 350° for 45 minutes.

All that is missing from the true derma is the section of beef gut.
6–8 servings.

Doughs

PITA (ISRAELI FLAT BREAD)

1 envelope yeast
1¼ cups warm water

2 teaspoons salt
3 cups flour

Dissolve yeast in water with salt. Work in the flour to make a big sticky ball. Knead on a floured board very smooth. Cut into 6 balls and knead each ball. Flatten with a rolling pin to a ¼-inch thickness. Cover with a towel for 45 minutes to rise. Preheat oven to 500°, and set dough on a greased baking sheet. Bake for 16 minutes until brown and puffed up. Remove and cool. Makes about 6 pitas.

KIBBUTZ BREAD

5½ pounds fine semolina
1 small slice lamb's tail fat or
    3 tablespoons olive oil or ¼
    cup cooking oil
1 tablespoon salt

1 yeast cake
1 quart warm water
2 tablespoons sesame seeds
1 tablespoon aniseed
1 egg

In the semolina make a well in the center. Add lamb fat (or cooking oil or olive oil) and salt. Knead the whole. Add the yeast, warm water. Work the dough for 5 minutes until smooth. Cover with a cloth to rise for 1½ hours. Mix seeds into dough. Knead again for 20 minutes. Divide dough in small loaves, leave them an hour to rise. Brush with beaten egg, bake in preheated oven at 375° for 45 minutes.
Makes about 3 small loaves.

Dessert

CHEESE CAKE

There has to be a cheese cake—but it's not pure Israeli—not the rich European variety. "It's our cheese cake now," a cantor who sang the chant Kol Nidre in the Negev city of Beersheba told us.

2 cups crushed, dampened
   graham crackers
4 eggs, beaten
1 cup sugar

2 teaspoons vanilla
1½ pounds cream cheese
½ pint sour cream

Line bottom of a spring-form pan with graham crackers. Mix together eggs, sugar, 1 teaspoon vanilla, and cream cheese. Pour over crust and bake 25 minutes at 375°. Remove from oven, cool for 15 minutes. Raise oven temperature to 475°. Take sour cream and 1 teaspoon vanilla, spoon over cheese filling; bake 5 minutes. Chill for 24 hours.
4 servings.

CARROT RING

½ cup vegetable shortening
½ cup brown sugar
2 eggs
3 carrots, grated
Juice of ½ lemon

1 cup flour
½ teaspoon salt
1 teaspoon baking powder
1 teaspoon ground cinnamon

Preheat oven to 350°. Mix shortening and sugar, add eggs, carrots. Add all other ingredients. Grease a medium-size ring mold, pour in mixture. Place in a pan of water in preheated oven. Bake 1 hour. Unmold and serve.
4 servings.

Israeli Wines for Cooking and Drinking

It's mostly new wine to the world, and from tasting and talking it over with wine "experts," it would appear some of it is excellent, a great deal good—and a lot of it, sweet bubbe (grandmother) stuff.

The Israelis have created dryer wines made from *Vitis vinifera* grapes. The traditional-tasting red wine is Carmel's Cabernet Sauvignon. For the white-wine drinker, there is Hock, a wine like a Riesling, and Sauvignon Blanc. Other dry types are Adom Atic, which is less complex than Carmel Cabernet Sauvignon. The Cabernet Sauvignon can be exciting wine. As for sweet wines, the Israelis make Grenache Rosé, a Concord grape wine; Almog Malaga; Topaz Tokay. Dessert wines are Partom Port, Sharrir Sherry, and muscatel. Champagne? Yes. Carmel Extra Dry Champagne, Carmel Demi Sec Champagne, and Carmel Pink Champagne. For wines for Passover: these are wines made from *Vitis vinifera* grapes in Israel, or if in a hurry, try it from *Vitis labrusca* grapes in New York.

MIDDLE EAST AND
NORTH AFRICA

If you die before dinner, at least eat a good breakfast . . .
Al Jolson, North Africa, 1944

Semitic people, Carthaginians, the Phoenicians, settled North Africa, the Middle East. To be followed by another Semitic group, the Arabs. Until the setting up of Israel, Middle East and North African Jews solidly existed there, rooted deeply as part of the landscape, pioneers going back to before recorded history. Little of that society or culture is now left in Egypt, Libya, Tunisia, Algeria, Morocco, Syria, Iraq, Lebanon.

Traveling just a generation ago in those countries, we were still able to find Jewish-North African food at its best, relating to its surroundings, ritual in its controls; respectful of the Orthodox rules of what was acceptable, and what was not to a faithful follower of the chosen, traveling out of ancient Egypt with Moses.

The North African Jews not only presented an Arab influence in their food, but produced the *only* clean, hygienic version of it, fully safe for the visitor to eat. They were the closest to the actual diet of the ancient Hebrews of Judea, eating grain, some lamb and mutton, dates, grapes, and a very few other fruits as the main part of their diets.

Couscous, in various versions, is the traditional Middle East and North African dish; some Jews claimed it went back to the days of the Old Testament. It is, in its basic form, a thick steamed semolina porridge, flavored with vegetables and meat, usually lamb or mutton. Jewish versions, with chicken and spices, are as good as any of the Muslim offerings.

The Middle East and North Africa, we found out, eats its party meals on *very* low tables, guests reclining on rugs, our poor joints helped out by cushions. The Jewish houses were a bit more up to date, and would sometimes have high tables and chairs, but the traditionalists kept the cuisine near the floor. At meals they kept the main dish in the center of the group, everyone directly feeding himself from it with his fingers. Jewish parties usually provided knives and forks, individual plates. There would be the thin pastilis, a pastry filled with eggs, chicken, liver, almonds, always baked crisp. Chicken cooked with peanuts and peppers. The Arab Muslim pilaf was adopted but the mutton stew was not too popular. Garlic, olive oil, wild mint, thyme, cinnamon, saffron, cumin, and pistachio nuts were widely used to season North African-Jewish cooking. Chickens were raised on rice and milk, and so had a special taste. Roast goat and kids, stuffed with nuts, seasoned with mint and cumin, were High Holiday delights. The Jews avoided the tasty squid, cuttlefish, lobsters, and shrimp of the Mediterranean, but they enjoyed the fish called the capitan. And while the Mohammedans were forbidden alcohol (from an Arab word alkuhul) the Moslems used it anyway, offering us date brandy and Bollinger champagne. The Jews drank Algerian wines, and a sip of hard stuff, but joined the native population in sipping Lakmi, a syrup beverage made from the sap of the young palm. Wrote Sir Aurel Stein, the great Jewish explorer, "Fresh, it's perfumed, fermented, it's a potent danger."

In Egypt the food, once lifted from the common dish on the table, is placed on a round of flat bread like the Israeli pita (here called siwan). The Egyptian Jews copied a fine white bean and spinach stew, the el bkeila; also dumyat tave with pine nuts and raisins. There was even a kind of strudel, either a baklava or a kounage, filled with walnuts, filberts, almonds, honey, and heavily oversugared. To the lover of the Vienna strudel, it was too sweet and *hardly* eatable.

The meal would end with the thick syrupy grounds of mocha coffee, and fruit; the guava melon, figs, grapes. Under various names the same cuisine is served in Libya, Algeria, Morocco, Syria, Lebanon. The Jews there adopted it according to their tastes. However, the more prosperous the Middle East and North African Jews became, the more they turned to Jewish versions of French, Italian, and Spanish dishes. But the average Middle East or North African Jew remained an Oriental, dressing like the natives, living in the same housing, respectful as they to his godhead's good graces, worshiping dressed in slippers and white robe, or sitting on his rug, smoking a water pipe. Keeping his women not veiled, but at least behind a curtain, separated from the males in his shul, as he recited from his old and sacred Torahs. Chanting and swaying in hope of a homeland, Eretz Yisroel.

The North African Jew was the farthest away, the remotest from the culture, the modern viewpoint of the Jews of the rest of the world. He removed his shoes before sitting at his dining mat, and often the women ate separately from the men. The wife was isolated at home, she lived to cook in an inner courtyard. The men went seeking masculine company in cafés, sipping black sweet coffee, nibbling on samak, the Tunisian fish appetizer, the filled cakes called maamoul; a sticky dough and walnut mess, the baklava.

The upper class Jews were usually different—lived in cooled villas, bought their Paquin gowns and Bond Street suits in Paris and London, owned an ice machine and electric fans. They could still serve guests a whole roast kid, and schorbo, a soup flavored with mint, a sweet couscous, el mistouf. But the wine would be imported from Europe. The caviar, Balkan. The truly Jewish dishes were North African versions of those of Russia, Germany, Austria.

Those houses we once visited have new tenants now. There are few shuls left with a minyan, the number needed to hold holy services. And the grandsons in Israel stand guard on the borders of a different world. All that remains, besides the notes of our visits to their parents' homes, are the recall of names; Marrakech, Casablanca, Alexandria, Bengasi, Tunis, Damascus, Beirut.

Meat

COUSCOUS
(NORTH AFRICA-JEWISH VERSION)

1 pint water
½ pound mutton shoulder cuts
¼ pound beef
2 chicken breasts
2 chicken gizzards
¼ teaspoon black pepper
2 onions, chopped
½ cup chick-peas
2 large carrots
Salt to taste
Pinch of saffron

4 tablespoons olive oil
1 pound semolina, rolled
3 drops hot red pepper sauce
3 ounces butter
1 cup raisins
2 turnips
¼ bunch coriander, chopped
2 sprigs parsley
1 cup broad beans
1 tomato
½ cabbage

In a pot put water, mutton, beef, and chicken breasts and gizzards, pepper, chopped onions, chick-peas, carrots, salt, saffron, olive oil. Boil for 1 hour. In another pot put the semolina and stack that pot on top of the first pot. Cook 45 minutes. Do *not* stir semolina. To broth pot add pepper sauce, butter, raisins, turnips, coriander, parsley, broad beans, tomato, cabbage and add to semolina, stirring to separate the grains. Toss gently so grains can swell, cook 30 minutes. Arrange couscous on large dish, set the pieces of meat on the rim.
6 servings.

MUSLIM-JEWISH LEG OF LAMB

2 tablespoons grated gingerroot
5 cloves garlic, crushed
1½ teaspoons salt
¼ teaspoon black pepper
½ cup margarine
Juice of 1 lime

1 (5-pound) leg of lamb, boned
1 tablespoon ground coriander
½ teaspoon cayenne
½ teaspoon ground cloves
½ teaspoon ground cardamom

Mix ginger, garlic, salt, black pepper, margarine, and lime juice. Make gashes in the leg of lamb. Spread margarine mixture over the surface. Put in roasting pan and put aside for 2 hours in refrigerator to marinate. Mix coriander, cayenne pepper, cloves, and cardamom in a skillet and stir over light heat 4 minutes. Sprinkle the combined mixture over lamb and put into a preheated 350° oven for 2 hours.
8 servings.

LAMB KEBABS

1 (5-pound) leg of lamb, boned, trimmed
1 tablespoon grated onion
¼ teaspoon oregano
¼ cup red wine vinegar
Salt, pepper to taste
½ cup palm oil or olive oil
12 bay leaves

Cut lamb into 1½-inch cubes. Cover with mix of onion, oregano, vinegar, salt, pepper, and oil. Marinate in refrigerator overnight. Drain and save marinade. Stab meat cubes onto 8 metal skewers, place a piece of bay leaf between each cube. Grill 4 inches from moderate heat, brushing with marinade.
8 servings.

NOTE: Palm oil is available at Fred Oliveira's Italian-American Delicatessen on Bleecker Street, New York City.

LIVER PÂTÉ TRIPOLI

1 pound beef liver, ground
2 tablespoons fat
Dash of cayenne
⅛ teaspoon ground nutmeg
½ teaspoon dry mustard
¼ teaspoon ground cloves
1 teaspoon curry powder
1 onion, minced
½ cup brandy

Fry liver in fat. Add seasonings and onion. Remove from fire. Pour on ½ cup palm brandy (or any brandy), and chill. Serve with toast.
6–8 servings.

BAR MITZVAH SNACK MINCED VEAL

1 pound veal   2 tablespoons chicken fat
1 onion, minced   Salt, pepper to taste

Cut veal into ¼-inch cubes. Sauté onion in fat until soft over medium heat. Raise heat high, add veal, salt, and pepper, stir until meat loses its color. Heat 10 minutes. Serve with lemon slices.
6 servings.

Fowl

HOT LIME CHICKEN

½ cup lime juice   1 teaspoon tomato sauce
1 teaspoon paprika   1 teaspoon sugar
2 teaspoons ground coriander   6 chicken breasts, boned, cut in
2 teaspoons ground cardamom   half
1 teaspoon salt   1 tablespoon chopped cilantro
1 cup Chicken Soup

Mix all ingredients except chicken breasts and cilantro. Slit chicken breasts on their smooth sides, ⅛ inch deep. Place chicken breasts in a pot, pour lime juice mixture over. Marinate the breasts 3 hours in cool place, turning 3 times. Take chicken from marinade and put pot on low heat. Bring liquid to simmering. Add chicken breasts. Simmer 15 minutes till just firm and on plates sprinkle with cilantro.
6 servings.

DUCK AND CABBAGE

2 tablespoons vegetable oil
2 large onions, quartered
1 (5-pound) duck, disjointed
1 teaspoon turmeric
1 teaspoon ground coriander
1 small green pepper, quartered
1 1-inch stick cinnamon
1 teaspoon salt

6 whole cloves
1/2 teaspoon chopped gingerroot
2 1/2 cups water
1 small cabbage, quartered
2 potatoes, peeled, halved
1 cup green peas, cooked
2 tablespoons vinegar

Preheat oven to 350°. Heat oil in a large casserole. Fry onions golden. Add duck. Sprinkle on turmeric and coriander, add the green pepper, cinnamon, salt, cloves, gingerroot, and water. Cover tightly, bake in oven 1 hour. Skim off excess fat. Add cabbage and potatoes. Cover, return to oven for 1 hour. Add peas and vinegar 4 minutes before taking out of oven.
6 servings.

HONEY-GLAZE CHICKEN

1/4 cup margarine
1/2 cup honey
3 tablespoons prepared mustard

2 teaspoons curry powder
3 pounds chicken pieces
1 cup shredded lettuce

Preheat oven to 375°. Heat margarine in roasting pan in oven until melted. Remove pan, add honey, mustard, curry powder. Stir, blend. Add chicken. Turn chicken to coat evenly. Return pan to oven. Bake, uncovered, 45 minutes until tender. Baste, turn pieces while baking. Spread lettuce on platter and set chicken on it.
4 servings.

CHICKEN LIVERS VERMOUTH

Every Jewish culture has its version of chicken livers.

1 pound chicken livers
2 tablespoons butter or chicken
   fat
½ teaspoon salt

Dash of pepper
1 tablespoon chopped parsley
½ cup dry vermouth

Remove connective tissue, and brown livers in fat in a skillet. Add salt, pepper, parsley, and vermouth. Simmer 10 minutes.
8 servings.

Fish

STEWED DRIED FISH WITH PUMPKIN LEAVES

3 pounds dried fish
1 quart water
1 level teaspoon salt
2 medium-size onions, chopped

2 tomatoes, chopped
½ pound pumpkin leaves
4 tablespoons palm oil or olive oil

Soak fish overnight in water. Drain. Place in a pot and add quart of fresh water, salt. Boil for 1 hour. Add vegetables and leaves to the fish. Add oil. Cook on medium flame, covered, for 40 minutes.
6 servings.

FRIED SPICED FISH

Juice of 1 lemon
1½ pounds sole fillets
½ teaspoon grated gingerroot
1 clove garlic, crushed
¼ teaspoon cumin

½ teaspoon paprika
½ teaspoon chili powder
¼ teaspoon turmeric
1½ teaspoons salt
½ cup vegetable oil

Rub lemon juice over fish. Dry, and mix gingerroot, garlic, cumin, paprika, chili powder, turmeric, and salt. Rub this mixture into fish fillets. Set aside for 2 hours to marinate in refrigerator. Heat oil to cover bottom of skillet. Fry fillets well.
4 servings.

BLACK JEWS' SKEWERED HERRING

2 salt herrings cut in 2-inch bits	Pinch of powdered pimento
2 tablespoons chopped coriander	1 teaspoon chopped parsley
1 blade sweet marjoram	1 onion, finely chopped
Salt, pepper to taste	

Put herring bits into a dish with the seasonings, including parsley and onion. Cover all parts of the fish. Marinate for 6 hours in cool place. Remove herring from marinade, skewer the herring, pack closely. Grill over hot flame. Serve hot.
4 servings.

CHANUKAH FISH WITH STUFFED DATES

1 (6-pound) fish	1/2 cup butter
1/2 pound large pitted dates	1/4 teaspoon powdered ginger
1/2 cup rice, cooked	Salt, pepper to taste
1/2 cup chopped almonds	1 onion, sliced
4 tablespoons sugar	1 tablespoon ground cinnamon

Wash fish (cleaned) in salt water. For date stuffing, mix boiled rice, almonds, sugar, 2 tablespoons butter, ginger, salt, and pepper. Stuff the dates with this. Pack fish with stuffed dates, skewer closed. Set fish on ovenproof dish with 3 tablespoons butter and onion. Cook slowly in preheated oven at 350°, until fish is soft and flaky. Remove dates from belly and set around platter, dust with cinnamon.
6 servings.

DRIED COD WITH CHILIES

2 pounds dry cod fillets
3 ancho chilies, boiled soft
¼ cup blanched almonds
1 tomato, peeled, chopped

½ teaspoon oregano
½ cup olive oil
Salt, pepper to taste
Pinch of sugar

Soak the cod in cold water 12 hours, changing the water 3 times. Drain. In a pot cover with fresh water, bring to a simmer, cook 15 minutes until fish flakes with a fork. Remove fish from pot. Put chilies, almonds, tomato, and oregano in a blender for a coarse purée. Heat the oil in a skillet, cook chili mixture 5 minutes, stir until the sauce is thick. Season to taste with salt and pepper and sugar. Add cod to sauce and heat thoroughly, serve.
6 servings.

Soup

CASSAVA SOUP

This may be hard to find in a market.

2 large cassavas, rind removed, diced
1 pint water
1 onion, minced
Salt, pepper to taste

¼ cup chopped celery
2 cups milk
Pinch of anise
1½ tablespoons butter

Cook cassavas in water until tender. Cook down the liquid almost to nothing. Add onion, salt, pepper, celery, milk, and anise. Simmer 5 minutes. Before serving, add butter.
4 servings.

MIDDLE EAST EGG-LEMON SOUP

6 cups Chicken Soup
½ cup raw rice
4 eggs

Juice of 4 lemons
2 cups diced, cooked chicken meat

Bring the chicken soup to a boil and add the rice. Cook, covered, until the rice is tender. Beat the eggs well, until frothy. Add the lemon juice to the eggs a little at a time; keep beating and add 1 cup of the soup to the mixture. Pour in the rest of the soup, and continue beating. Add the chicken meat and heat, do not boil.
6 servings.

Vegetables

BAKED ONIONS AND TOMATOES

Enjoyed as a side dish on Rosh Hashonah—New Year—both by the rigid sectarian faithful and the secular Jews.

2 large red onions, sliced thick   ½ teaspoon chopped basil
Salt, pepper to taste   2 hard-cooked eggs, sliced
⅔ cup olive oil   12 anchovies
2 tomatoes   1 tablespoon capers
½ teaspoon sugar   ½ cup chopped parsley

Preheat oven to 375°. Put onion slices in a baking dish, add salt and pepper. Pour a little olive oil over each slice. Place a thick slice of tomato on each large slice of onion. Add salt, pepper, sugar, and basil. Add some olive oil on tomatoes. Put vegetables in the oven, bake 45 minutes until the onions are tender. Baste with oil. Take from oven and place a slice of hard-cooked egg on top of tomatoes, also 2 anchovies, crossed, on each egg slice. Add capers and parsley.
6 servings.

DEEP FRY PLANTAINS

To try some exotic dishes said to have originated with the Falasha Jews of Ethiopia, and carried north—try a dish of plantain (bananalike fruit obtainable in some big-city special markets). If unobtainable, use bananas.

6 large plantains   1 teaspoon ground pepper
1 teaspoon powdered ginger   ½ cup water
½ teaspoon salt   1 cup vegetable oil

Wash, then peel plantains. Slice into 1-inch cubes. Mix ginger with salt, pepper, and water. Add plantains to mixture, deep fry in oil until brown. Drain off excess fat, serve hot.
4 servings.

Doughs

HONEY OAT BREAD

1 cup boiling water
1½ cups oatmeal, quick-cooking
   or regular
⅓ cup honey
¼ cup butter, soft
3 tablespoons salt

1 cup sour cream
2 envelopes dry yeast
½ cup warm water
2 eggs
6 cups flour

Mix boiling water, oats, honey, butter, and salt. Stir. Add sour cream. Soften yeast in warm water and add it and eggs, 2 cups of flour to oat mixture. Beat smooth. Add enough flour to make dough stiff. On a floured board, knead smooth. Cover dough with bowl and let it stand for ½ hour. Cut into 2 equal portions and shape each into a loaf. Place in medium-size greased loaf pans. Cover. Refrigerate overnight. Bake in preheated oven at 375° for 40 minutes. Remove from pans, cool on rack. Makes 2 loaves.

DATE-NUT LOAF

½ pound dates, chopped
1½ cups hot water
2½ cups pastry flour
2 teaspoons baking powder
Pinch of salt
2 tablespoons butter, melted

½ cup honey
1 teaspoon vanilla
1 egg
½ cup chopped walnuts
½ cup chopped almonds

Add chopped dates to the hot water, and boil for 5 minutes. Set aside. Mix together all the dry ingredients. Beat them well, add to the date mixture, and combine. Add the butter, honey, vanilla, egg, and mix well; then add the nut meats. Mix again and turn into a medium-size greased loaf pan. Bake for 1 hour 15 minutes in a preheated 325° oven. 8 servings.

Dessert

APPLE SPICE CAKE

2½ cups flour
3 teaspoons ground cinnamon
1½ teaspoons baking soda
1 teaspoon ground cloves
2 teaspoons allspice

½ cup butter
1½ cups sugar
2 cups applesauce
2 eggs
1½ cups white raisins

Preheat oven to 350°. Mix together flour, cinnamon, baking soda, cloves, allspice, butter, and sugar. Add applesauce, eggs, and raisins. Pour into a medium-size greased pan. Bake for 1 hour. Let cool 30 minutes before serving.
6 servings.

SWEET POTATO CUSTARD

½ cup sugar
½ cup butter
2 eggs, beaten
2 cups milk

3 cups mashed sweet potatoes
1 tablespoon vanilla
½ tablespoon grated nutmeg

Mix sugar and butter together until fluffy. Add eggs, milk, potatoes, vanilla, and nutmeg. Stir smooth. Pour into greased dish and bake at 350° until brown. Serve cold or warm. Top with fruit.
4 servings.

BANANA DELIGHT

2 cups flour
1 teaspoon sugar
1 teaspoon salt

2 tablespoons butter
2 bananas, mashed
½ cup vegetable oil

Mix together flour, sugar, and salt. Add butter and bananas and mix well. Add enough water to make a stiff dough. Cover with a cloth, let rest ⅛ hour. Roll out very thin. Cut in 3-inch squares and fry in oil. Serve with sugar.
4 servings.

REPUBLIC OF SOUTH AFRICA

As for traveling: when I was at home I was in a better place.

The Talmud

South Africa is really Zulu and Kaffir country, but for the moment it is held by the Boers. The minority population is Cape Dutch, English, Indian, some Germans, and a large group of South African Jews. Mostly the Jews came from England in the days of the first great diamond discoveries, the opening of the gold mines on the Rand. Today they are brokers, doctors, lawyers, and clerks and artisans.

There is very little of what can be called South African-Jewish cooking. The best of the cuisines, from upper class to dock workers' tables, are inclined to the Russian-German-Jewish dishes.

But one can find an exploratory use of the tamarind or saffron from the native Indian population. A cooking of the rolpens, the paunch of an ox filled with beef (the Jews skip the pork filling) and pickled in vinegar; bobotie, a combination of beef, almonds, lemon juice, curry, eggs. Appleoffertje is an apple and raisin fritter. The Cape sheep has a fat tail weighing six pounds, and is used like oil in frying.

The fish have odd names; the snolk, seventy-four, the kabeljou (cod), and best of all, Cape salmon. The gooseberry is yellow and the fruits grenadillo and mango are as common as our peaches and pears. Kongyt is a pickled watermelon rind. But none of these are particularly Jewish. Nor Jewish is the holiday called Braaivleisaand, Roast Meat Night, which is a kind of outdoors cookout orgy.

The wines are fair. Drankenstein, Constantia, La Gratitude, are found in most South African-Jewish homes; the well-to-do get their wines from Germany and France, and drink a Dutch liqueur, Van der Hum. Happily, the English Jews serve tea at 4 o'clock in the afternoon. And dinner in the back country on a trek can have a saddle of reedbuck, hartebeest, grouse, partridge, wild dove, cooked kosher.

Meat

BOBOTIE

The cook is usually black, but aware of the dietary laws if the household is Orthodox.

2 pounds ground meat	Salt, pepper to taste
2 slices bread	1/2 cup pounded almonds
2 cups chicken or beef broth	Juice of 1/2 lemon
2 eggs, beaten	2 onions, chopped
1 teaspoon curry powder	2 tablespoons chicken fat
1 tablespoon sugar	6 lemon leaves, if handy

Preheat oven to 350°. Soak beef and bread in half the soup. Beat in 1 egg, add curry, sugar, salt, pepper, almonds, lemon juice. Sauté onions in fat, but not too brown. Add to meat mixture. Set out in a greased baking dish 3 lemon leaves, add mixture with 3 lemon leaves in mix. Bake in oven at 350° for 35 minutes. Mix 1 egg with rest of soup and put on top of bobotie, bake 15 minutes.
6 servings.

DURBAN BAKED STEW

2 pounds beef stew meat	8 white onions
Salt, pepper to taste	3 carrots, sliced
1 onion, sliced	2 cups Chicken Soup
1 teaspoon chopped tamarind	1/2 cup dry sherry
6 medium-sized potatoes, peeled	

Preheat oven to 300°. Mix meat with salt, pepper, onion, tamarind. Place in Dutch oven; add whole potatoes, onions, and carrots. Blend soup with wine, pour over meat. Cover, bake in slow 300° oven 5 hours.
6 servings.

REEDBUCK (OR BEEF) SAUERKRAUT

3 pounds reedbuck chuck
3 onions
2 tablespoons chicken fat
Salt, pepper to taste

1 teaspoon paprika
1½ pounds sauerkraut
1 bay leaf
1 cup hot water

Slice beef in 2-inch cubes; sauté it and onions in fat. Add salt, pepper, paprika. Cover and simmer on low heat 30 minutes. Add the sauerkraut. Cook 12 minutes. Add bay leaf, water. Cover and cook 1½ hours. Discard bay leaf.
12 servings.

SOUTH AFRICA PETCHA

Based on the Russian-Jewish dish—but with a flavor all its own.

2 calf's feet, cleaned, chopped up
2 onions
4 cloves garlic
½ teaspoon fennel
3 quarts water

½ teaspoon salt
1 teaspoon black pepper
4 hard-cooked eggs, sliced
1 tablespoon mango juice

Set feet, onions, 2 cloves garlic, fennel, water, salt, and pepper in a saucepan. Bring to a boil and simmer over low heat 3½ hours. Strain soup. Slice meat from bones and divide in 2 pie plates. Crush remaining garlic and mix in soup. Pour soup into pie plates. Let set in refrigerator for 1 hour. Put eggs in the plates. Sprinkle with more black pepper and mango juice. Chill.
6 servings.

Fowl

ORANGE-GLAZED CHICKEN AND PEARS

3 canned pears, halved	¼ teaspoon ground ginger
3 tablespoons orange jam	1 (4-pound) broiler-fryer, cut up
1 tablespoon lemon juice	Salt, pepper to taste
1 tablespoon honey	Pinch of paprika
Pinch of grated lemon peel	¼ cup margarine

Preheat oven to 350°. Drain pears, save ½ cup syrup. Mix syrup with orange jam, lemon juice, honey, lemon peel, and ginger. Powder chicken with salt, pepper, and paprika. Set skin side up in a baking pan and dot with margarine. Bake 45 minutes. Set pears around edge of pan. Brush chicken, pears, with orange jam mixture. Bake 15 minutes with glaze. 6 servings.

HAVURAT (FELLOWSHIP) DUCK WITH LENTILS

1 (6-pound) duck, cleaned
Salt, pepper to taste
3 tablespoons olive oil
2 tablespoons chicken fat
½ clove garlic, minced
1 onion, chopped

1 bay leaf
1 teaspoon chopped parsley
½ cup chopped celery
½ cup dry white wine
3 cups lentils, cooked

Caress inside of duck with salt and pepper. Set duck in deep pot and add all ingredients but the wine and lentils. Brown duck on all sides. Add wine and simmer until wine is evaporated. Add water just to cover duck. Cover and cook over medium heat 50 minutes until duck is tender. Skim fat from pan and pour remaining juice over lentils and duck. Serve hot. 6 servings.

Fish

DEVILED CAPE SALMON

1 onion, minced
½ cup butter
2 tablespoons flour
1 cup milk
1½ teaspoons salt
1 teaspoon dry mustard

2 teaspoons Worcestershire sauce
Juice of ½ lemon
1 egg, beaten
2 cups flaked cooked salmon
½ cup matzo meal

Preheat oven to 350°. Sauté the onion in the butter, light brown, for 5 minutes. Add the flour and milk, stir until mixture boils. Add salt, mustard, Worcestershire sauce, lemon juice, egg, and salmon. Mix well and set in buttered baking dishes. Sprinkle on the matzo meal. Bake in 350° oven 20 minutes. 6 servings.

CAPE LOBSTER TAILS

For some reason, South African Jews do not consider lobster tails forbidden by dietary laws.

3 pounds lobster tails	Paprika to taste
½ cup butter	2 egg yolks
½ cup brandy	½ cup heavy cream
Salt to taste	¼ cup dry white wine

Parboil lobster tails 5 minutes. Take meat from shells, slice. Sauté lobster in butter 5 minutes. Warm brandy, and flame over lobsters. As flame dies, add salt, paprika. Beat egg yolks in cream and wine, and mix with pan juices; stir over low heat 5 minutes until sauce thickens. 4 servings.

Soup

CREAM OF PEANUT SOUP

Try a new taste.

1 onion, chopped	2 quarts Chicken Soup
2 stalks celery, chopped	1 cup peanut butter
¼ cup margarine	½ cup chopped peanuts
1 tablespoon flour	

Fry onion and celery in margarine until soft, *not* brown. Mix in flour, blend well. Add chicken soup, stir, bring to a boil. Remove from heat, press through a sieve. Add peanut butter and blend. Return to low heat, remove at start of boil. Garnish with peanuts. 8–10 servings.

COLLARD GREENS SOUP

1 bunch collard or turnip greens
2 quarts water
2 cups raw beef in bits
2 cups cooked navy beans
1 onion, minced

1 green pepper, minced
1 tablespoon oil
3 potatoes, peeled, cubed
Salt, pepper to taste

Wash greens. Chop coarsely. Put in kettle with 1 quart water, beef bits. Cover and simmer 30 minutes. Add beans and cook slowly 30 minutes. Cook onion and green pepper in oil, tender, *not* browned. Add to soup along with potatoes, 1 quart water, salt and pepper to taste. Cover, simmer 30 minutes until potatoes are done.
6 servings.

Dessert

SOUTH AFRICA APPLE KUCHEN

2 cups sifted flour
1/4 teaspoon salt
2 1/2 teaspoons baking powder
2/3 cup sugar
1/2 cup melted butter
1 egg, beaten
1/2 cup water

1 slice candied citron
4 apples peeled, cored, cut in
  wedges
1/2 cup dried currants
3/4 cup sugar
1 tablespoon grated lemon peel

Preheat oven to 375°. Mix flour, salt, baking powder, and 2/3 cup sugar. Add 2 tablespoons butter and knead until crumbly. Add egg, water. Work until dough clings. Knead hard on floured surface. Roll dough out and put into a greased medium pan. Brush on half of melted butter, add citron. Take apples and arrange in overlapping rows on dough. Sprinkle with currants. Blend remaining butter with sugar and lemon péel, sprinkle on apples. Bake at 375° for 40 minutes. Serve warm.

About 12 servings.

DUTCH-JEWISH SESAME RICE

2 tablespoons cashew nuts
½ cup butter
1 cup sesame seeds
½ teaspoon cayenne
1 bay leaf, crumbled

4 cups hot, cooked rice
1 teaspoon salt
1 tablespoon rose water or juice
   of ½ lemon

Fry cashews brown in 1 tablespoon butter. Remove from pan. Add remaining butter to pan, fry sesame seeds, cayenne, and bay leaf until seeds are brown. Mix cashew nuts, fried sesame seeds. Mix into the hot rice with salt. Combine well. Sprinkle on rose water or lemon juice.

6 servings.

BUBALEH PASSOVER PAN CAKE

2 eggs, separated
½ teaspoon salt
2 tablespoons sugar
¼ cup matzo meal

2 cups mashed potatoes
1 teaspoon grated lemon peel
2 tablespoons oil

Beat egg whites and salt. Add sugar, beat until egg whites are firm. Now beat yolks and add to whites. Sprinkle matzo meal and mashed potatoes over mixture, add lemon peel, and fold in. Place oil in a hot skillet. Pour in batter. Brown on both sides, turn with a spatula. Remove, cut in quarters. Sprinkle with sugar and serve.

4 servings.

CARROT CORN BREAD

3 carrots, cut in bits	2 cups yellow corn meal
2 eggs	½ teaspoon salt
4 tablespoons oil	1 teaspoon baking soda
2 cups buttermilk	1 teaspoon baking powder

Preheat oven to 450°. Set carrots, eggs, oil, and buttermilk in blender, and whirl smooth. Mix corn meal, salt, soda, and baking powder in bowl, stir to blend. Add carrot mixture and mix with a fast beat. Pour batter into a greased baking pan and bake 25 minutes until mixture shrinks away from side of pan. Knife into squares.
About 6 servings.

Note on the Marula Cocktail

This drink was offered to us by a Johannesburg South African rabbi. It's half marula juice, half Dutch gin. Powerful, it even affects elephants, according to the press. The marula fruit ripen in Kruger National Park and elephants go on their annual spree. The berry is green, about the size of a plum. Its taste, we'd say, is between that of a lime and a mango. After dining on a marula tree, an elephant goes to a stream for water, can easily gulp more than 50 gallons. The fruit ferments in the beast's belly as it is digested with water; the elephant acts as a four-legged still. More fruit is eaten and more water follows. The result: a drunken pachyderm. A blood sample analyzed by medical researchers showed a "highly volatile substance closely corresponding to alcohol."

LATIN AMERICA

Better a dinner of herbs where love is, than a stalled ox and hatred . . .

Proverbs 15:17

There is no Latin-American Jewish cooking of any vast proportions. The Jewish population in various countries there is small, and in most cases it has submerged itself into the native culture and the native eating habits and ways of preparing food. However, with the rise of the Nazis since the 1930s, there have been migrations of European Jews to Latin-American countries, and so one finds beach heads, clusters of such families in Mexico City, Buenos Aires, Rio de Janeiro, Montevideo, Panama, Lima. They are engaged in trade, some in farming, cattle, others in importing, exporting. There is an old colony of Jews in Entre Rios near Buenos Aires, a Baron de Hirsch project of long ago.

The second generation, born in Latin America, is mainly moving toward assimilation, intermarrying, taking Latinized names. The food they eat is more and more like the native Spanish-Indian dishes. Only among the older people does one find the European-Jewish cooking still in use. Often on our trips, we ate Latin-American versions of German and Austrian dishes. In Mexico, a former Viennese hostess served us cauahtemoc, that fine dish of eggs and beans. In one house with a mezuzah (Hebrew prayer box) on the door, we got nixtamalina, our old Jewish friend ground corn meal, related to the mamaliga of Romania, Russia, and Poland.

The Mexican Jews have tamed the mole de guajolote—the turkey with the hot pepper sauce, and they are beginning to be able to stand the hot peppers, marjoram, cilantro, ground anise, and chimaja (a wild cherry root) in their food. In Costa Rica we found Jews serving salpicon, meat and mustard greens; in El Salvador, a robalo a la Española, haddock Spanish style; in Guatemala, sopa de pan, bread soup; in Brazil, canjoquinha de miho verde, green corn mush; in Argentina, carbonada a la criolla, stew with peaches and pears. And so it went in Latin America. Almost no Jewish Latin-American cuisine coming alive. As guests at dinners of European-Jewish dishes, we ate the fine food of the country.

Of the few items where the infiltration of Jewish cooking ideas into Latin-American dishes was palatable we give recipes, those we found, and ate, with relish.

All was not lost. Leo Rosten reported a sandwich sign in a Jewish delicatessen in Mexico City as reading:

Pastrami por Fressers	10 pesos
Pastrami (Double Decker) por Grandes Fressers	15 pesos
Pastrami (Triple Decker) por Grandisimo Fressers	20 pesos

A fresser, in Yiddish, is a greedy eater, a gourmand, a hasty and vulgar feeder.

Meat

FAMILY SURPRISE (BAKED MEATS)

An amazing Jewish dish with no history we could discover.

2 pounds garlic beef sausages,
 sliced
½ pound veal, cubed
½ pound beef, sliced
2 chickens, cut in frying pieces
½ cup olive oil
4 cloves garlic, crushed
2 onions, cut fine

8 tomatoes, peeled
4 cups rice
2 cups water
2 sweet red peppers, sliced
3 cups peas
10 artichoke hearts
15 asparagus tips
2 tablespoons saffron

Preheat oven to 350°. Sauté sausage, veal, beef, and chickens in the olive oil with 2 cloves garlic and onions. Add tomatoes, and simmer 10 minutes. In a casserole, with all this, set rice and water, red peppers, peas, artichoke hearts, and asparagus tips. Mix saffron powder and 2 cloves garlic. Stir into the rice. Cook covered in oven 10 minutes. Take off cover, cook 10 more minutes.
6–8 servings.

JEWISH-CHATEAUBRIAND MONTEVIDEO

1 (2-pound) club steak
½ cup margarine
Salt, white pepper to taste
2 teaspoons mustard
2 tablespoons chopped parsley
2 teaspoons dry sherry

2 teaspoons Worcestershire sauce
2 ounces cognac, heated
½ cup catsup
½ cup Chicken Soup
10 mushrooms, sliced, sautéed

On a grill do the steak rare. Add margarine, salt, white pepper, mustard, chopped parsley, sherry, and Worcestershire to a pan, heat. When hot add steak, pour on cognac, and flambé. Remove steak and slice. Mix catsup, soup, and mushrooms in the sauce, heat, and stir. Pour on steak.

4 servings.

Fowl

SPICY DUCK

3 tablespoons vegetable oil	1 teaspoon chopped gingerroot
1 onion, sliced	1 (4-pound) duck, disjointed
2 cloves garlic, crushed	1 teaspoon salt
2 pickled green chilies, chopped	1 cup water
2 tablespoons ground coriander	1 cup coconut milk
½ teaspoon cumin	Juice of 1 lemon
1 teaspoon cayenne	

In oil sauté onion light brown. Add garlic, green chilies, coriander, cumin, cayenne, and gingerroot. Sauté for 4 minutes. Add duck, salt, and water. Cover, simmer 40 minutes or until duck is tender. Spoon off excess fat, add coconut milk. Simmer 10 minutes, uncovered. Remove from heat, add lemon juice.

6 servings.

CHICKEN RICE (PERU)

1 (3-pound) chicken, boned	¼ teaspoon ground cloves
1 cup margarine	¼ teaspoon cardamom
2 onions	¼ teaspoon saffron
2 cups rice	¼ cup raisins
2 cups Chicken Soup	

Preheat oven to 350°. Cut chicken into 3-inch pieces. Brown in margarine in ovenproof pan. Remove chicken from pan. Slice onions and fry brown. Add rice to the onions. Pour the soup over rice and simmer. When nearly all the soup has evaporated, mix chicken with the rice, cloves, cardamom, saffron, and raisins. Stir and bake in oven 30 minutes. 6 servings.

CHICKEN, TOMATOES, OLIVES ARGENTINA

When in the 1930s Europeans went into exile in South America, they soon made a chicken part of the main meal—with a Latin-American flavor.

1 (4-pound) roasting chicken	2 tablespoons butter or margarine
½ dozen taco corn sheets	½ cup dry white wine
1 tablespoon cooking oil	½ clove garlic, minced
2 tomatoes, chopped	Pinch of saffron
2 shallots, minced	8 olives
Salt, pepper to taste	

Roast and carve chicken according to the established way. Fry taco sheets cut into small squares in oil. Simmer tomatoes and shallots, seasoned, over moderate heat with margarine until soft. Add wine, garlic, saffron, olives and simmer. Arrange chicken on a hot platter, pour sauce around, and garnish with the fried taco bits.
6 servings.

Fish

BAKED FISH EL SALVADOR

There are a few Jews in San Salvador, in the export business, and they have cooks who are trained in Latin-American Jewish cuisine cross-pollination.

1 (4-pound) whole fresh fish
   (barracuda, bonita)
Juice of 1 lemon
Salt, pepper to taste
½ teaspoon chili powder
4 parsley leaves
2 onions, minced

2 stalks celery, minced
1 onion, sliced
4 tablespoons olive oil
½ pound fresh mushrooms, thinly
   sliced
½ cup white wine
2 tablespoons chopped parsley

Preheat oven to 350°. Wash and split fish. Rub inside and out with the lemon juice, salt, pepper, and chili powder. Mix and place parsley leaves, half the minced onion, and celery in cavity. Place sliced onion on bottom of oiled baking dish with half of the mushroom slices; top with fish. Bake, uncovered, in oven 20 minutes. Heat remaining oil; slowly brown rest of onions, add remaining mushrooms, wine, and parsley. Pour on fish; bake 45 minutes; baste frequently. Add more wine during cooking if needed. Serve with added fresh chopped parsley and lemon wedges. 8 servings.

BAKED FISH IN BANANA LEAVES (OR FOIL)

1 teaspoon chili powder
1 teaspoon crushed aniseed
1 teaspoon salt
2 pounds sea bass fillets

Banana leaves or aluminum foil
2 tablespoons white vinegar
1 tablespoon melted butter

Preheat oven to 400°. Mix chili powder, aniseed, and salt. Rub well into fillets. Place fillets side by side on banana leaves on large baking sheet. Pour on vinegar and melted butter. Fold up the leaves and tie securely. Bake in 400° oven 45 minutes.
4 servings.

POMPANO IN PAPER

3 fresh pompano
1 quart water
2 green onions, chopped
¼ cup butter
2 cups dry white dinner wine
1 clove garlic, crushed

2 red onions, chopped
1 bay leaf
Pinch of thyme
2 tablespoons flour
2 egg yolks
Paper or parchment sheets

Preheat oven to 450°. Cut fish into fillets. Simmer heads and bones in salted water, reduce to 2 cups of fish stock. Fry green onions and fillets in 3 tablespoons butter. Add wine and garlic, cover, and simmer 8 minutes until tender. Drain, save wine stock. Sauté in butter the red onions. Cook 10 minutes. Add fish and wine stock, bay leaf, and thyme. Cook 10 minutes. Discard bay leaf. In a skillet mix 2 tablespoons butter, flour. Beat egg yolks; add to skillet, mix thoroughly. Chill sauce. Use paper bags or six 1-foot-square parchment paper sheets, oiled. Put on a tablespoon of sauce, top with a fillet. Fold, press to seal. Place on oiled baking sheet; bake in the hot oven until brown. Serve in paper.
6 servings.

Soup

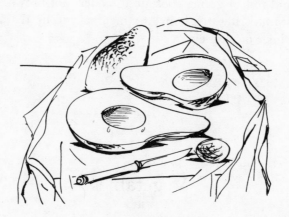

AVOCADO SOUP

2 large avocados, peeled, pitted, diced
4 cups Chicken Soup
1 tablespoon lemon juice
1 teaspoon minced cilantro
1 teaspoon salt

½ cup slivered, toasted almonds
⅛ teaspoon pepper
¼ teaspoon ground nutmeg
3 drops Tabasco sauce

In a blender mix diced avocados, soup, and remaining ingredients. Cover, blend 40 seconds until nuts are finely crushed. Heat to boiling. Do *not* boil.
4 servings.

ALBONDIGAS (MEATBALL) SOUP

½ pound garlic beef sausage	1 egg, beaten
1½ pounds ground beef	½ cup olive oil
2 cloves garlic, minced	1 onion, minced
1 tablespoon minced parsley	½ cup tomato sauce
Salt to taste	2 quarts beef or chicken broth
½ cup bread crumbs	Chopped parsley to garnish

Grind sausage, mix with beef, 1 clove garlic, parsley, salt, bread crumbs, and egg. Mix, form into balls 1½ inches in size, and sauté brown in 2 tablespoons oil in a skillet. Heat remaining oil in a large saucepan, add onion and rest of garlic, cook until tender, not brown. Add tomato sauce and broth. Bring to a boil. Add meatballs to broth, cover, simmer ½ hour. Sprinkle on parsley.
8 servings.

Vegetables

MEXICAN PEPPERS IN CHICKEN FAT

8 Mexican frying peppers, cut in half lengthwise	1 teaspoon oregano
2 tomatoes, sliced	1 teaspoon basil
1 onion, sliced	Salt, pepper to taste
2 cloves garlic, sliced	8 tablespoons chicken fat
4 anchovy fillets	½ cup chopped parsley

Preheat oven to 400°. Remove stem and seeds from peppers, place hollow sides up on a baking sheet. In each place a slice of tomato, slice of onion, 3 slices of garlic—top with ½ anchovy. Sprinkle on oregano, basil, salt, pepper, very lightly. Pour 1 tablespoon fat on each pepper. Bake in oven 40 minutes until peppers wrinkle and vegetables are soft. Sprinkle on chopped parsley to serve.
8 servings.

LATIN-AMERICAN LATKES (POTATO PANCAKES)

5 potatoes, peeled	1 cup matzo meal
2 eggs	1 cup drained, diced sweet
2 onions, grated	peppers
1½ teaspoons salt	4 tablespoons oil
½ teaspoon pepper	

Grate the potatoes. Drain. Stir in all ingredients except oil. Heat half the oil in a skillet. Drop mixture 2 tablespoons at a time on skillet to make 1 latke. Brown, turn, brown on other side. Add more oil as needed.
6–8 servings.

REFRIED BEANS

A Mexican dish—the Jewish version uses chicken fat instead of bacon drippings.

1 pound dried pinto beans	1 clove garlic, crushed
½ cup chicken fat	2 teaspoons salt
¼ cup chopped onion	1 teaspoon chili powder
¼ cup finely chopped green	
pepper	

Soak beans overnight. Put beans and liquid into a saucepan. Bring to a boil, reduce heat, and simmer, covered, 1½ hours until tender. Drain, reserving liquid; add water to liquid to make 1 cup. In fat, sauté onion, green pepper, and garlic 5 minutes. Stir in beans, salt, and chili powder. Fry in a skillet after mashing mixture until beans are well heated.
2–4 servings.

BLACK RADISH SALAD

The large black radish came to Latin America with the Jews from Russia.

2 cups sliced black radishes	1 teaspoon sugar
½ cup vinegar	1 teaspoon coarsely ground black
1 tablespoon salt	pepper

Salt and sweat radish for half an hour. Mix radishes with vinegar, salt, and sugar. Allow to marinate 2 hours. Drain, press the liquid out of radishes. Add pepper and toss radishes.
4 servings.

BROILED SHERRIED TOMATOES

4 large tomatoes	1 teaspoon dried dill
1 cup dry sherry or ½ cup	½ cup mayonnaise
Guatemala Tecolote	½ cup grated hard cheese
Salt, pepper to taste	

Cut tomatoes in halves. Pierce with a fork. Soak with sherry. Season with salt and pepper, dill. Broil 7 minutes. Mix equal amounts of mayonnaise and cheese. Pack 1 tablespoon or more on each tomato half. In broiler brown *lightly*.
4–6 servings.

Dessert

APPLE CRUMB

1½ pounds tart apples	¾ cup oatmeal
½ cup butter	½ cup flour
½ cup brown sugar	1 teaspoon ground cinnamon

Preheat oven to 350°. Peel and core apples, slice. Arrange in a buttered 6-cup baking dish. Melt butter in a saucepan. Add brown sugar, oatmeal, flour, and cinnamon. Stir mixture crumbly. Sprinkle over apples and bake in a moderate oven 35 minutes until crumbs are golden and apples tender. Serve warm or cold with thick cream.
6 servings.

SHADCHEN (WEDDING BROKER) SANGRIA

A tribute from a dying profession.

1 quart dry red wine
⅓ quart soda water
Juice of ½ lemon
3 tablespoons sugar

2 ounces vodka
1 ounce South American cognac
8 slices orange
8 slices lemon

Combine all ingredients except the orange and lemon in a large glass bowl. Add orange, lemon slices, chill well. Before serving, add ice, and wish the wedding celebration well.
8 servings.

RIO RUM COFFEE COCKTAIL

1 cup dark Jamaica run
1 cup cold black coffee
1 cup skim milk

Freshly grated nutmeg
Sugar to taste

Collect your ingredients. Shake with cracked ice. It's very easy to make a batch at a time. A pinch of nutmeg to each glass. Most luncheon meetings serve it.
6–8 servings.

MEXICAN-JEWISH CHEESECAKE

12 graham crackers
2 pounds cream cheese
1¾ cups sugar
3 tablespoons flour
¼ teaspoon salt
Grated rind of 1 lemon

Grated rind of ½ orange
5 eggs
2 egg yolks
2 tablespoons papaya juice
1 cup heavy cream

Preheat oven to 475°. Dampen a dozen graham crackers, crush, use as crust in medium cake pan. Beat cheese. Mix in sugar, flour, and salt, keep mixture smooth. Add rinds, eggs and egg yolks, and papaya juice. Add ¼ cup cream. Turn into crust. Bake for 15 minutes. Reduce heat to 200°, bake 1 hour more. Let stand 15 minutes and cool. Top with rest of cream, whipped.
10 servings.

WINE BANANAS

Served at a Mexico City bar mitzvah.

6 bananas, peeled
2 tablespoons melted butter
½ cup muscatel
Juice of 1 lemon

2 tablespoons brown sugar
¼ teaspoon ground cloves
Pinch of salt

Set bananas in shallow pan. Mix all other ingredients. Pour over bananas. Bake under broiler, baste until fruit is a *pale* brown.
6 servings.

BLUE GRAPE PIE

2 quarts Concord grapes
½ cup sugar
½ tablespoon cornstarch

1 tablespoon tequila
1 tablespoon butter, melted
Pie pastry for 2 (9-inch) crusts

Remove and save skins from grapes. Heat pulp and strain to remove seeds. Mix sugar and cornstarch, add to pulp along with skins, also the tequila, butter, and mix well. Pour on lower crust, and then put on top, making slits for steam. Bake in preheated 450° oven 10 minutes, then at 350°, 45 minutes. Cool. Serve with ice cream.
6 servings.

THE UNITED STATES

Only in cooking does the end justify the means . . .

Tante Longstrasse

There is the wrong impression, usually given by American-Jewish novelists, ghetto-raised television gag men, and Tin Pan Alley song writers, that the Jewish-American food was the cookery of the poor on the Lower East Side, New York. In their memories, it consisted of barrel-herring, corned beef sandwiches, stew meat, a Friday-night chicken and challah, a kitchen dominated by garlic, clarified fat, and corn meal mush.

Our hunt for accuracy and lucidity shows that actually the best of the European cuisines came to America first in the seventeenth century with the Spanish and Portuguese Sephardic Jews. And in 1825, the Yehudim, (the German Jews) began to come over. After which, starting in 1880, came the huge migration of the Eastern European Ashkenazic Jews.

The German-American Jews, the Deutsche Yehudim, were *not* ghetto folk, they prospered. Kuhns, Warburgs, Seligmans, Kahns, Schiffs, Lehmans, Loebs, Guggenheims, Strausses. As did some who left Judaism, such as the Belmonts, the Dillons, the Mark Clarks. . . . Leo Rosten speaks of the Yehudims' "pride, philanthropy, snobbery . . ." but he doesn't go into their delight in fine food, their splendidly set tables. They improved the chicken and goose dishes, did wonders in civilizing some American items. (One of Lillian Russell's Jewish banker lovers introduced to her the delight of chopped liver.) The Yehudim combined the best of the German cooking with some additions from Austria and a touch of the French with an American dish.

Whether moving to the Bronx *or* Southampton, settling as farmers in Texas (there is a town, Seligman, Arizona), seeing the Middle West, taking part in the Gold Rush (where in San Francisco, a Levi Strauss invented Levi's, pants out of tent cloth, copper riveted at the seams), Jewish cooking spread across the nation, often in wild isolated areas. But it moved about and took on some American notions; improved the native dried fruit pie, extended the range of the schnitzel.

The Russian and Polish Jews, and their Galician and Lithuanian cousins, who were called Galitzianer and Litvak, they, until the second and third generation, kept the ritual Orthodox dietary laws fairly pure. But the young, the grandsons, after a deluge of changes, invasions of other ethnic cookery, saw L. A. Feuerbach's words of 1850 come true, "Der Mensch ist, was er isst . . . Man is what he eats." And the young generations tasted whatever they felt like, from pizza to Laredo chili.

Today, American-Jewish cooking is either the surviving old dishes of Europe, or improvised adaptations to fit the processed foods, the TV trays, the deep freeze, the breakdown of the Orthodox faith of Moses and Abraham into the Conservative and the Reform temple versions of Judaism. It was still true to many, the advice of the Talmud, "He who eats and drinks, but does not bless the Lord, is a thief."

The bagel and lox (and cream cheese) is New York Jewish-American—a native *not* an immigrant. Just as the hot pastrami sandwich is Romanian-Jewish, the kosher garlic pickle is Polish. The Jewish-German delicatessen from coast to coast in the United States educated several generations of Americans to the potato salad, sauerkraut, pumpernickel, spiced meats, pickled herring, smoked goose, the art of the use of sour cream, leberwurst, salami, and wrinkled black olives (maslinas).

In American-Jewish kitchens were found adoptions and changes in recipes; but, unlike jazz (the one pure American art form native to the United States, created and brought to perfection there), American-Jewish cooking, with its vast memory bank of already tested European dishes, did little to invent a new cuisine—as assimilation, intermarriage, a desire to move with the Joneses, and not with the Jacobses, dominated the new generations.

What this book sets down as Jewish-American recipes are samples of some attempts to experiment, to merge with the native food habits. The inventor of the Western story, Bret Harte (he added an "e" to his name, but was of the Hart, Shaffner, and Marx clothing family) and Judah P. Benjamin of the Confederacy, added nothing to Jewish-American cuisine. Louis B. Mayer, the raucous rajah of the MGM film studios, insisted that his mother's chicken soup with matzo balls be served in the studio dining room. We ate it there, during a screen writing period; it was among the firm's better products. Bernard Baruch, until age slowed his digestion, liked a slice of roast goose; Otto Kahn and Mrs. Kahn (nee Addie Wolff) insisted on a chef who could produce a Fleischbruhe mit Markklosschen (a clear soup with marrow dumpling). Emma Lazarus, whose stirring words, a bit too romantic (GIVE ME YOUR TIRED, YOUR POOR . . .), are engraved on the base of the Statue of Liberty, was, according to a newspaper item in *Di Yiddishe Velt* (*The Jewish World*), inclined to enjoy majaz gomboc (Hungarian liver dumplings).

While the élite German-Jewish group stood for banking, philanthropy, and a certain amount of gaudy sinful living (mostly missing from Stephen Birmingham's *Our Crowd; The Great Jewish Families of New York*), Jews among the less endowed (as pictured in Mike Gold's *Jews Without Money,* and Milt Gross's *Nize Baby*) were busy over their cooking pots. Emma Goldman, the anarchist free-love advocate, cooked, and ran a marvelous Jewish eating place for a time, when not engaged in debates. Life was minyans in store-front shuls, striking at the sweat shops, pushcart peddling, patronizing the shvitzbuds, the Jewish theaters on Second Avenue, the tangy Yiddish downtown restaurants. Or going to gawk at the great actor families of the Thomashefskys, Maurice Schwartz, Ben Ami ("kosher Stanislavsky"), and the Adlers, all at the Café Royal, where the waiters spoke three crisp dialects of Yiddish and could insult in all. The Jews took their pots to the Catskills, as boarders doing their own cooking; carried gefilte fish and horseradish to the Gentiles.

In later years, their children, grandchildren—scientists, movie tycoons, Ph.D.s, Nobel Prize winners, hoodlum chiefs, ambassadors and ward heelers, presidential advisers, Las Vegas stickmen, would think back to their mother's hockfleish, mandlen soup.

We were once at a party with a famous California judge when he broke into tears speaking of his mother's Simchath Torah spiced prune-and-apple cake.

Meat

KASHA (BUCKWHEAT GROATS) CHOLENT U.S.A.

1 cup dried lima beans
4 pounds beef brisket
2 onions, sliced
1 tablespoon chicken fat
1 tablespoon salt

½ teaspoon pepper
1 teaspoon paprika
1 clove garlic, minced
5 cups hot water
1 cup dry kasha

In water soak beans 12 hours. Sauté the meat and onions brown in fat. Add salt, pepper, paprika, garlic, water, and drained beans. Cover, not too tightly; cook over low heat 2 hours. Add kasha and, if needed, a little water. Cook 1 hour until meat and beans are tender. Slice meat, serve with beans and kasha.
8 servings.

TAFELSPITZ (BOILED BEEF)

4 pounds chuck beef
2 beef bones, cracked
2 teaspoons salt
6 whole black peppercorns
2 parsley roots

2 carrots
2 stalks celery
1 leek
2 onions

Set beef and bones in kettle with water to cover. Add salt, pepper-corns, vegetables, and bring to a boil. Simmer 3 hours until beef is tender. Strain off the bouillon. Slice beef and serve with horseradish and chopped chives.
6 servings.

LENNIE BERNSTEIN MEATBALLS

Served at a Toronto, Canada, fête—after a concert—by some of the Jewish community.

1 onion, finely chopped

3 tablespoons margarine

2 cups bread crumbs

½ cup Chicken Soup

2 pounds twice ground meat

1½ teaspoons salt

¼ teaspoon ground black pepper

¼ teaspoon ground cinnamon

½ cup grated raw potato

2 eggs, beaten

1 cup flour

1½ cups beef broth

¼ cup tomato purée

½ cup drained pickled onions

⅛ teaspoon marjoram

⅛ teaspoon paprika

½ teaspoon sugar

Salt, pepper to taste

Fry onion in margarine. Wet bread crumbs with soup. Mix meat with salt, pepper, and cinnamon. Add onion, crumbs, potato, and eggs. Mix and form into balls. Dredge in flour, brown in a skillet. Set in casserole, save drippings in skillet. Pour off fat, add broth and purée. Add remaining ingredients, cook 3 minutes. Pour over meatballs, serve very hot.

12 servings as an hors d'oeuvre.

B'NAI B'RITH SEAFOOD CANAPÉS

Served at a party in Detroit, honoring our last cookbook.

6 slices white bread

1 cup butter

8 big boneless sardines

Juice of ½ lemon

Salt, pepper to taste

6 tablespoons ground fish

Cut crusts from bread and slash into diamond shapes. Fry lightly on both sides in butter, cool. Mash and mix together 5 teaspoons of butter with sardines. Season with lemon juice, salt, pepper. In another bowl, blend the fish with remaining butter to a smooth paste. Spread the fried bread with a layer of sardine mixture. A pastry bag with a small opening will pattern a line of fish butter on the edge of canapés. Chill before serving with cocktails.

Makes about 2 dozen canapés.

STUFFED CABBAGE TEMPLE EMANUEL

This is *not* the New York City temple, but an outpost in the Southwest. It is the only Jewish recipe we found for stuffed cabbage made with sausage and grapes.

1 head cabbage
2 pounds kosher beef sausage
1 clove garlic, minced
2 cups stewed tomatoes, sieved
    after measuring
½ teaspoon oregano

¼ cup olive oil
¼ teaspoon chopped parsley
Salt, pepper to taste
1 cup halved seedless grapes
½ pint Chicken Soup

With care, separate big leaves and parboil until soft enough to bend. Wrap and roll 1 sausage into 1 leaf—tuck in ends and place in casserole. Mix garlic in with tomatoes, oregano, olive oil, parsley, salt, and pepper. Pour over cabbage rolls. Simmer on stove 1 hour. Remove from stove and refrigerate. Tastes best after 2 days' chilling. Remove fat from top and reheat, cook ½ hour. Before serving, add grapes and chicken soup and heat.
6 servings.

Fowl

DUCK LIVERS ARMAGNAC

5 duck livers
1 cup flour
2 tablespoons margarine
4 (3-inch) pastry shells
1 cup seedless grapes

5 mushrooms, sliced
1 cup armagnac
5 tablespoons Chicken Soup
Salt, pepper to taste
Freshly ground nutmeg

Cut up duck livers in 2-inch bits. Dip livers in flour and sauté in margarine on medium heat 5 minutes. Remove and place in pastry

shells. Put grapes in the pan with mushrooms, sauté 4 minutes. Light to flambé with armagnac heated in a spoon. Add soup, mix. Season and pour sauce over livers, then dust with nutmeg.
4 servings.

RICH MISHPOCHEH (RELATIVES) CHICKEN

This is a very fancy dish as to contents, and was usually produced to impress on West End Avenue and Lake Shore Drive.

1 (4-pound) frying chicken	Salt, pepper to taste
1 cup chicken fat	2 oranges, sliced
4 tablespoons brandy	1 clove garlic, crushed
1 tablespoon meat glaze	3 mushrooms, sliced
1 teaspoon tomato paste	1 teaspoon lemon juice
1 tablespoon potato flour	½ red bell pepper, diced
2 cups Chicken Soup	1 green pepper, diced
½ cup dry white wine	2 tablespoons olive oil
1 teaspoon red currant jelly	2 tomatoes, skinned, cut up

Slice chicken in serving pieces. Fry in fat until browned. Heat brandy, ignite, pour over chicken. Remove chicken. Add to pan meat glaze, tomato paste, flour. Cook and stir smooth; add soup, wine, jelly, salt, and pepper; bring to a boil. Put chicken in a casserole, pour sauce on. Simmer, covered, 25 minutes. Peel oranges, sauté shredded peel; add garlic, salt, and pepper; cook 2 minutes. Add mushrooms, lemon juice; cook 3 minutes. Add peppers, cook 2 minutes. Add olive oil, tomatoes, oranges. Put chicken on serving dish. Top with hot mixture.
4 servings.

PHEASANT WITH WILD RICE

Lord Duveen sold expensive paintings to Western millionaires. His Jewish chef prepared 2 dishes wealthy West Coast Jewish families relished.

4 pheasants	2 cups chicken fat
1 cup flour	1 pound wild rice, cooked
Salt, pepper to taste	1 cup chopped parsley to garnish
3 eggs, beaten	

Slice each pheasant into 8 serving pieces. Remove skin. Dredge in flour, salt, and pepper. Dip in eggs, then again in flour. Brown in fat 8 minutes. Steam in stove-top roaster 15 minutes. Serve ½ cup wild rice with each plate. Garnish with parsley.
8 servings.

DUVEEN DUCK AU VIN

1 (5-pound) duck	1 large onion, thinly sliced
Salt, pepper to taste	1 tablespoon grated lemon rind
2 tablespoons olive oil	1 mixed teaspoon majoram and
1 cup orange juice	rosemary
1 cup dry burgundy	Pinch of oregano
1 tablespoon lemon juice	2 tablespoons orange curaçao

Preheat oven to 275°. Slice duck into serving pieces, season with salt and pepper. Brown in olive oil and remove to a casserole with lid. To skillet, add orange juice, wine, lemon juice, onion, rind, herbs. Bring to boil, scrape up browned bits off pan. Pour over duck; bake, covered, in a slow oven 3 hours, until tender. Remove duck to platter. Strain pan juices. Add orange curaçao. Cook, stir. Pour over duck. Serve on rice.
6 servings.

Fish

LOX WITH EGGS (SMOKED SALMON)

1 large onion, chopped	8 eggs
1 green pepper, chopped	¼ cup heavy cream
2 cups sliced mushrooms	1 tablespoon chopped parsley
½ cup butter	¼ teaspoon basil
½ pound smoked lox (salmon), cut into bits	2 drops Tabasco sauce
	½ teaspoon pepper

Mix the onion, green pepper, and mushrooms in a skillet. Put on lid, let vegetables steam without butter until they stick to the pan. Begin to add butter, stir. Add salmon, cook 2 minutes, stir until salmon turns light pink. Beat eggs with cream, parsley, basil, Tabasco. Add to skillet, cook over low heat, stir constantly until eggs set.
6 servings.

SMOKED SALMON IN CREAM-HORSERADISH SAUCE

A Beverly Hills Sunday brunch dish at David Selznick's during the making of *Gone With the Wind*.

½ cup finely minced shallots	2 tablespoons freshly grated horseradish
3 teaspoons chopped dill	
½ pound smoked salmon, shredded	1 tablespoon mayonnaise
	Salt, pepper to taste
1 cup sour cream	

Mix shallots and 2 teaspoons dill with salmon. In separate bowl, mix sour cream, horseradish, mayonnaise, salt and pepper. Combine well. Add to salmon. Toss. Garnish with remaining dill. Serve on pumpernickel.
6 servings.

Soup

JEWISH-AMERICAN CHICKEN SOUP

Notice the short-cut use of bouillon cube, seasonings, garlic salt. Does it taste as good as Mama's? Try it.

1 (5-pound) chicken, cut in sections	1 teaspoon poultry seasoning
1 onion, chopped	Pinch of garlic salt
6 cups water	Pepper
1 bouillon cube	¼ cup uncooked rice, sautéed 2 minutes in margarine

Set chicken parts with onion in a pot and cover with water. Add bouillon cube, seasonings, cover, cook 2 hours. Remove all meat from bones. Return meat to pot, add rice. Cook until rice is tender.
4 servings.

LOX (SMOKED SALMON) POTATO SOUP

2 large onions, chopped	1½ quarts water
2 tablespoons butter	1 cup milk
½ pound Nova Scotia lox, diced	½ teaspoon ground black pepper
4 potatoes, peeled, diced	

Fry onions in butter until golden, *not* brown. Add lox, potatoes, and water. Cook 1 hour. Add milk and pepper; reheat, do *not* boil.
4 servings.

SOUR CREAM NOODLES (VERY NON-KOSHER)

½ pound medium noodles
1 pound ground beef
3 tablespoons butter
1 pound tomato sauce
1 teaspoon salt
⅛ teaspoon pepper

½ clove garlic, minced
1 cup cottage cheese
1 cup sour cream
6 green onions, chopped
¾ cup shredded Cheddar cheese

Boil noodles in salted water. Drain. Sauté the meat in butter. Add tomato sauce, salt, pepper, and garlic. Simmer 5 minutes. Combine noodles, cottage cheese, sour cream, and onions. In a casserole place alternate layers of noodle mix, meat mix, start with noodles. Top with the shredded cheese. Bake for 25 minutes in preheated oven at 350°.
8 servings.

JEWISH NEW ENGLAND BOILED DINNER

Said to be Norbert Weiner's favorite dish.

3 cups beef soup
3 cups Chicken Soup
2 pounds beef brisket
1 (4-pound) roasting chicken, cut up
1 onion, diced
2 sprigs parsley
1 bay leaf

1 stalk celery, with top
4 potatoes, peeled, quartered
2 carrots, halved
½ pound green beans, sliced
2 zucchini, sliced
4 beets, cooked
1 teaspoon chopped fresh parsley

Bring beef and chicken soups to a boil in a kettle, add brisket and chicken. Bring to a boil again being sure liquid covers beef and chicken. Add onion and the sprigs of parsley, bay leaf, celery. Reduce heat, simmer 1½ hours. Add potatoes and carrots. Simmer 25 minutes, add green beans. Simmer 8 minutes and add zucchini. Continue to simmer for 10 minutes. Slice beets and heat in a saucepan. Set up meat and chicken on a platter surrounded by vegetables. Drain beets and arrange around the beef. Sprinkle with fresh parsley.
6–8 servings.

Doughs

EGG BAGELS

The purist bagel hound does *not* like his bagel tampered with. But the egg bagel is popular. There is also a pumpernickel bagel, even a bagel with baked onion bits on top, also poppy seed dustings are in demand.

2 packages dry yeast
1 cup warm water
2 tablespoons sugar
5 cups sifted flour

2 teaspoons salt
3 tablespoons vegetable shortening
2 eggs, beaten
½ cup poppy seeds

Dissolve yeast in 1 cup of warm water, let stand 10 minutes, add sugar. In a large bowl put down the flour, make a well and place the salt and shortening in it. Pour in yeast and beaten eggs. Mix with flour until thoroughly blended. Knead dough in bowl. Cover with cloth and let stand until dough is doubled in bulk, 1½ hours. Punch several

times—knead, letting it rise again for 1 hour. On lightly floured board, roll out pieces of dough to make round strips 10 inches long and ¾ inch wide. Join ends to make rings. Heat oven to 400°, grease wire racks. Place rings 3 at a time into boiling water for 2 minutes. As bagels rise to surface of water, remove, sprinkle with poppy seeds and place on oven racks. Bake 20 minutes until golden brown. Reduce heat to 350°, and bake 15 minutes.
Makes 24 bagels.

AMERICAN FARFEL (BAKED DOUGH)

3 cups matzo farfel	1 teaspoon vanilla
1 cup hot water	¾ teaspoon salt
4 eggs	2 cups milk
½ cup sugar	3 apples, peeled, sliced
½ teaspoon ground cinnamon	2 tablespoons butter

Preheat oven to 350°. Set farfel in bowl, add water, stir until absorbed. Set to cool. Beat eggs lightly with sugar, cinnamon, vanilla, and salt. Add milk, farfel mixture, blend well. Add apples, put into buttered casserole. Dot with butter, bake at 350° for 1 hour. Stir last 30 minutes.
10 servings.

MRS. RABBI WEISS'S CHEESE BLINTZES (ST. LOUIS)

FOR THE BLINTZ:

¾ cup flour	1 cup milk
½ teaspoon salt	1 tablespoon butter, melted
2 eggs, beaten	

FOR THE FILLING:

½ pound cottage cheese	2 tablespoons sugar
2 egg yolks	Pinch of salt
¼ teaspoon ground cinnamon	

Mix flour and salt. Combine with eggs, milk, and butter. Beat smooth. Pour into small, hot, greased skillet enough batter to make a thin cake, tilting pan for batter to spread evenly. Cook until top is dry. Cook only 1 side. Mix filling ingredients and put 1 tablespoon on each pancake. Fold over edges and press firmly. Fry both sides until brown. Serve with sour cream.

4–6 servings.

Dessert

AMERICAN-JEWISH CHEESECAKE

There are those who claim the cheesecake was invented in New York City. Certainly this recipe has items that could not be found in Russia or Austria. It comes from an old California Jewish family whose great-grandfather came out with the Gold Rush of '49. They were kosher until twenty years ago, now cook Jewish, and have endowed a temple window.

3 eggs
1 pound Hoop cheese
½ cup sugar
1 can condensed milk, small size
1 tablespoon lemon juice
Pinch of salt
1 teaspoon sugar
¼ pound butter, melted

18 graham crackers, crushed to crumbs for cake
1 tablespoon brown sugar
1 pint sour cream
1 teaspoon vanilla
6 graham crackers crumbed for topping

Separate eggs and beat yolks with cheese, ½ cup sugar, condensed milk, lemon juice until blended. Beat egg whites with a pinch of salt, 1 teaspoon sugar. Fold beaten egg whites into yolk mixture and pour into ordinary piecrust (see below).

FOR CRUST: Add melted butter to crumbs, 1 tablespoon of brown sugar. With this fill bottom, sides of 9-inch ovenproof glass pan. Reserve some crumbs for top. Bake 10 minutes in oven preheated to 350°.

Add cake mixture. Bake cake 25 minutes at 350°. Spread hot cake with sour cream mixed with vanilla. Sprinkle with reserved crumbs. Bake 10 minutes more. Serve cold, not chilled.
6 servings.

LA COUPE BARUCH
(VANILLA ICE CREAM, TANGERINES, KIRSCH)

Hedda Hopper spoke of this to us as an invention of Barney Baruch.

3 tangerines   ½ cup slivered blanched almonds
1 quart vanilla ice cream   ½ cup kirsch

Peel tangerines, separate into sections, remove filaments and seeds. Fill a bowl with vanilla ice cream, scoop out a baseball-size hole on top. Arrange tangerine sections in a circle on top of the ice cream. Sprinkle with almonds. Pour kirsch into center and serve at once.
4 servings.

STRAWBERRIES WITH COINTREAU

A dish Sarah Bernhardt remembered from a St. Louis Jewish family fête.

1 quart fresh wild strawberries   4 tablespoons port
1 cup currant jelly   2 teaspoons Cointreau liqueur

Clean and chill the berries. Mix all other ingredients in a china bowl until jelly dissolves and sauce is smooth. Chill for 2 hours. Serve berries with sauce poured on. Do *not* add whipped cream. That is Chozzerish (in bad taste).
4 servings.

GUGGENHEIM CHAMPAGNE ZABAGLIONE

4 cups champagne sec
4 cups dry white wine
4 egg yolks

1 cup granulated sugar
1 tablespoon grated grapefruit
rind

Mix all the ingredients in a saucepan. When mixture is frothy, place pan over moderate heat, continue to beat till it swells, thickens, and bubbles form on the top. Remove at once from the heat. Do *not* stop beating while on heat. Pour zabaglione into glasses, serve immediately.
8 servings.

INDEX